Adaptable Crochet

Written and illustrated by Claire Bojczuk

Front Cover *Pioneer Sampler Quilt*
page 52

Left *Navaho Inspired Throw*
page 100

Pottage Publishing

Dear Reader

Thank you so much for taking the time to read **Adaptable Crochet**.

The aim of this book is to offer you designs and techniques that can be adapted to your own creative needs.

Colour trends come and go, so various colour combinations are included to help you envisage how flexible the designs here can be. Likewise, sizing options and advice about yarn quantities are given allowing you adjust the patterns according to your own particular requirements.

Some of the techniques may be familiar to you, while others are less mainstream, but in both cases there are plenty of step-by-step exercises and tips to help you. It has been difficult to get this level of information just right; so please forgive me if you find some techniques too obvious and easy, or others too perplexing and challenging. Either way, I sincerely hope you find something new and interesting to use in your crochet. I'd love to see what you can make.

Claire

For Elizabeth

Acknowledgements

I would like to thank Lee Lawrence and the late Bruce Robertson who taught me the little I know about graphic design. I must thank Joe Loboda, and my brothers, Jeremy and William, for their unfailing support, despite their utter ignorance of crochet. Thank you to my dear friends, Sarah Daniels and Paula Marvelly for always taking such kind and genuine interest in this and all my other endeavours. Thank you to my daughter, Elizabeth, for being wonderful, helpful and kind. This book would not have come about were it not for the encouragement and enthusiasm of all Pottage Publishing's amazing customers both large and small. Thank you to everyone at Focuscraft and Habico for distributing my first book, ***Crochet Unravelled*** to wool and craft shops far and wide. Thank you to Sew-In of Marple, and Dave Bluff in particular for his insider knowledge about yarn and retailing. Thank you, too, to all the other bricks and mortar retailers who took the trouble to reply to my pesky emails and stock ***Crochet Unravelled***, and to those of you who encouraged me to write another book. Without you all this book would not have come to fruition, and for that I am very grateful.

First published in Great Britain in 2018.

British Library Cataloguing-in-Publication Data. A catalogue record for this book is available from the British Library.
ISBN 978-09548296-2-9
Photography: Andy Rose (andyrosephotography.co.uk).
Illustrations: Claire Bojczuk.
Printed in the UK.
Published by Pottage Publishing, PO Box 202, South Ockendon, Essex, RM15 6WZ www.pottagepublishing.co.uk.

Contents

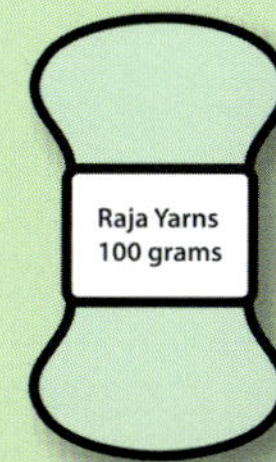

What you need to know

Basic crochet stitches and techniques are illustrated on pages 5–7 in case you need to refresh your knowledge.

However, ***Adaptable Crochet*** is not a beginner's book. If you are at all unsure about stitches, techniques or pattern reading, our sister book, ***Crochet Unravelled****: a clear and concise guide to learning crochet* is full of step-by-step exercises to get you started in crochet.

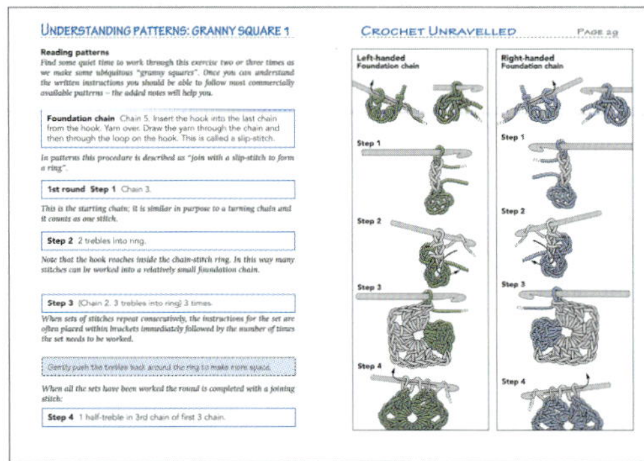

Above *Sample pages from* ***Crochet Unravelled: a clear and concise guide to learning crochet.***

How to use this book

1 ***Adaptable Crochet*** is divided into six chapters. Each chapter is based around a different crochet technique. The chapters stand on their own; in other words, you do **not** need to work through one chapter in order to understand the next.

Right *The six techniques: Log Cabin Crochet, Pioneer Quilt, Geo-filet, Texture Technique, Triangular Crochet, and Bruges Crochet.*

2 There are sections within the chapters giving explanations or exercises about that chapter's technique. Always read and work through these before embarking on a project; not only will you get to practise the technique but you will also discover how much that particular technique suits your style of crochet.

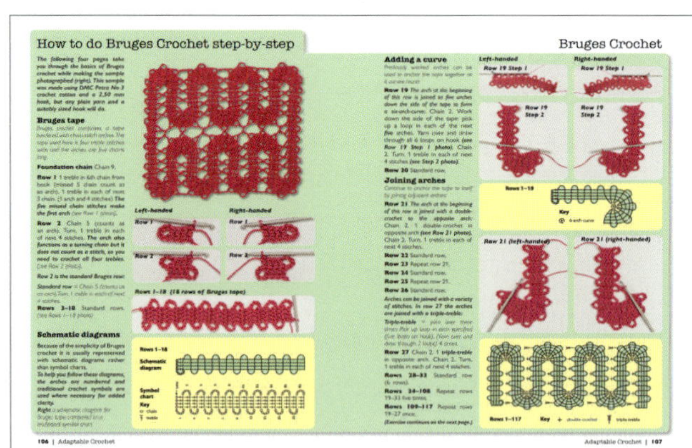

Right *A step-by-step exercise from the Bruges Crochet chapter.*

3 Before starting a project, take time to look through the whole chapter, because some projects have colour alternatives, or design options. If the yarn suggested isn't available, refer to the yarn substitution section on pages 10–11.

Right *Colour alternatives from the Pioneer Quilt chapter.*

Basic Stitches & Techniques

Chain stitch

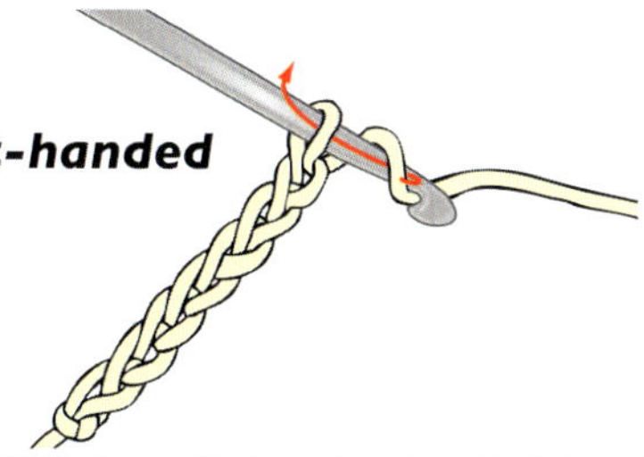

Left-handed

Yarn over and draw through loop on hook.

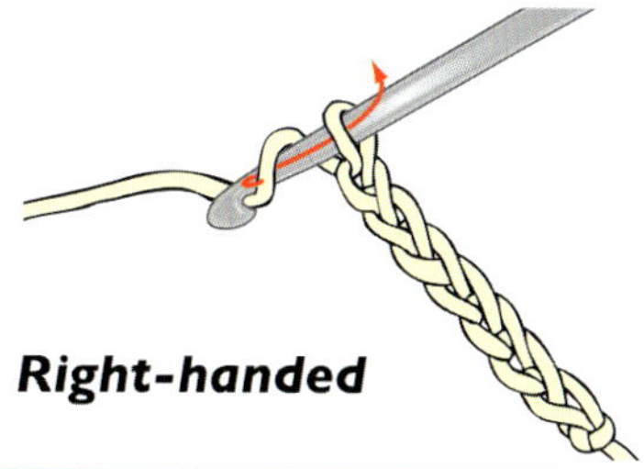

Right-handed

Counting chains

Count chains by counting backward from the hook. Omit both the loop on the hook, and the slip-knot.

Foundation chains

Spending time getting the foundation chain right can make a big difference to a finished project. If the first couple of rows of a project are narrower than the subsequent rows, the foundation chains were probably too small. If this happens, try using a larger sized hook, and swap back to the recommended hook for the first row.

To check your foundation chain is the correct tension, lay it against a sample of the project's stitch pattern. The width of the chains should closely match that of the stitches.

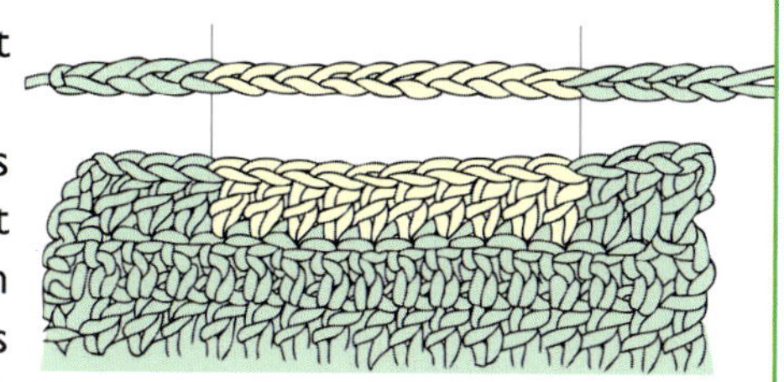

Above *Comparing a foundation chain to a sample of the project's stitch pattern.*

Turning chains

Alter the number of turning chains to suit your particular style.

Stitch	slip-stitch	double-crochet	half-treble	treble
No of chains	0 or 1 chain	1 or 2 chain	1 or 2 chain	2 or 3 chain

UK/USA Crochet terms

Adaptable Crochet uses standard UK terminology.

Right: *An approximate conversion guide for UK and USA yarns and hook sizes.*

UK Yarn	Metric Hook size	USA Yarn	Alternate Yarn Description	USA Hook size
20s thread	1.00 mm			11 or 10
	1.25 mm			9 or 8
10s thread	1.50 mm	0/Lace	Fingering, 2 ply	7
	1.75 mm			6 or 5
	2.00 mm		Cobweb, 3 ply	0
4 ply (thread)	2.50 mm	1/Super fine	Sock, Fingering	B or C
4 ply (yarn)	3.00 mm		Baby	C or D
	3.50 mm	2/Fine	Sport, 5 ply	E or F
Double knitting	4.00 mm	3/Light	Light worsted, 8 ply	F or G
	4.50 mm		Worsted	G or H
Aran	5.00 mm	4/Medium	Afghan, Worsted	H
	5.50 mm		10–12 ply	I
Chunky	6.00 mm	5/Bulky	Chunky, Craft, Rug	J

Below *UK/USA crochet terms.*

UK Terminology	USA Equivalent
slip-stitch	slip-stitch
double-crochet	single-crochet
half-treble	half-double-crochet
treble	double-crochet
double-treble	treble
triple-treble	double-treble

Basic Stitches & Techniques

Left-handed ***Right-handed***

"yarn over"

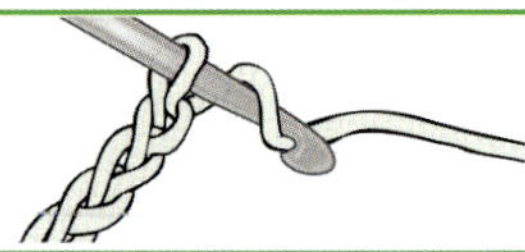

Scoop the yarn over the hook.

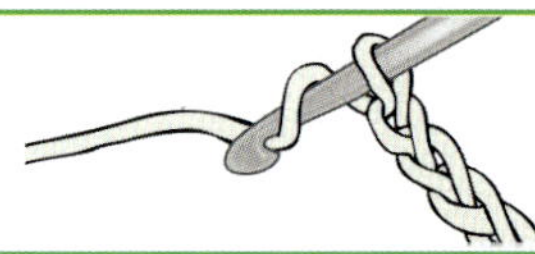

"draw through"

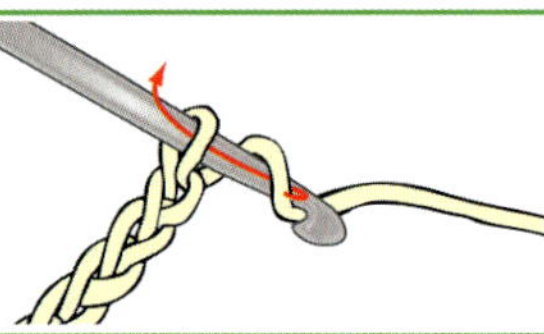

Draw the yarn which has just been scooped through the loop or loops which are already on the hook.

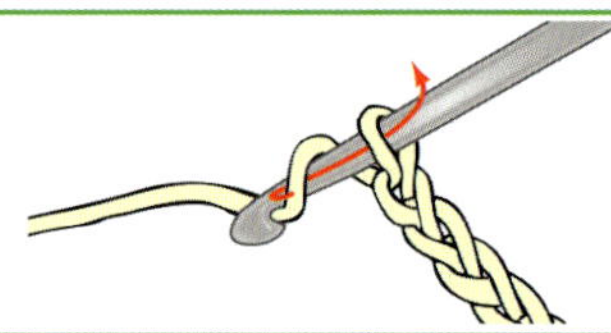

"in next stitch"

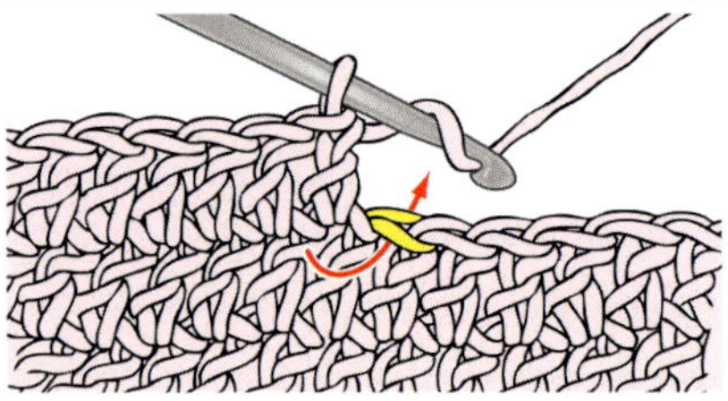

Insert the hook under the top two threads of the next stitch.

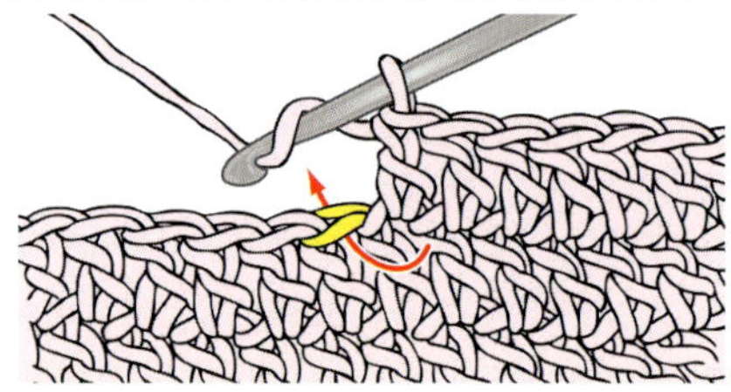

Identifying a stitch

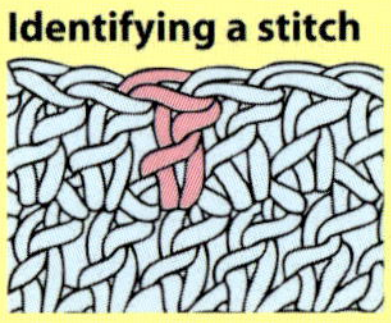

front view of a treble stitch

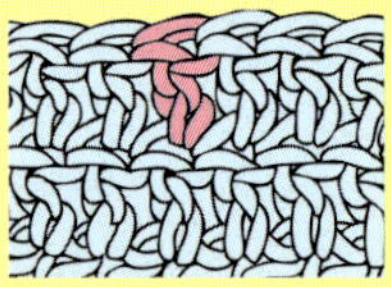

back view of a treble stitch

TIP The top of a stitch has a teardrop shape, the wider end of which sits over the post of the stitch. When crocheting rounds you will see the front of the stitch, when crocheting rows you will see the back of the stitch.

Identifying a stitch

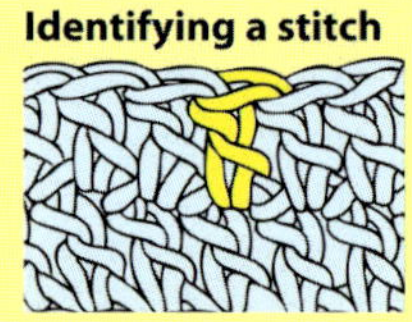

front view of a treble stitch

back view of a treble stitch

"in next space or chain-space"

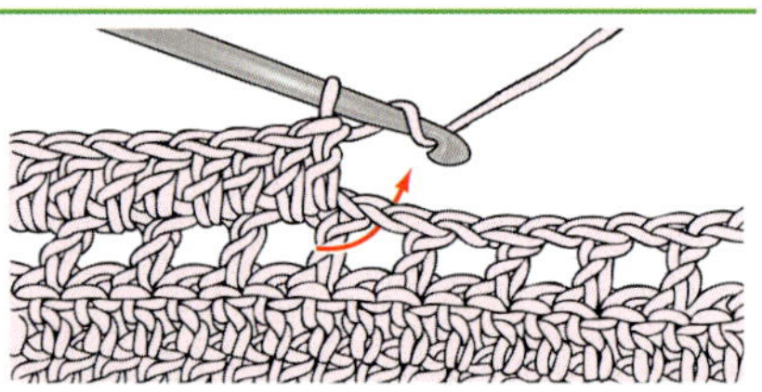

Insert hook *underneath* the chain or chains of the row below.

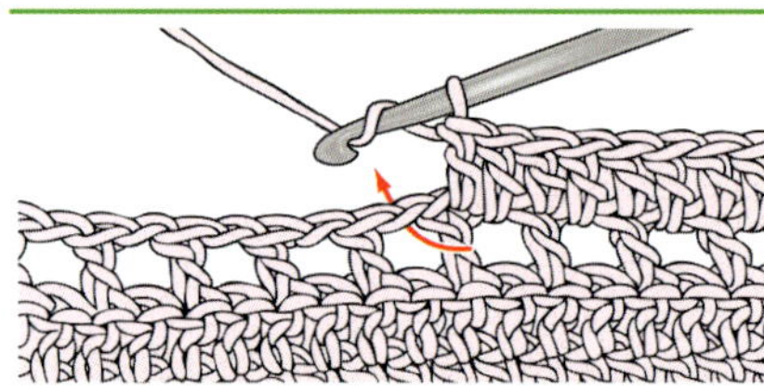

"pick up a loop"

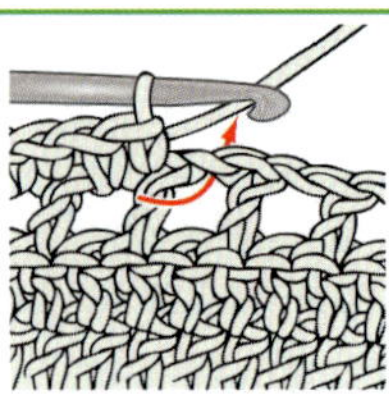

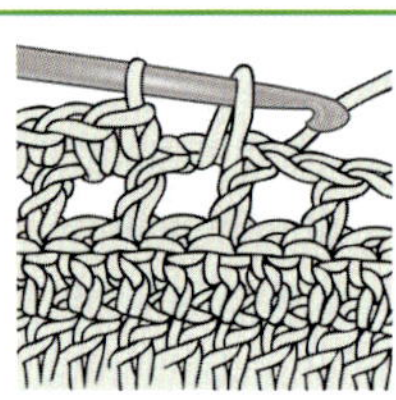

Insert hook into stitch or space specified. Yarn over and bring back through the stitch or space.

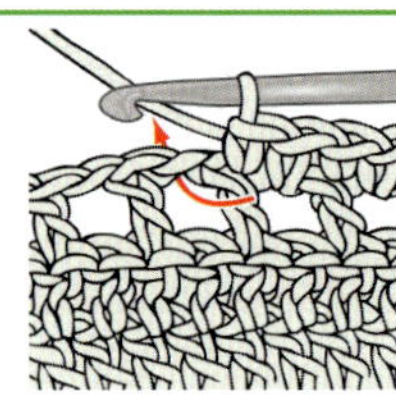

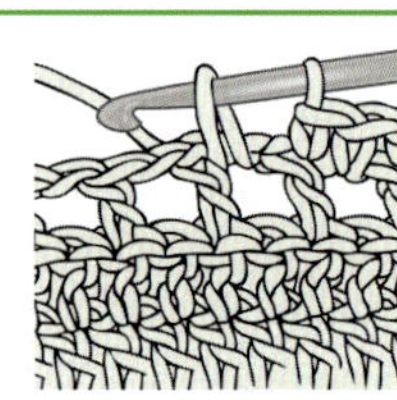

slip-stitch

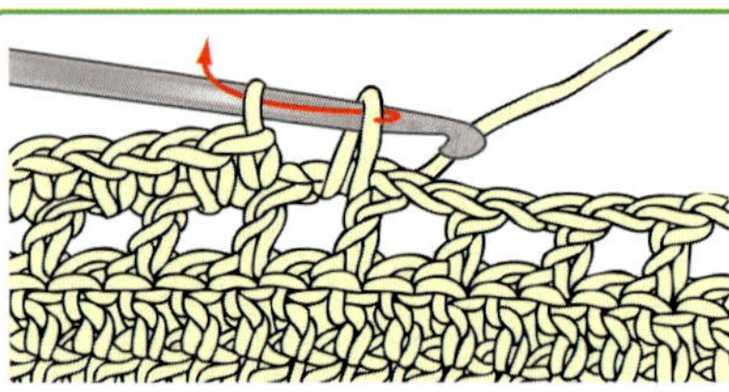

Pick up a loop in stitch or space indicated. Draw this loop through the loop on that is already on the hook.

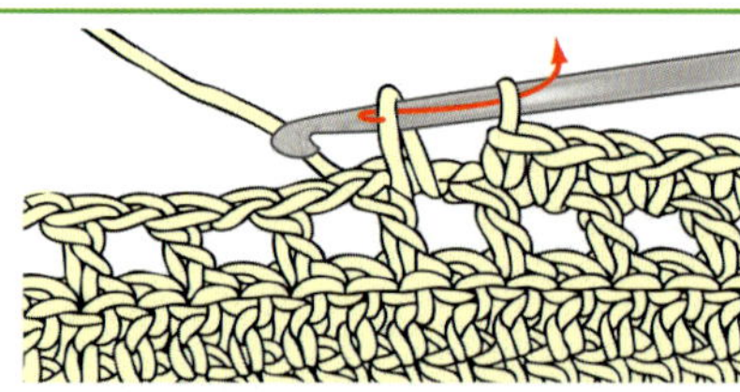

"slip-stitch to form ring"

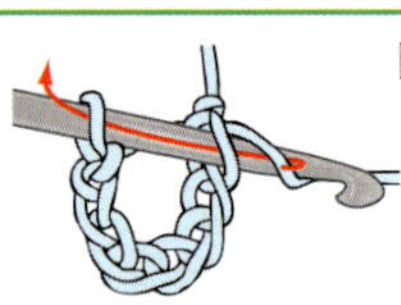

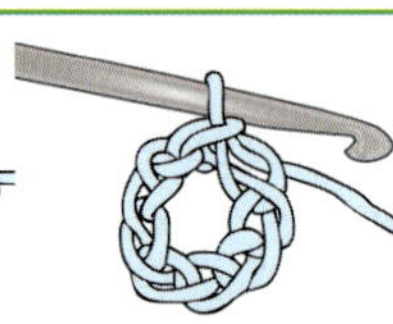

Join a length of chain by slip-stitching into the chain furthest from the hook.

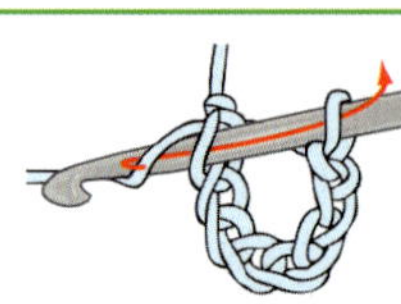

Basic Stitches & Techniques

Left-handed — ***Right-handed***

double-crochet

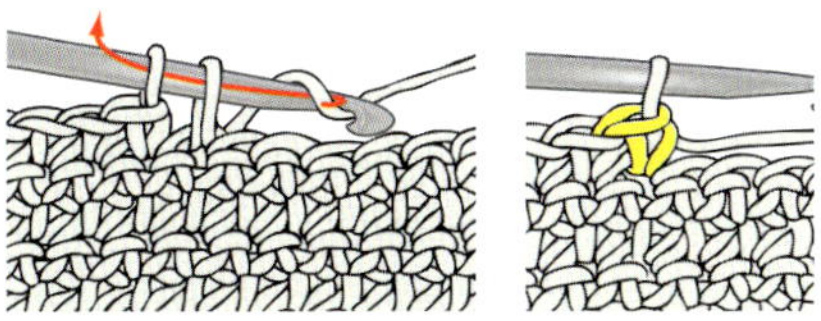

Pick up a loop in stitch or space indicated. Yarn over and draw through both loops on hook.

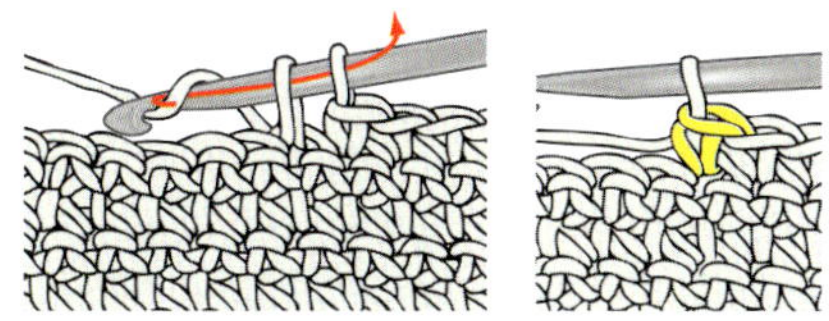

half-treble

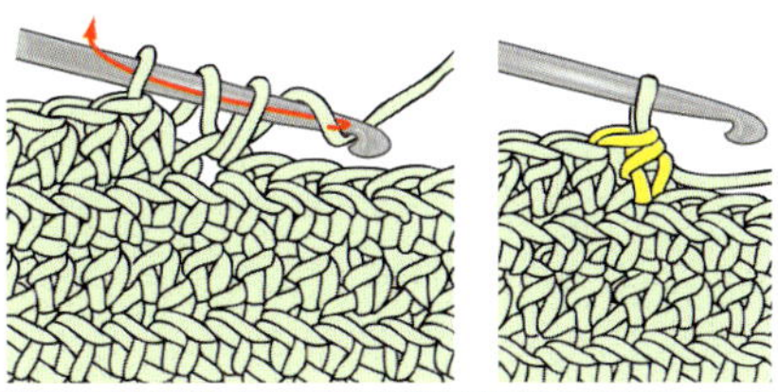

Yarn over. Pick up a loop from stitch or space. Yarn over and draw through all three loops on hook.

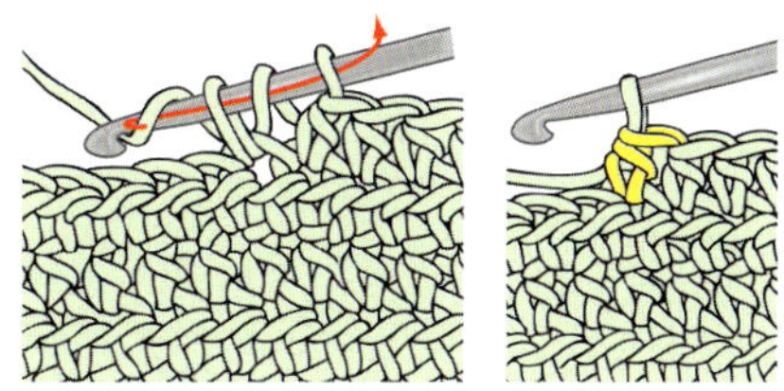

treble

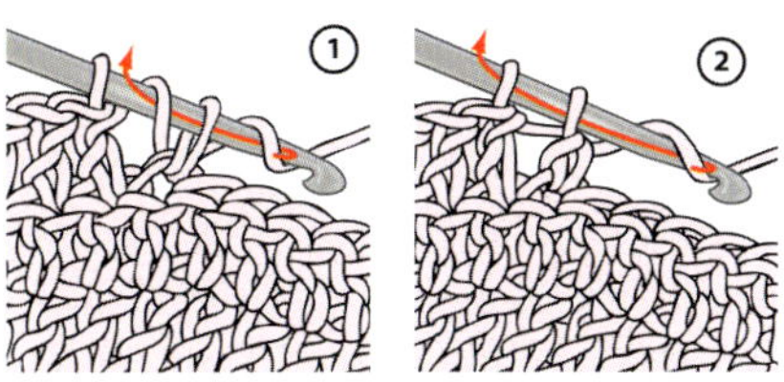

Yarn over. Pick up a loop from stitch or space. Yarn over and draw through two loops ***(step 1)***. Yarn over and draw through remaining two loops ***(step 2)***.

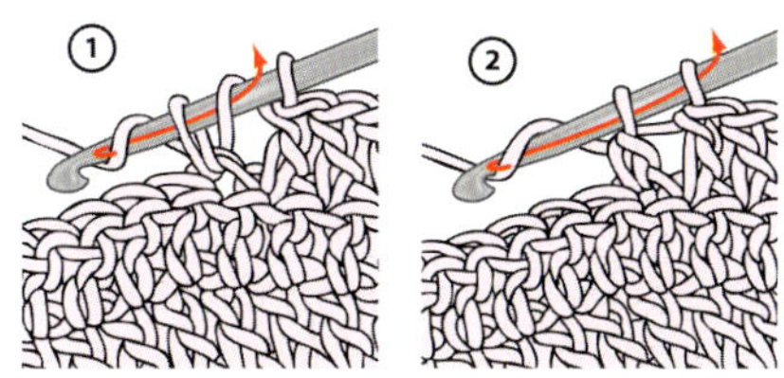

extended-treble

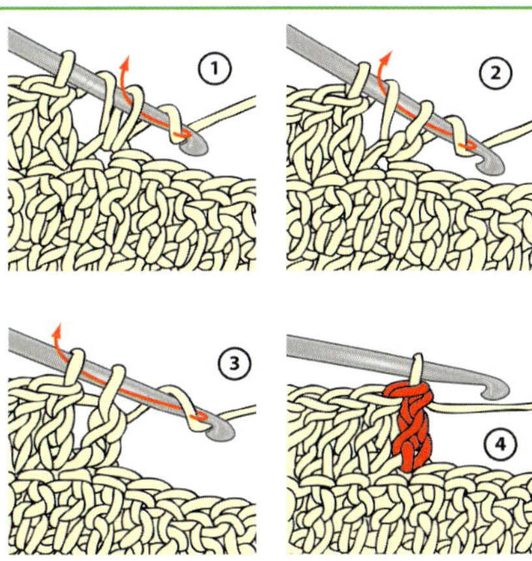

Yarn over. Pick up a loop from stitch or space. Yarn over and draw through one loop ***(step 1)***. Yarn over and draw through two loops ***(step 2)***. Yarn over and draw through remaining two loops on hook ***(step 3)***.

Step 4 shows completed extended-treble.

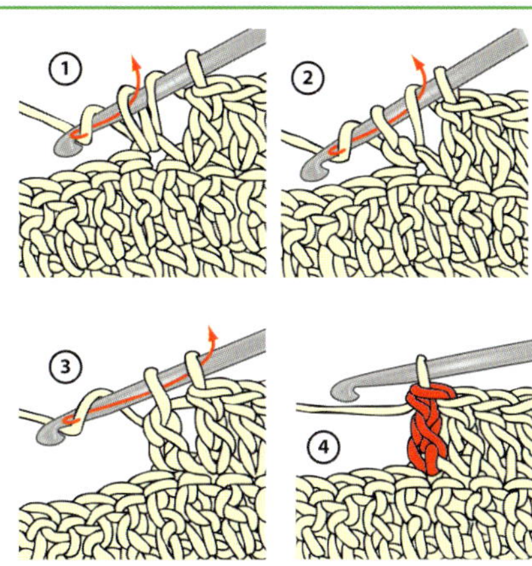

"swap yarn"

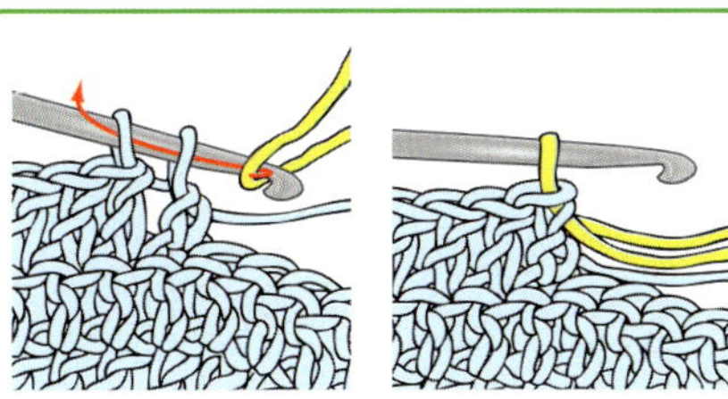

Undo the last draw through of the previous stitch and re-do draw through with yarn specified.

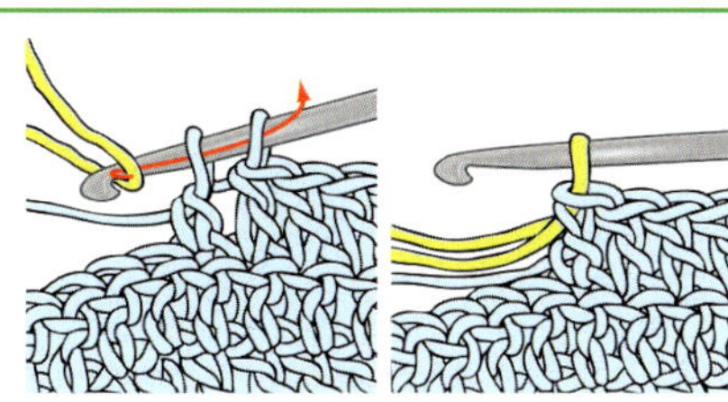

"fastening off"

Fasten off provisionally

Fasten off provisionally if you need to swap to another colour yarn at a later time.

Cut yarn leaving at least a 15 cm yarn-tail (leave more if using yarn-tail for sewing-up), and draw yarn-tail loosely through final stitch.

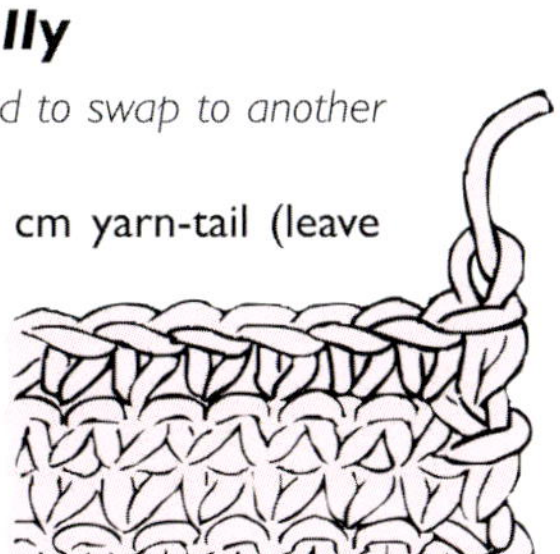

Fasten off

Follow instructions for ***fasten off provisionally*** (left), but tighten yarn-tail. Thread yarn-tail onto yarn needle, bring yarn-tail to back of work and weave through the ridges until well secured. Carefully snip yarn-tail close to work.

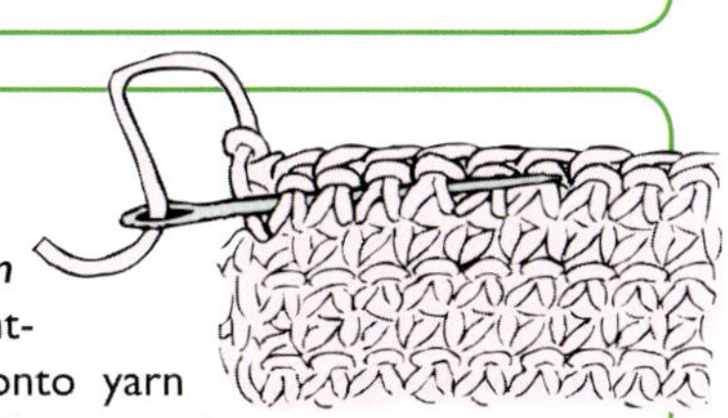

Sewing up

***Adaptable Crochet** includes some designs which involve sewing pieces of crochet together. You can, of course, use any sewing method you like, but the running stitch and weaving stitch techniques shown here are very versatile and were used for the projects photographed in this book.*

Materials

As well as a blunt ended wool needle you will need a length of yarn. This can either be a yarn-tail or a separate length of yarn.

Length of sewing yarn

The length of yarn required to sew a seam might be anywhere between 2½–4 times the distance being sewn depending on your choice of stitch and your personal tension. Bear in mind that a length of yarn that is longer than the distance between your nose and your arm's length will become unwieldy, so for longer seams you may need to use more than one length.

Yarn-tails

Plan ahead if you intend to use yarn-tails to sew your crochet together. Think about which tails you might need for sewing up and leave enough yarn on these tails before cutting. You can leave extra long tails at either the beginning or the end of the crochet, or both.

Tension

Perhaps the most important aspect of sewing crochet together is achieving a good "tension", in other words the degree of tightness or looseness of the stitches. There is really no hard and fast rule to tension; just practice first and decide for yourself how tight or loose you want the stitching to be.

Experiment first!

Running stitch, weaving stitch, single seam or double seam, tight or loose tension — what you choose will depend upon your personal choice and the type of item you are making. The only rule here is to experiment with different methods project by project.

How many threads?

At the top edge of a piece of crochet you will see pairs of threads forming a teardrop shape. With the methods shown here, only sew through ***one*** of these threads.

Running stitch

Running stitch is suitable for joining smaller pieces of crochet together, eg granny squares. It is usually worked on the wrong side of the crochet.

Running stitch instructions

Place the two pieces of crochet right sides together. Sew through the threads in the following sequence:

1 Downwards through a single thread of piece A.
2 Downwards through the corresponding single thread of piece B.
3 Upwards through the next single thread of piece B.
4 Upwards through the corresponding single thread of piece A.
5 Downwards through the next single thread of piece A.

Repeat steps 2–5.

Below *Right side view of two granny squares sewn together with running stitch.*

Below *Wrong side view of the same two granny squares sewn together with running stitch.*

Below *A contrasting yarn is used to illustrate how to sew two granny squares together with running stitch.*

Left-handed

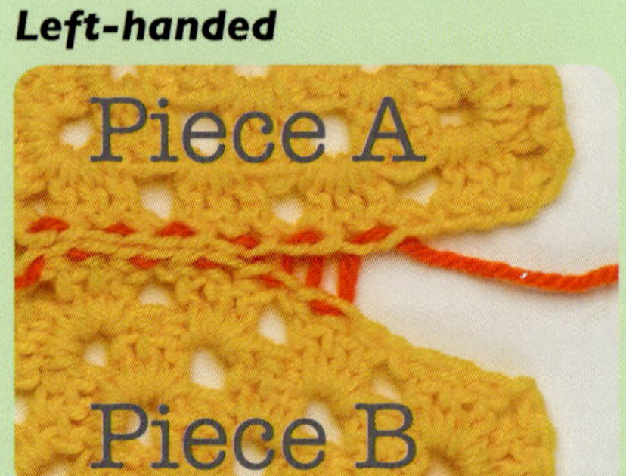

Right-handed

Sewing Up Techniques

Weaving stitch

Weaving stitch makes a sturdier seam than running stitch. From the front it looks very similar to running stitch, but a weaving stitch seam is fairly visible on the reverse. It is generally worked on the wrong side.

Below *Right side view of two granny squares sewn together with weaving stitch.*

Below *Wrong side view of same two granny squares sewn together with weaving stitch.*

Weaving stitch instructions

Place the two pieces of crochet right sides together. Sew through the threads in the following sequence:

1 Downwards through a single thread of piece A.
2 Downwards through the corresponding single thread of piece B.
3 Upwards through the next single thread of piece B.
4 Upwards through the most recently worked thread of piece A.
5 Downwards through the next single thread of piece A.
6 Downwards through the most recently worked single thread of piece B.

Repeat steps 3–6.

Left-handed

Left and right *A contrasting yarn is used to illustrate how to sew two granny squares together with weaving stitch.*

Right-handed

Sewing a top edge to a side edge

Left-handed

Both running stitch and weaving stitch can be used to join top and side edges of crochet together.

Left and right *weaving stitch joining a top edge to a side edge of crochet.*

Right-handed

Single and Double Seams

Single seam

All the illustrations on these pages show a single seam being made. In other words only one of the teardrop shaped threads from each piece is sewn through.

Double seam

After sewing a single seam, a double seam can be made by turning the work over and sewing through the remaining teardrop shaped threads from each piece.

Either running stitch or weaving stitch can be used for a double seam, but bear in mind that double seams can generally only be made when both edges feature teardrop shaped threads.

Substituting yarn

The yarns recommended in *Adaptable Crochet* are simply that — recommendations. If they are not to your taste or budget use the information on these pages to find substitutions.

Fibre content

Fibre content (see panel below) is the single most important thing to consider when substituting yarn. Look for a substitute yarn whose fibre content most closely matches the recommended yarn.

If the pattern suggests a yarn made from 100% cotton, but you use a yarn that is 100% acrylic, the finished article will probably not resemble the original, and may not even serve the intended purpose!

Sampling

Using a completely different fibre content may have a good outcome, of course, so whatever yarn you choose, always start by buying one ball of each shade you need and make samples to assess whether the shade and quality achieve the effect you are looking for. You can also launder your sample according to the ball band instructions to test how well it will withstand wear, tear and washing.

Discontinued yarns

It's a sad fact that as new yarns are developed, old ones are discontinued, so it is almost inevitable that you will need to find alternatives to the yarns suggested in *Adaptable Crochet* (and this is true of any crochet pattern you might like to try).

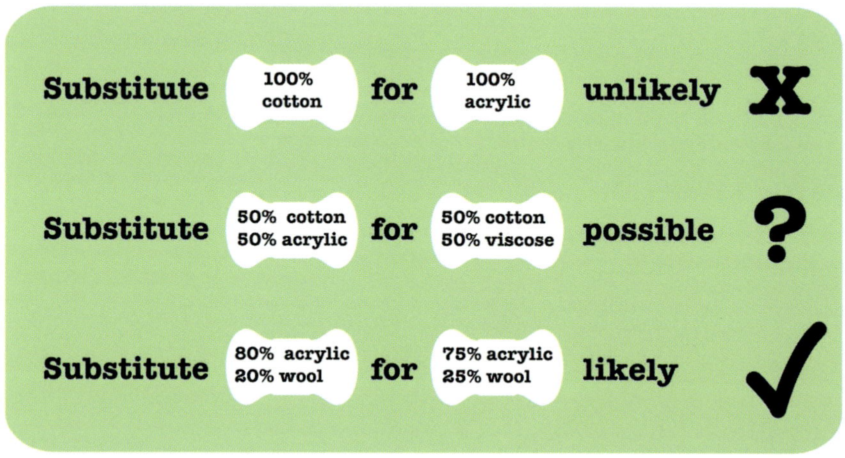

Right *When substituting yarn, try to find a similar fibre content.*

Fibre content

Information about the fibre content of yarn is listed on its ball band. The fibre content of your projects is always worth some thought.

Acrylic

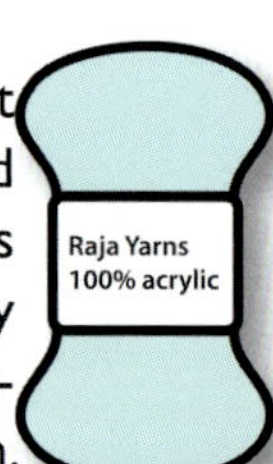

Acrylic is the most frequently found man-made fibre. It is economical, brightly coloured, and lightweight yet warm. Cheaper brands can feel scratchy to work with and may flatten after several washes. Nowadays spinners (yarn manufacturers) often use the prefix "premium" to denote a higher quality acrylic.

Wool

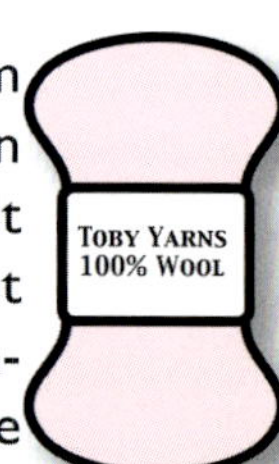

Wool makes a warm fabric with a certain amount of stretch. It dyes wonderfully but needs careful washing. Unless otherwise specified "wool" on a ball band refers to sheep's wool.

Cotton

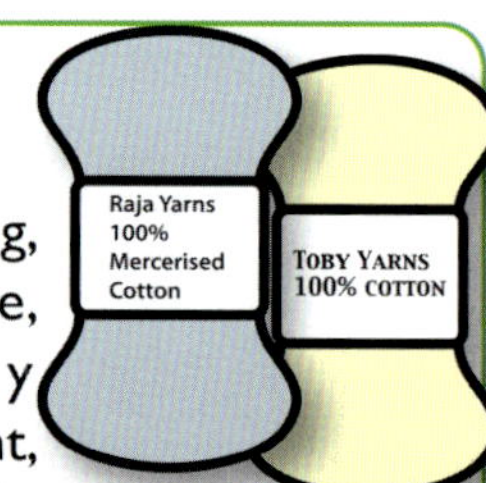

Cotton is strong, cool, durable, non-stretchy and absorbent, making it suitable for summer clothing and bags. Mercerised cotton has been specially treated to give it extra strength and a silky appearance.

Blend

Two different fibres are combined in one yarn for flexibility of use, eg a yarn that is 50% wool and 50% cotton would be both warm and absorbent.

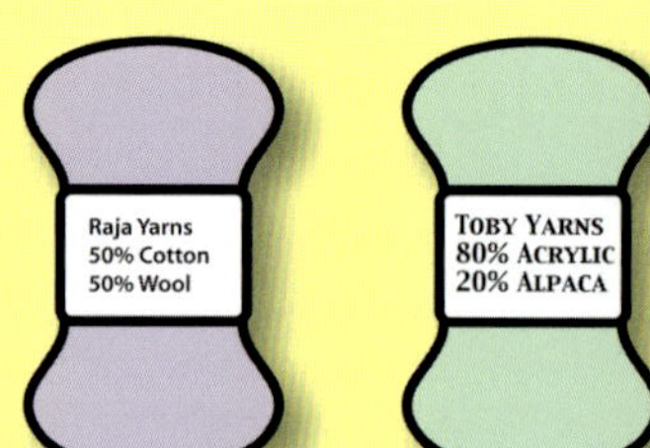

Substituting Yarn

Shades

Different colours of the same yarn are called **shades**. *All yarn will have a shade number listed on the ball band. Some will also give a shade name. (The "lot number" refers to a batch of yarn that was dyed at the same time.)*

In *Adaptable Crochet*, if a manufacturer has given a shade a name, it will be listed before the shade number:

***Shade** Fondant (510)*

If a yarn only has a shade number, an approximate description of the colour is given in swirly brackets after the shade number:

***Shade** (510) {white}*

Substituting Shades

Bear in mind that while some colours like black, navy, cream and white, will tend to be very similar from brand to brand, other shades, eg "red", may vary greatly.

Right *The Navy shades are very similar, but the Red shades look different.*

TIP The more shades in a project, the harder it will be to find substitutions.

Yarn thicknesses

The majority of projects in this book have been made in double-knitting, because there is such a vast choice in this thickness compared to 4 ply or aran.

The suggested thickness can be substituted, but bear in mind that this will affect the size of the finished project. Remember also to use an appropriate hook size (see yarn and hook sizes on page 5).

Below *Granny squares crocheted in three different thicknesses of Patons Merino Extrafine.*

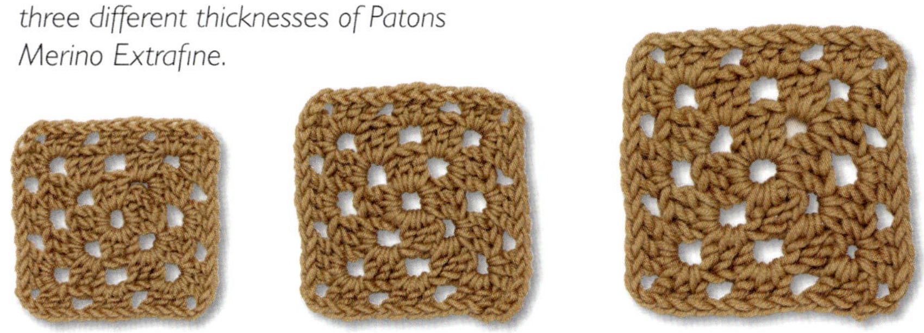

4 ply
3.5 mm hook
(7 x 7 cm)

double-knitting
4 mm hook
(7.75 x 7.75 cm)

aran
4.5 mm hook
(9.5 x 9.5 cm)

Yarn quantity

Yarn quantities in the *Adaptable Crochet* patterns are approximate because each crocheter will use differing amounts of yarn for the same project.

Below. *Six 50g balls would only need to be substituted with three 100g balls.*

Take care if your substitute yarn is sold in a different weight, for example, if a pattern specifies 3 x 100g balls of yarn, you would need up to twice as many 50g balls.

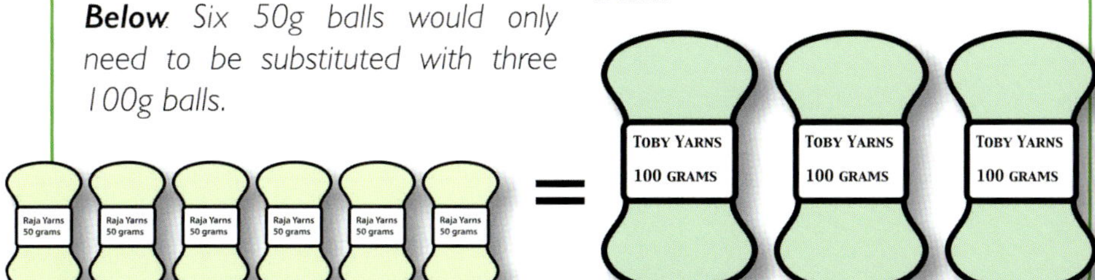

Classic v Fashion

Yarns are sometimes referred to as either *classic* or *fashion*. *Classic* yarns are those which have stood the test of time, and are likely to be available in the long term.

Fashion yarns have unusual qualities like added sparkles, innovative colour, integral stripes, slubs or "eyelashes". Once such novelties have worn off, these yarns are quickly discontinued!

Log Cabin Crochet is an easy technique that imitates traditional patchwork quilts of the same name. Little or no sewing is involved here though, because the coloured blocks are added by crocheting across the edges of previous blocks.

There are two versatile log cabin patterns to choose from: **Log Cabin Central** (photographed here), which is worked in one piece, and **Log Cabin Corner** (photographed on page 27) where seven coloured blocks are crocheted-as-you-go to make square sections which are then sewn together.

Log Cabin
Crochet

What is Log Cabin Crochet?

1 Log Cabin Crochet

Log Cabin Crochet imitates patchwork quilts of the same name. These quilts are characterised by square or rectangular blocks of different colours radiating outward from a central or corner block.

There are two different Log Cabin Crochet designs in this chapter.

TIP Before attempting either design, work through the step-by-step Log Cabin Exercise on pages 16–19.

Above *The Log Cabin Exercise is crocheted-as-you-go from the centre outwards. There is no sewing up. This exercise can be crocheted with any double knitting scrap yarn of different colours.*

Log Cabin Central

In the ***Log Cabin Central*** design pairs of colour blocks radiate outwards from a single central block. To increase the size of the design, simply add more pairs of colour blocks.

Above *The entire **Log Cabin Central** design is crocheted-as-you-go, from the centre outwards. There is no sewing up.*

Right *Individual **Log Cabin Corner** sections are crocheted-as-you-go and then sewn or crocheted together.*

Log Cabin Corner

In the ***Log Cabin Corner*** design, rectangular colour blocks stack against the corner of a square block to create a section. Sections are then sewn or crocheted together. This pattern can be used to make square or rectangular designs. The size of the design can be easily altered by changing the number of sections.

Left *A Log Cabin Corner section.*

2 The Log Cabin Crochet Stitch Pattern

Both Log Cabin Crochet designs use the same stitch pattern. This is a simple repeat of 3 trebles and 1 chain. The stitch pattern is staggered on alternate rows.

Top right *A symbol chart showing the Log Cabin Crochet stitch pattern of 3 trebles and 1 chain.*

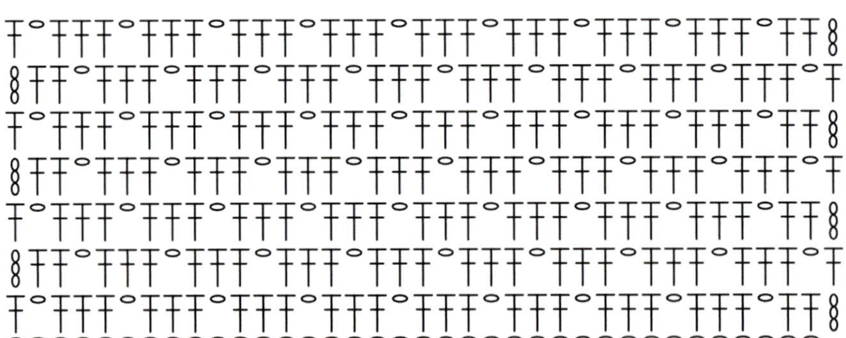

Bottom right *The chain-spaces are staggered on alternate rows to create a light and supple fabric.*

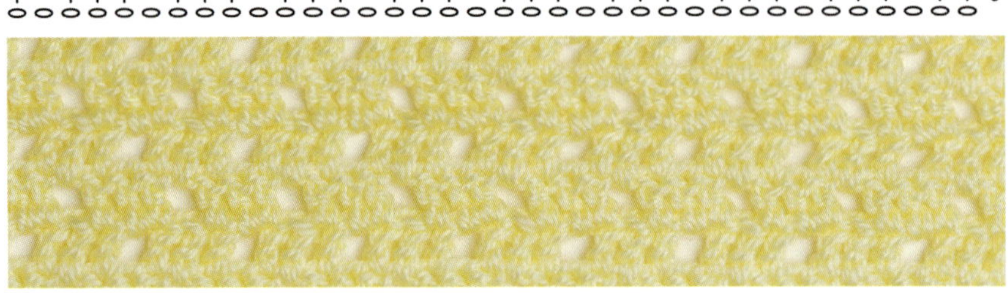

3 The Log Cabin Crochet Block numbers

Each colour block is allocated a number. Start by crocheting Block 1 and continue adding colour blocks in numerical order.

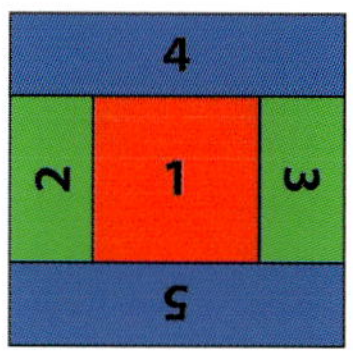

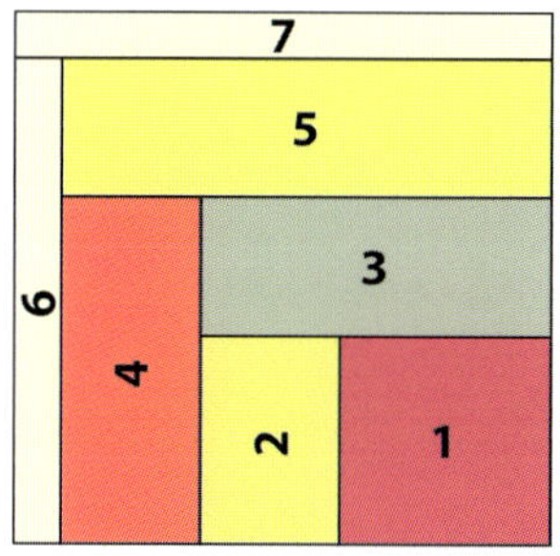

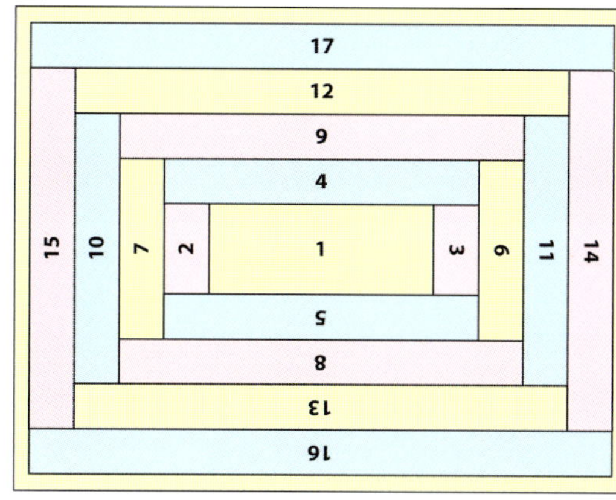

4 Rotating the work

New colour blocks are added by working across the edges of one or more previous colour blocks. In order to do this, the work is rotated at the start of a new colour block.

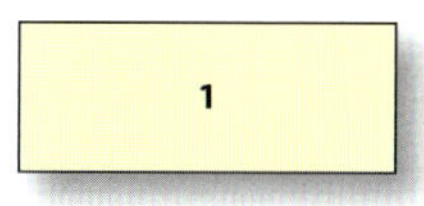

Top and right *Colour Block 1 is rotated so that Colour Block 2 can be worked along the side edge.*

5 Left-handed crocheters

The Log Cabin Crochet instructions, symbol charts, and colour block diagrams can be used by both right-handed and left-handed crocheters. But since left-handed crocheters will rotate their work in the opposite direction to right-handers, they may find it easier to refer to the colour block diagrams here.

Below *Log Cabin Exercise colour block placement diagram for left-handers (see page 16).*

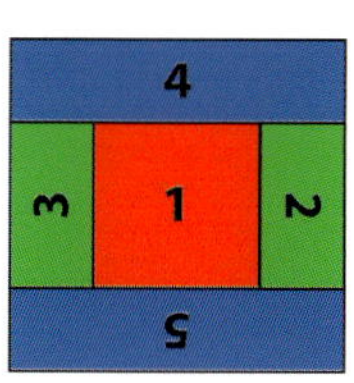

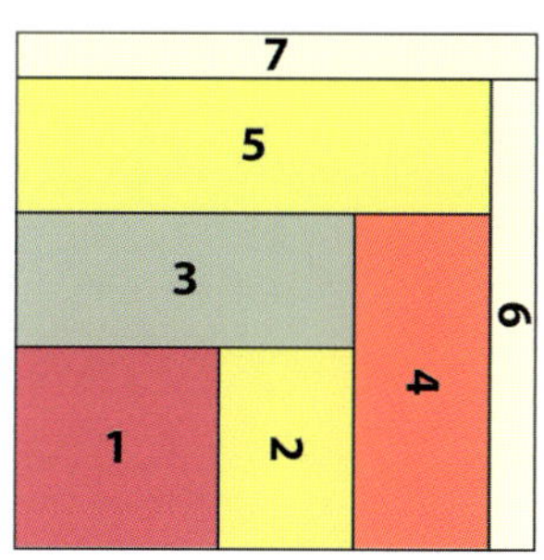

Above *Log Cabin Corner colour block diagram for left-handers (see page 26).*

Below *Log Cabin Central colour block diagram for left-handers (see page 20).*

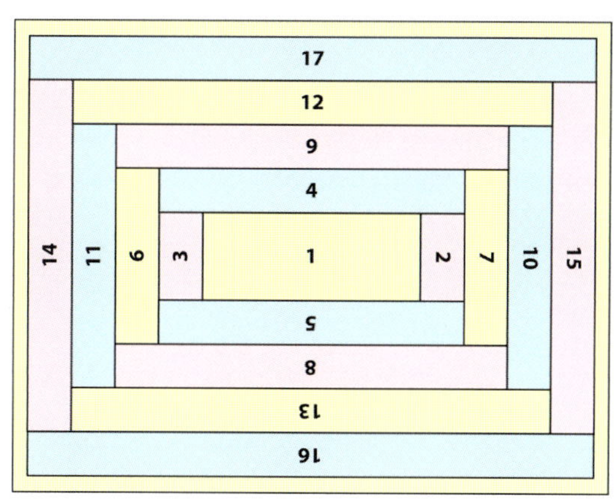

Log Cabin Crochet step-by-step exercise

Working through this step-by-step exercise will give you all techniques you need to complete the two Log Cabin designs. (Left-handed crocheters can also refer to the colour block diagram at the bottom left of page 15.)

TIP The instructions refer to red, green and blue yarn, but you can use any three colours. Use a hook appropriate for your yarn.

Below *Log Cabin Exercise Colour Block placement diagram.*

Below *Log Cabin Exercise symbol chart for Colour Block 1.*

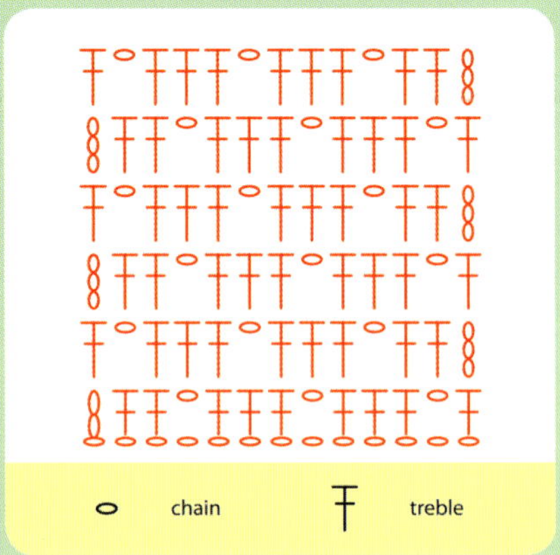

Colour Block 1

TIP All log cabin colour blocks should have rows consisting of groups of 3-trebles, plus one final treble at the end of the row.

Foundation chain With red yarn, chain 15.

Row 1 1 treble in 4th chain from hook (missed 3 chain counts as 1 treble). 1 treble in next chain. (Chain 1. Skip next chain. 1 treble in each of next 3 chains.) 2 times. Chain 1. Skip next chain. 1 treble in last chain. (3 groups of 3-trebles plus one final treble)

Rows 2–6 Chain 3 (counts as 1 treble). Turn. 1 treble in next chain-space. 1 treble in next stitch. (Chain 1. Skip next stitch. 1 treble in next stitch. 1 treble in next chain-space. 1 treble in next stitch.) 2 times. Chain 1. Skip next stitch. 1 treble in last stitch. (3 groups of 3-trebles, plus one final treble.)

The side facing you as you work row 6 is the right side.

Swap to green yarn at end of 6th row (see page 7).

Rotating colour blocks

Left-handed

After swapping to green yarn, rotate the work so that you can continue to crochet along the side edge of colour block 1.

Left *Left-handed crocheters will rotate a quarter turn anti-clockwise.*

Right *Right-handed crocheters will rotate a quarter turn clockwise.*

Right-handed

Understanding the terms "edge-spaces" and "row-joints"

A common challenge when working across the side edge of crochet is ensuring that you end up with the correct number of evenly spaced stitches. To help you place your stitches evenly, two features of the side edge have been given names: "edge-spaces" and "row-joints".

Left-handed

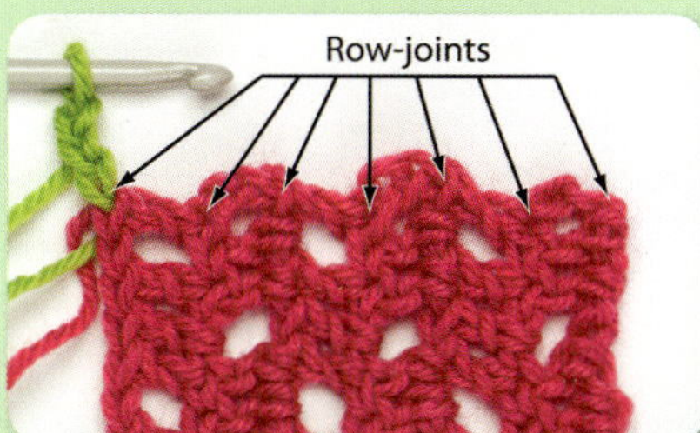

"edge-space"

The edge-spaces are the large holes formed by the final chain-space in a row. There are 3 edge-spaces along the side edge of colour block 1.

The hook is inserted inside the edge-space when making a treble.

"row-joint"

The row-joints are the places where the rows meet. There are 7 row-joints along the side edge of colour block 1. The starting chain sits over the first row-joint.

Right-handed

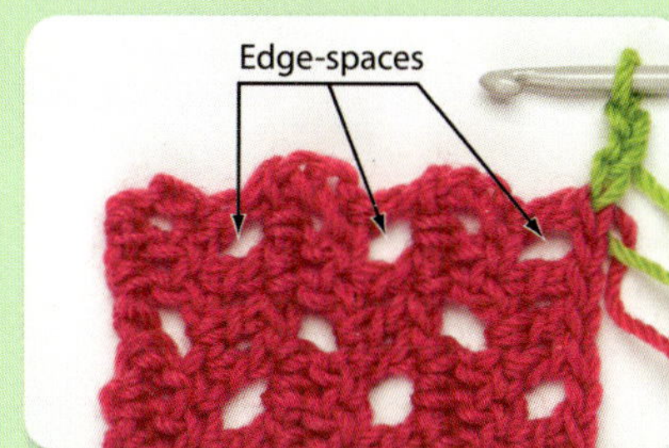

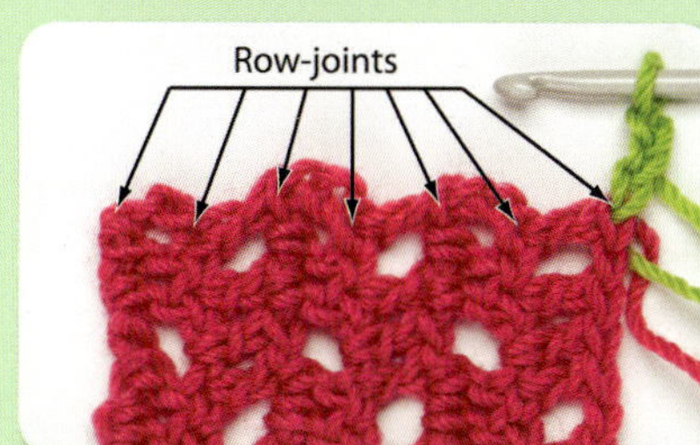

Take a look at the side edge of your Colour Block 1 and identify the three edge-spaces and seven row-joints so that you know where to place the trebles for the first row of Colour Block 2.

Edge-spaces are relatively easy to identify whereas row-joints are harder to find. It doesn't matter exactly where you place the hook in a row-joint; simply massage the hook into the row-joint to find an opening.

Colour Block 2

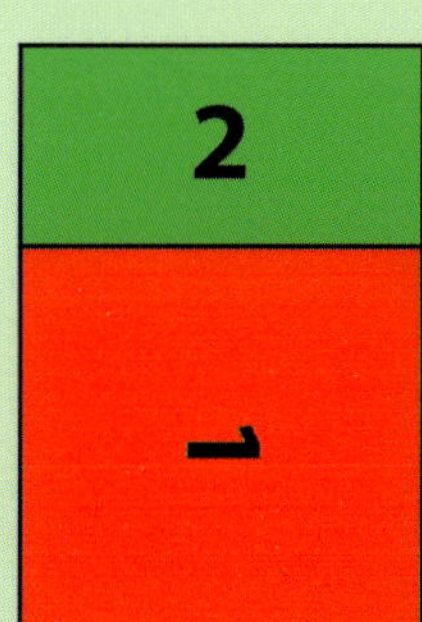

With right side still facing, rotate the work and crochet across edge of Block 1 with green yarn as follows:

Row 1 Chain 3 (counts as 1 treble). 1 treble in next edge-space ***(see above)***. 1 treble in next row-joint ***(see above)***. (Chain 1. 1 treble in next row-joint. 1 treble in next edge-space. 1 treble in next row-joint.) 2 times. Chain 1. 1 treble in last row-joint. (3 groups of 3-trebles, plus 1 final treble)

Rows 2–5 Chain 3 (counts as 1 treble). Turn. 1 treble in next chain-space. 1 treble in next stitch. (Chain 1. Skip next stitch. 1 treble in next stitch. 1 treble in next chain-space. 1 treble in next stitch.) 2 times. Chain 1. Skip next stitch. 1 treble in last stitch. (3 groups of 3-trebles, plus one final treble.)

Fasten off provisionally at end of row 5 (see page 7).

TIP The stitch pattern may not be apparent after crocheting the first row of a new colour block, but rest assured that it will emerge after a few rows.

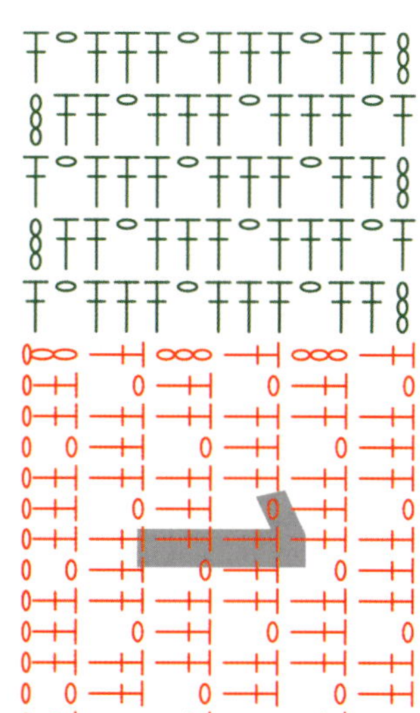

Log Cabin Square exercise continued

Colour Block 3

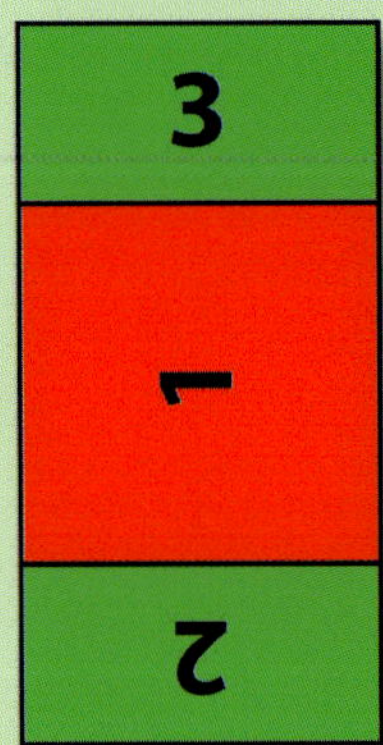

With the right side facing, join green yarn with a slip-stitch to corner-space of opposite side edge of Block 1 and repeat instructions for Block 2.
Swap to blue yarn at the end of row 5.

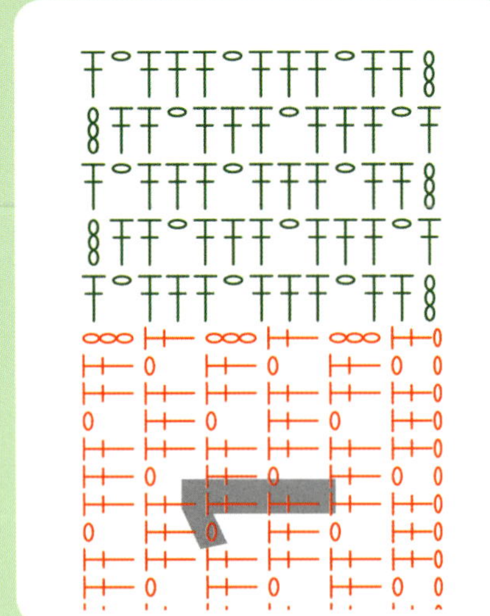

Working across two or more colour blocks

The first row of Block 4 is crocheted across Blocks 3, 1, and 2 in that order. Take extra care when crocheting across previously joined blocks. Check at the end of row 1 that you have 8 groups of 3-trebles plus one final treble. Refer to the symbol chart if necessary.

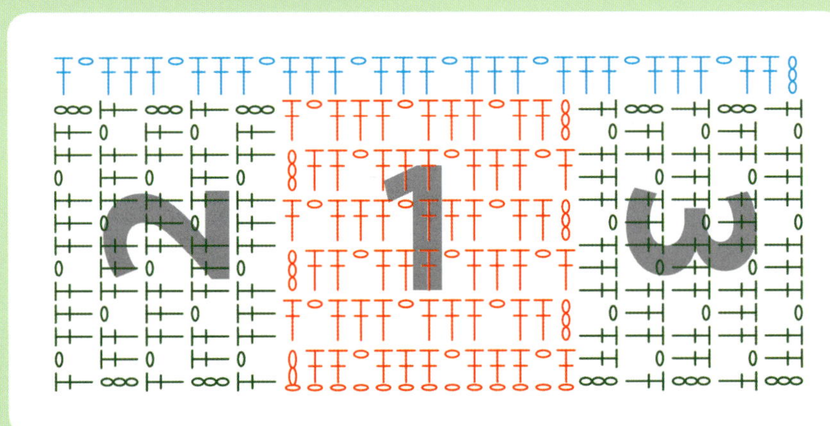

Right *Log Cabin Square symbol chart showing first row of Block 4 worked across Blocks 3, 1 and 2.*

Colour Block 4

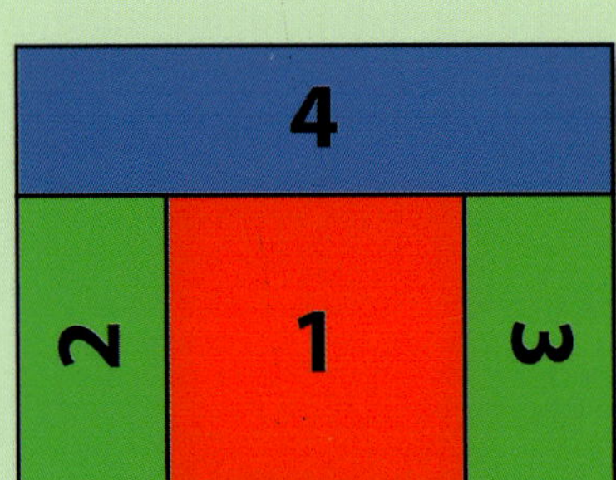

With right side facing, rotate work and crochet across edges of Blocks 3, 1 and 2 with blue yarn as follows:

Row 1 Chain 3 (counts as 1 treble). 1 treble in next edge-space. 1 treble in next row-joint. (Chain 1. 1 treble in next row-joint. 1 treble in next edge-space. 1 treble in next row-joint.) 2 times. *Now work across the top of Block 1. (Study the symbol chart if you are not sure where to place the trebles.)* (Chain 1. Skip next stitch. 1 treble in next stitch. 1 treble in next chain-space. 1 treble in next stitch.) 3 times. *Now work across the edge of Block 2.* (Chain 1. 1 treble in next row-joint. 1 treble in next edge-space. 1 treble in next row-joint.) 2 times. Chain 1. 1 treble in last row-joint. (8 groups of 3-trebles, plus 1 final treble)

Rows 2–5 Chain 3 (counts as 1 treble). Turn. 1 treble in next chain-space. 1 treble in next stitch. (Chain 1. Skip next stitch. 1 treble in next stitch. 1 treble in next chain-space. 1 treble in next stitch.) 7 times. Chain 1. Skip next stitch. 1 treble in last stitch. (8 groups of 3-trebles, plus one final treble.)

Fasten off provisionally at end of row 5.

Foundation chain trebles

Left-handed

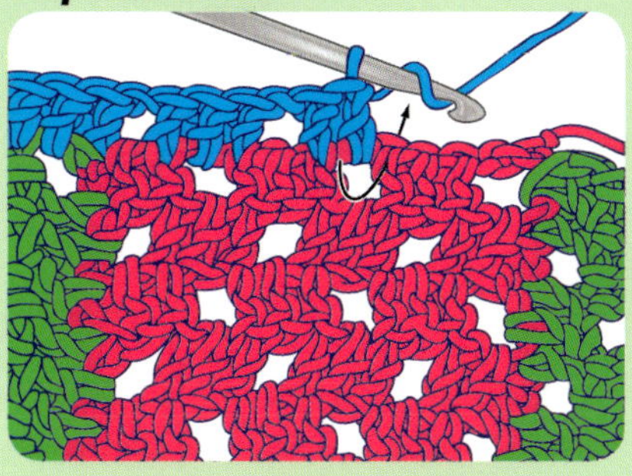

The middle of the first row of Block 5 is worked across the foundation chain edge of Block I.

Work these trebles by inserting the hook between the bottom two strands of the foundation chain trebles (see illustration)

This technique is used in all the Log Cabin patterns.

Right-handed

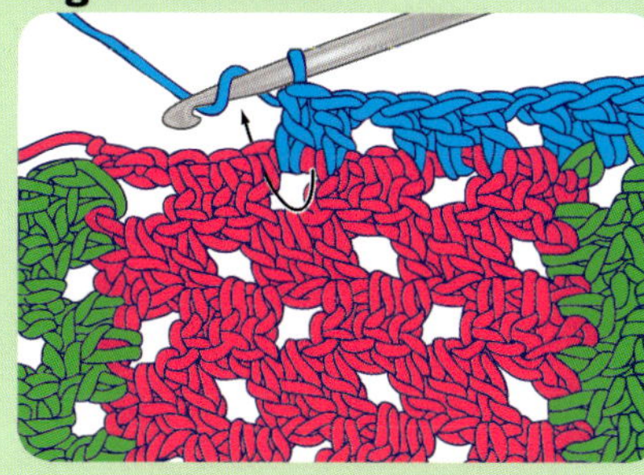

Colour Block 5

FCT = *Foundation Chain Treble*

With right side facing, undo provisional fasten off from block 2 and swap to blue yarn. Rotate work and crochet across edges of Blocks 2, I and 3 as follows:

Row I Chain 3 (counts as 1 treble). 1 treble in next edge-space. 1 treble in next row-joint. (Chain 1. 1 treble in next row-joint. 1 treble in next edge-space. 1 treble in next row-joint.) 2 times. *Now work across the bottom of Block I*. (Chain 1. Skip next FCT. 1 treble in next FCT. 1 treble in next chain-space. 1 treble in next FCT.) 3 times. *Now work across the edge of Block 3.* (Chain 1. 1 treble in next row-joint. 1 treble in next edge-space. 1 treble in next row-joint.) 2 times. Chain 1. 1 treble in last row-joint. (8 groups of 3-trebles, plus 1 final treble)

Rows 2–5 Chain 3 (counts as 1 treble). Turn. 1 treble in next chain-space. 1 treble in next stitch. (Chain 1. Skip next stitch. 1 treble in next stitch. 1 treble in next chain-space. 1 treble in next stitch.) 7 times. Chain 1. Skip next stitch. 1 treble in last stitch. (8 groups of 3-trebles, plus one final treble.)

Adding More Colour Blocks

You can either fasten off at the end of Block 5, or swap to another yarn and continue adding colour blocks. A symbol chart showing another four colour blocks is provided to help you.

When you add a new block, check that the first row has the right number of 3-treble groups, as well as one final treble at the end of the row. ***In this particular design***, the number of 3-treble groups increases by 5 with each additional two pairs of blocks.

Colour Block	Number of 3-treble groups
I, 2 & 3	*3*
4, 5, 6 & 7	*8*
8, 9, 10 & II	*13*

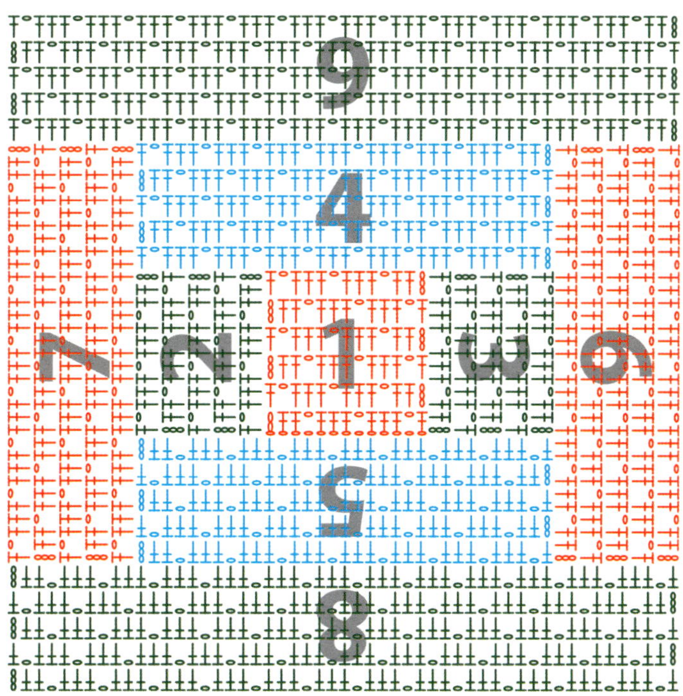

Log Cabin Central Design

This Log Cabin Central Design (photographed at the start of the chapter) has been worked in traditional "baby" shades. Of course you do not have to restrict yourself to pastels; any three colours will do. Some "grown up" colour combinations, and general advice about adapting this design can be found on pages 24–25.

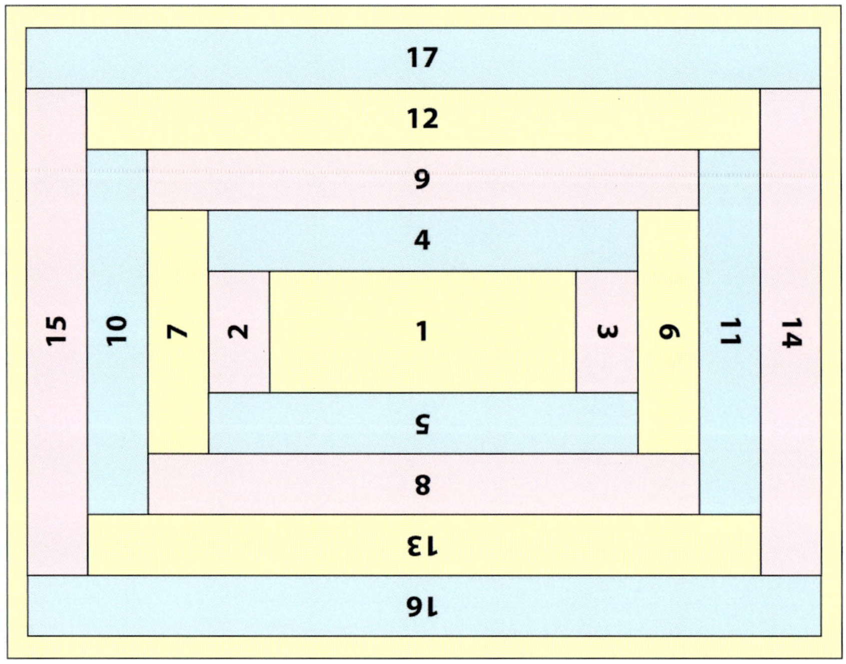

Right The Log Cabin Central Colour Block Diagram. (Left-handed crocheters can also refer to the colour block diagram at the bottom right of page 15.)

Lemon
Blocks 1, 6, 7, 12, 13 & edging

Baby Pink Marl
Blocks 2, 3, 8, 9, 14 & 15

Baby Denim Marl
Blocks 4, 5, 10, 11, 16 & 17

Materials

***Yarn** Bernat Softee Baby*
***Composition** 100% acrylic*
***Yardage** 331 metres (362 yards) approx*
Shades

- *2 x 140g balls Lemon (2003)*
- *1 x 140g balls Baby Pink Marl (30301)*
- *2 x 140g balls Baby Denim Marl (30300)*

***Hook** 4.00 mm*
***Finished size** 110 x 85 cm (43 x 33")*
***Tension** The centre block (Block 1) measures approximately 40 x 16 cm (16 x 6")*

TIP Unusually, this yarn is sold in 140g balls. Refer to page 25 to work out how much you would need for each set of colour blocks if you choose a different yarn.

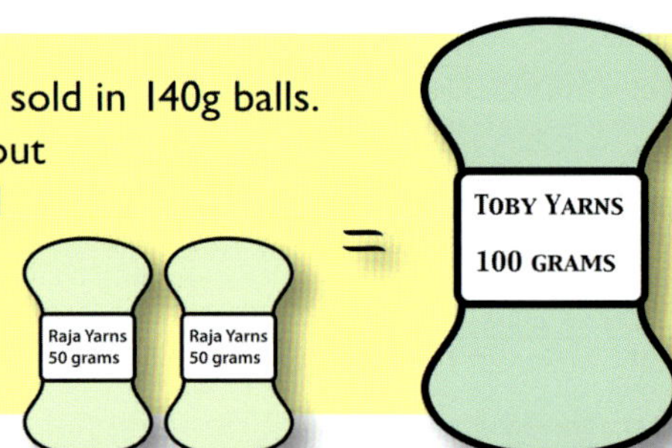

Instructions

*Familiarise yourself with **all** the information on pages 14–15 and crochet the Log Cabin Square exercise on pages 16–19 before starting this lengthy project.*

TIP Blocks 2–17 all start with the right side facing.

Colour Block 1

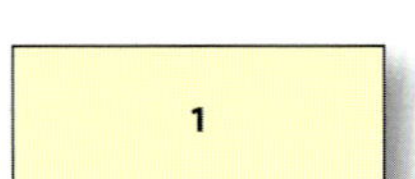

Foundation chain With yarn specified, chain 71.

Row 1 1 treble in 4th chain from hook (missed 3 chain count as 1 treble). 1 treble in next chain. (Chain 1. Skip next chain. 1 treble in each of next 3 chains.) 16 times. Chain 1. Skip next chain. 1 treble in last chain. (17 groups of 3-trebles plus one final treble)

Rows 2–14 Chain 3 (counts as 1 treble). Turn. 1 treble in next chain-space. 1 treble in next stitch. (Chain 1. Skip next stitch. 1 treble in next stitch. 1 treble in next chain-space. 1 treble in next stitch.) 16 times. Chain 1. Skip next stitch. 1 treble in last stitch. (17 groups of 3-trebles plus one final treble.)

(The side facing you as you work the 14th row is the right side of the work.)

Swap to yarn specified for Block 2 at end of 14th row.

Colour Block 2

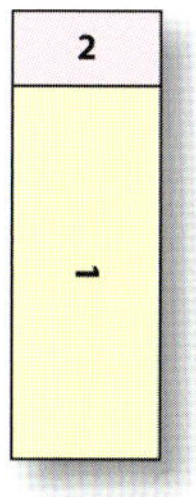

Rotate the work and crochet across edge of Block 1 with yarn specified for Block 2 as follows:

Row 1 Chain 3 (counts as 1 treble). 1 treble in next edge-space. 1 treble in next row-joint. (Chain 1. 1 treble in next row-joint. 1 treble in next edge-space. 1 treble in next row-joint.) 6 times. Chain 1. 1 treble in last row-joint. (7 groups of 3-trebles, plus 1 final treble)

Rows 2–7 Chain 3 (counts as 1 treble). Turn. 1 treble in next chain-space. 1 treble in next stitch. (Chain 1. Skip next stitch. 1 treble in next stitch. 1 treble in next chain-space. 1 treble in next stitch.) 6 times. Chain 1. Skip next stitch. 1 treble in last stitch. (7 groups of 3-trebles, plus one final treble.)

Fasten off provisionally at end of row 7.

Colour Block 3

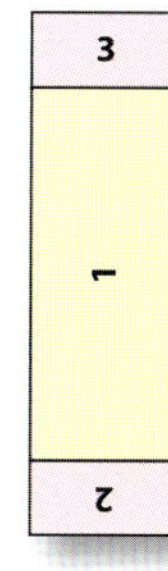

With the right side facing, join yarn with a slip-stitch to corner space of opposite side of Block 1 and repeat instructions for Block 2.

Swap to yarn specified for Block 4 at the end of row 7.

Colour Block 4

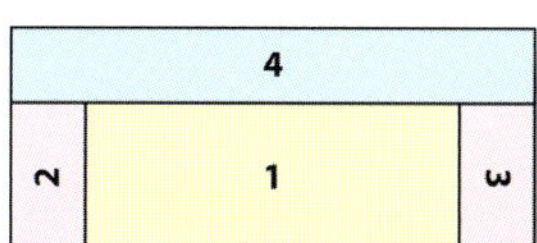

Rotate work and crochet across edges of Blocks 3, 1 and 2 with yarn specified for Block 4 as follows:

Row 1 Chain 3 (counts as 1 treble). 1 treble in next edge-space. 1 treble in next row-joint. (Chain 1. 1 treble in next row-joint. 1 treble in next edge-space. 1 treble in next row-joint.) 3 times. *Now work across the top of Block 1.* (Chain 1. Skip next stitch. 1 treble in next stitch. 1 treble in next chain-space. 1 treble in next stitch.) 17 times. *Now work across the edge of Block 2.* (Chain 1. 1 treble in next row-joint. 1 treble in next edge-space. 1 treble in next row-joint.) 3 times. Chain 1. 1 treble in last row-joint. (24 groups of 3-trebles, plus 1 final treble)

Rows 2–7 Chain 3 (counts as 1 treble). Turn. 1 treble in next chain-space. 1 treble in next stitch. (Chain 1. Skip next stitch. 1 treble in next stitch. 1 treble in next chain-space. 1 treble in next stitch.) 23 times. Chain 1. Skip next stitch. 1 treble in last stitch. (24 groups of 3-trebles, plus one final treble.)

Fasten off provisionally at end of row 7.

Colour Block 5

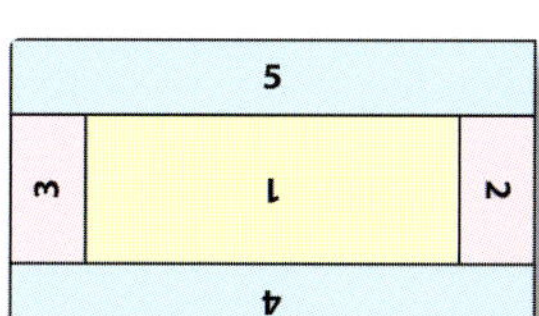

FCT = Foundation Chain Treble

With right side facing, undo provisional fasten off from Block 2 and swap to yarn specified for Block 5. Rotate work and crochet across edges of Blocks 2, 1 and 3 as follows:

Row 1 Chain 3 (counts as 1 treble). 1 treble in next edge-space. 1 treble in next row-joint. (Chain 1. 1 treble in next row-joint. 1 treble in next edge-space. 1 treble in next row-joint.) 3 times. *Now work across the bottom of Block 1.* (Chain 1. Skip next FCT. 1 treble in next FCT. 1 treble in next chain-space. 1 treble in next FCT.) 17 times. *Now work across the edge of Block 3.* (Chain 1. 1 treble in next row-joint. 1 treble in next edge-space. 1 treble in next row-joint.) 3 times. Chain 1. 1 treble in last row-joint. (24 groups of 3-trebles, plus 1 final treble)

Rows 2–7 Chain 3 (counts as 1 treble). Turn. 1 treble in next chain-space. 1 treble in next stitch. (Chain 1. Skip next stitch. 1 treble in next stitch. 1 treble in next chain-space. 1 treble in next stitch.) 23 times. Chain 1. Skip next stitch. 1 treble in last stitch. (24 groups of 3-trebles, plus one final treble.)

Swap to yarn specified for Block 6 at the end of row 7.

Log Cabin Central Design (continued)

Colour Block 6

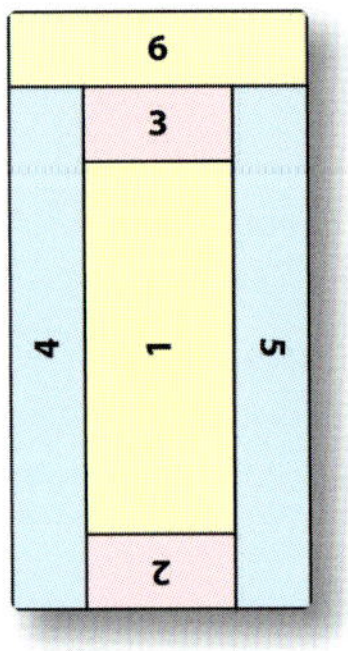

Rotate work and crochet across edge of Blocks 5, 3 and 4 with yarn specified for Block 6 as follows:

Row 1 Chain 3 (counts as 1 treble). 1 treble in next edge-space. 1 treble in next row-joint. (Chain 1. 1 treble in next row-joint. 1 treble in next edge-space. 1 treble in next row-joint.) 3 times. *Now work across the top of Block 3.* (Chain 1. Skip next stitch. 1 treble in next stitch. 1 treble in next chain-space. 1 treble in next stitch.) 7 times. *Now work across the edge of Block 4.* (Chain 1. 1 treble in next row-joint. 1 treble in next edge-space. 1 treble in next row-joint.) 3 times. Chain 1. 1 treble in last row-joint. (14 groups of 3-trebles, plus 1 final treble)

Row 2–7 Chain 3 (counts as 1 treble). Turn. 1 treble in next chain-space. 1 treble in next stitch. (Chain 1. Skip next stitch. 1 treble in next stitch. 1 treble in next chain-space. 1 treble in next stitch.) 13 times. Chain 1. Skip next stitch. 1 treble in last stitch. (14 groups of 3-trebles, plus one final treble.) *Fasten off provisionally at end of row 7.*

Colour Block 7

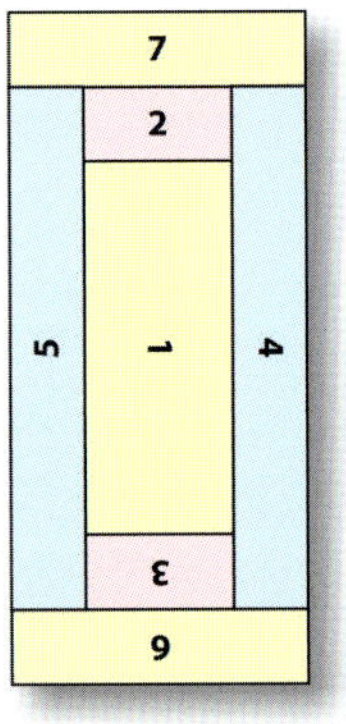

With right side facing, undo provisional fasten off from Block 4 and swap to shade specified for Block 7. Rotate work and follow instructions for Block 6, working instead across Blocks 4, 2 and 5. Swap to shade specified for Block 8 at the end of row 7.

Colour Blocks 8–17

The remaining blocks are worked in the same way. Refer to the block placement diagram on page 20 to get the right shade yarn for each pair of blocks, and check that you have the correct number of groups of 3-trebles at the end of each first row of a new block.

Blocks 8 & 9

31 groups of 3-trebles, plus one final treble.

Blocks 10 & 11

21 groups of 3-trebles, plus one final treble.

Blocks 12 & 13

38 groups of 3-trebles, plus one final treble.

Blocks 14 & 15

28 groups of 3-trebles, plus one final treble.

Blocks 16 & 17

45 groups of 3-trebles, plus one final treble.

Edging

The blanket has a simple edging of four rounds of a (1 double-crochet. Chain 1) pattern repeat.

1st round ***With right side facing swap to shade specified for edging at the end of the last row of Block 17.*** Chain 1, 1 double-crochet in same corner-space. Continue to work along the side edge of the block as follows: ◊(Chain 1. 1 double-crochet in next row-joint.) 7 times. *(Chain 1. Skip next treble. 1 double-crochet in next treble. Chain 1. Skip next chain-space. 1 double-crochet in next treble.)* 28 times. (Chain 1. 1 double-crochet in next row-joint.) 6 times. (Chain 1. 1 double-crochet. 2 chain. 1 double-crochet) in next corner, ie the space formed by the turning chain at beginning of last row of the block. Repeat from * to * 44 times. Chain 1. Skip next treble. 1 double-crochet in next treble.◊ (Chain 1. 1 double-crochet. 2 chain. 1 double-crochet) in next corner-space. Repeat from ◊ to ◊ once. Chain 1. 1 double-crochet in next corner-space. Join with a half-treble to first double-crochet.

2nd round Chain 1. 1 double-crochet in same corner-space. ◊*(Chain 1. Skip next stitch. 1 double-crochet in next chain-space)* 71 times. Chain 2. 1 double-crochet in same corner-space. Repeat from * to * 91 times.◊ Chain 2. 1 double-crochet in same corner-space.◊ Repeat from ◊ to ◊ once. 1 half-treble in first double-crochet.

3rd round Follow instructions for 2nd round adding an extra repetition of the stitch pattern for each side.

4th round Repeat instructions for 3rd round adding an extra repetition of the stitch pattern for each side. Replace final half-treble with 2 chain. Slip-stitch into first double-crochet and fasten off.

Log Cabin Central Symbol Chart

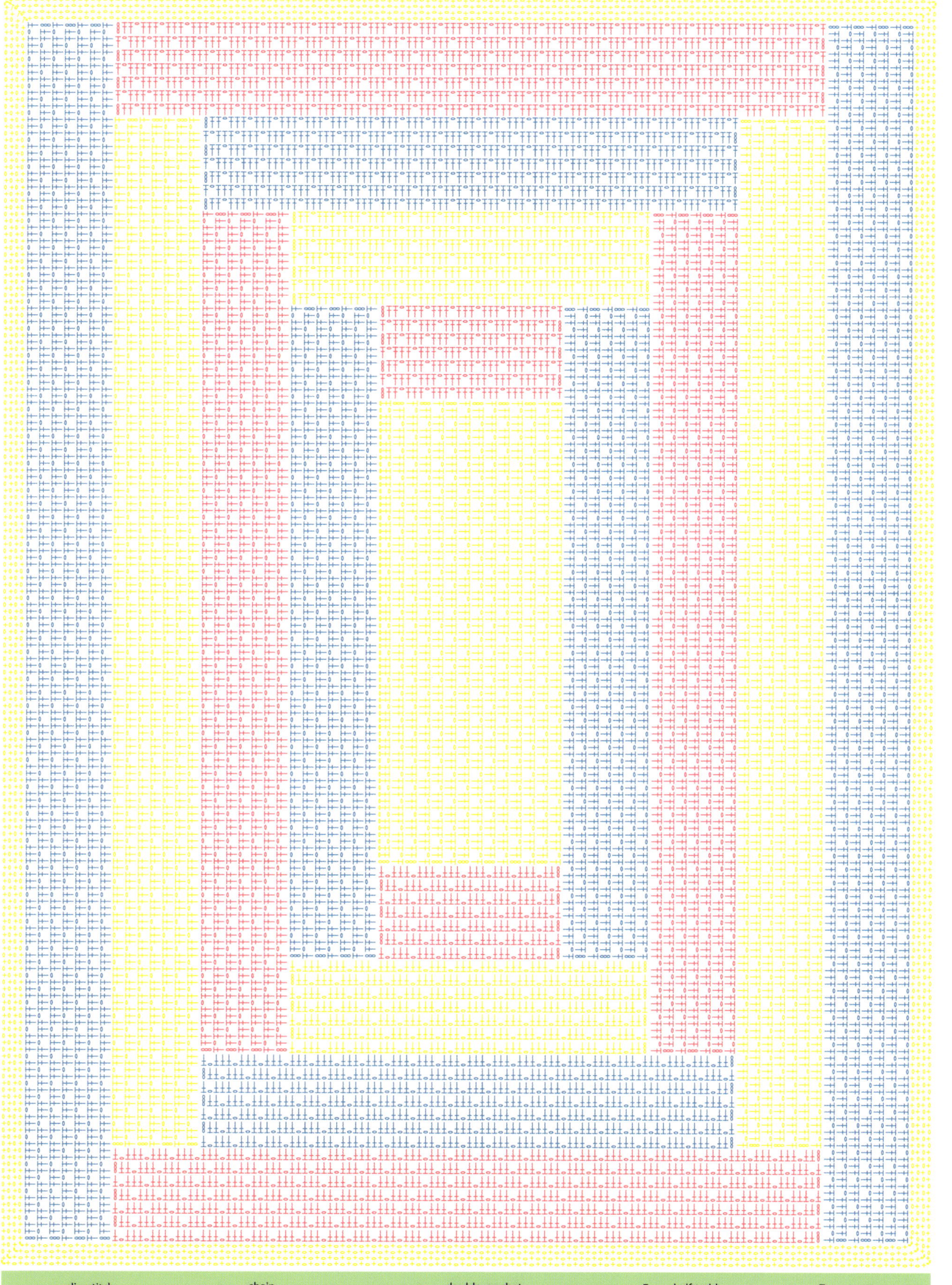

• slip-stitch ∘ chain + double-crochet T half-treble Ŧ treble

Log Cabin Central Adaptations

Although Log Cabin Crochet works with most yarns, it is particularly suited to marled, speckled and tweedy type yarns like the one used in these three colour combinations.

Below *These three Log Cabin Central colour combinations all use Stylecraft Alpaca Tweed DK (100g). Composition: 77% acrylic, 20% alpaca, 3% viscose. Yardage: 240 metres {262 yards} (approx). Hook: 4.00 mm*

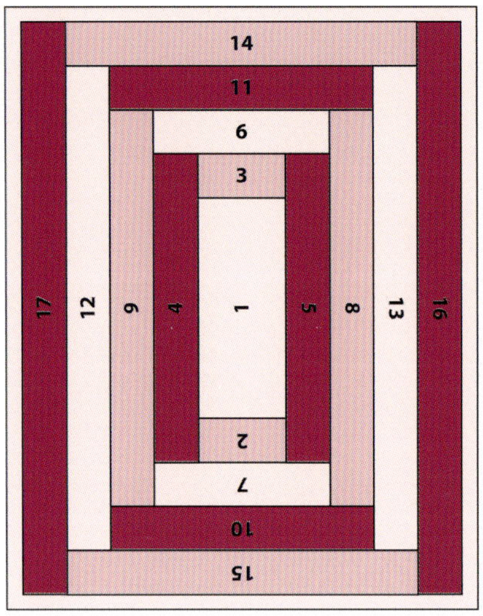

Blush (1668) ***Dusky Pink (1647)*** ***Cherry (1664)***

Sea Breeze (1659) ***Duck Egg (1646)*** ***Ocean (1660)***

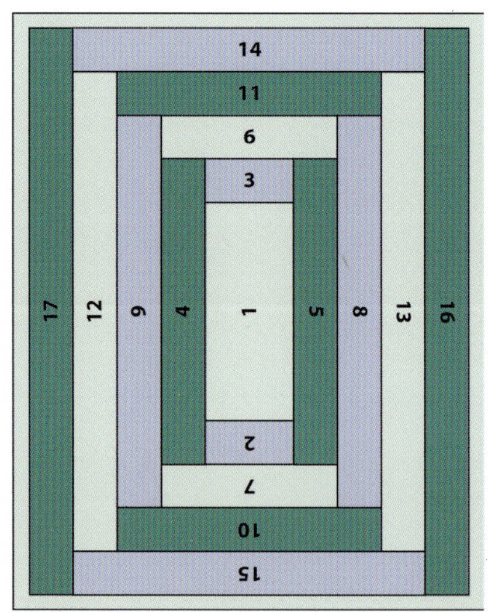

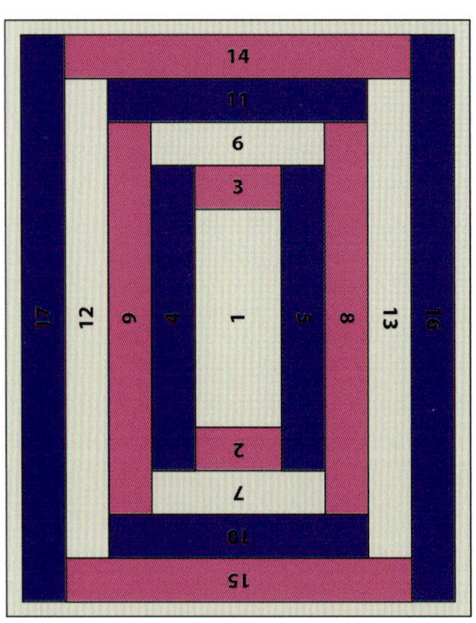

Aran (1658) ***Orchid (1669)*** ***Emperor (1666)***

Calculating Yarn Quantities

When creating your own designs, use these tables to work out how much yarn you need for each colour block. These weights (based on an acrylic yarn) are ***approximate*** only, but offer an idea of the ***proportions*** required for each shade.

Three colour version

Colour Blocks	Approx weight of yarn	Approx no of 50g balls	Approx no of 100g balls
1, 6, 7, 12, 13 & edging	190 g	4 balls	2 balls
2, 3, 8, 9, 14 & 15	140 g	3 balls	2 balls
4, 5, 10, 11, 16 & 17	160 g	4 balls	2 balls

Multi-colour version

Colour Blocks	Approx yarn weight	Approx no of 50g balls	Approx no of 100g balls
1	33 g	1 ball	1 ball
2 & 3	20 g	1 ball	1 ball
4 & 5	44 g	1 ball	1 ball
6 & 7	34 g	1 ball	1 ball
8 & 9	58 g	2 balls	1 ball
10 & 11	48 g	1 ball	1 ball
12 & 13	72 g	2 balls	1 ball
14 & 15	62 g	2 ball	1 ball
16 & 17	86 g	2 balls	1 ball
Edging	50g	1 ball	1 ball

Above *For an even more colourful version of the Log Cabin Central design you can use a different shade for each pair of blocks. This is a great way to use up a yarn stash. The table (left) will help you calculate how much yarn you need.*

TIP You could also experiment with your own colour combinations. Making a small swatch like the ones photographed on the opposite page is a great way to discover if colours work well together.

Adapting the size

For a smaller version of the Log Cabin Central design, omit one or more pairs of colour blocks. To increase the size, add one or more pairs of colour blocks.

13 Colour Blocks 70 x 95 cm

17 Colour Blocks 85 x 110 cm

21 Colour Blocks 100 x 125cm

Log Cabin Corner Design

The throw photographed opposite is made from individual crochet-as-you-go Log Cabin Corner sections which are then sewn together. A final edging along two sides is added to balance the design.

Instructions

Familiarise yourself with ***all*** the information on pages 14–15 ***and*** crochet the Log Cabin Square exercise on pages 16–19 before starting this lengthy project. You will also need to use the sewing techniques on pages 8–9.

Look at the size guide below and decide how many sections you require.

The instructions for crocheting the sections, sewing them together and adding an edging start on page 28.

Materials

The quantities here are for 24 sections. See page 30 for calculating yarn quantities for fewer sections. Other colour combinations are given on pages 32–33.

***Hook** 4.00 mm*
***Finished size** 117 x 145 cm*
***Tension** Colour Block 1 measures approximately 14 x14 cm (5.5 x 5.5")*
***Yarn** Stylecraft Life DK*
***Composition** 75% acrylic, 25% wool*
***Yardage** 298 metres (326 yards) approx*
Shades

- *2 or 3 x 100g Lily (2417) {bright pink}*
- *4 x 100g Zing (2356) {yellow}*
- *2 x 100g Mint (2342) {mint green}*
- *2 x 100g Melon (2359) {salmon pink}*
- *1 or 2 x 100g Cream (2305)*

Key to shades

- 1 *Lily (2417)*
- 2 *Zing (2356)*
- 3 *Mint (2342)*
- 4 *Melon (2359)*
- 5 *Zing (2356)*
- 6&7 *Cream (2305)*

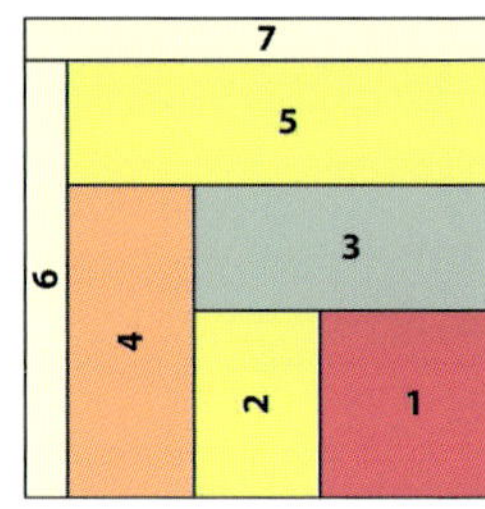

Size Guide

The Log Cabin Corner sections can be sewn together in various permutations to make square or rectangular designs.

(The sizes given here are for sections made in double knitting yarn, and are approximate only.)

***Left** 24 Log Cabin Corner sections 117 x 145 cm*

***Above** Six Log Cabin Corner sections 60 x 90 cm*

***Above** 12 Log Cabin Corner sections 90 x 117 cm*

***Right** Four Log Cabin Corner sections 60 x 60 cm*

Log Cabin Corner Section

Instructions

A Log Cabin Corner section is made from seven crochet-as-you-go colour blocks. Before making a Log Cabin Corner section please familiarise yourself with all the information and exercises on pages 14–19.

> **TIP** Border Block 7 can be omitted until after the sections have been sewn together into rows. (See note on page 30)

Below *Log Cabin Corner section symbol chart*

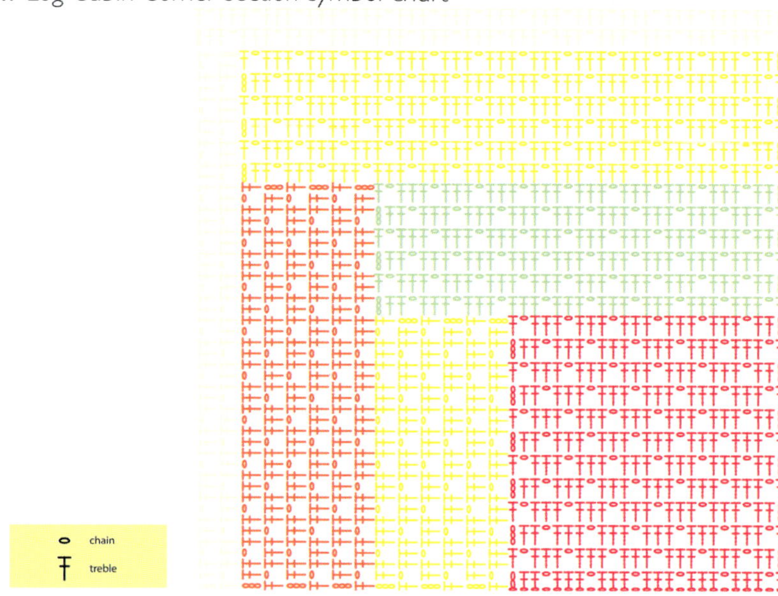

Colour Block 1

Either side can be the right side.

Foundation chain With shade specified for Block 1, chain 27.

Row 1 1 treble in 4th chain from hook (missed 3 chain count as 1 treble). 1 treble in next chain. (Chain 1. Skip next chain. 1 treble in each of next 3 chains.) 5 times. Chain 1. Skip next chain. 1 treble in last chain. (6 groups of 3-trebles plus one final treble)

Rows 2–12 Chain 3 (counts as 1 treble). Turn. 1 treble in next chain-space. 1 treble in next stitch. (Chain 1. Skip next stitch. 1 treble in next stitch. 1 treble in next chain-space. 1 treble in next stitch.) 5 times. Chain 1. Skip next stitch. 1 treble in last stitch.

At the end of row 12, swap to shade specified for Block 2.

Colour Block 2

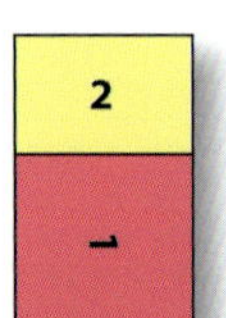

Rotate the work and crochet across side edge of Block 1 with shade specified for Block 2 as follows:

Row 1 Chain 3 (counts as 1 treble). 1 treble in next edge-space. 1 treble in next row-joint. (Chain 1. 1 treble in next row-joint. 1 treble in next edge-space. 1 treble in next row-joint.) 5 times. Chain 1. 1 treble in last row-joint. (6 groups of 3-trebles, plus 1 final treble)

Rows 2–6 Chain 3 (counts as 1 treble). Turn. 1 treble in next chain-space. 1 treble in next stitch. (Chain 1. Skip next stitch. 1 treble in next stitch. 1 treble in next chain-space. 1 treble in next stitch.) 5 times. Chain 1. Skip next stitch. 1 treble in last stitch.

At the end of row 6 swap to shade specified for Block 3.

Colour Block 3

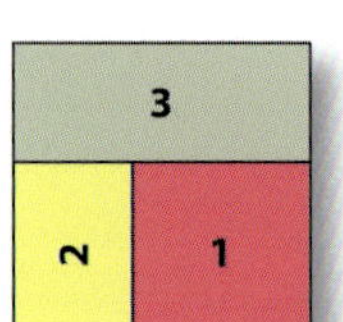

Rotate work and crochet across edges of Blocks 2 and 1 with shade specified for Block 3 as follows:

Row 1 Chain 3 (counts as 1 treble). 1 treble in next edge-space. 1 treble in next row-joint. (Chain 1. 1 treble in next row-joint. 1 treble in next edge-space. 1 treble in next row-joint.) 2 times. Chain 1. *Now work across the top of Block 1.* (1 treble in next stitch. 1 treble in next chain-space. 1 treble in next stitch. Chain 1. Skip next stitch) 6 times. 1 treble in last stitch. (9 groups of 3-trebles, plus 1 final treble)

Rows 2–6 Chain 3 (counts as 1 treble). Turn. 1 treble in next chain-space. 1 treble in next stitch. (Chain 1. Skip next stitch. 1 treble in next stitch. 1 treble in next chain-space. 1 treble in next stitch.) 8 times. Chain 1. Skip next stitch. 1 treble in last stitch.

At the end of row 6 swap to shade specified for Block 4.

Colour Block 4

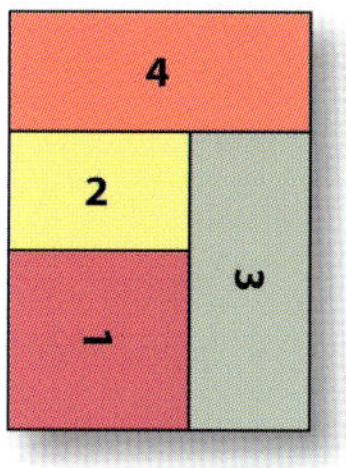

Rotate work and crochet across edges of Blocks 3 and 2 with shade specified for Block 4 as follows:

Row 1 Chain 3 (counts as 1 treble). 1 treble in next edge-space. 1 treble in next row-joint. (Chain 1. 1 treble in next row-joint. 1 treble in next edge-space. 1 treble in next row-joint.) 2 times. Chain 1. *Now work across the top of Block 2.* (1 treble in next stitch. 1 treble in next chain-space. 1 treble in next stitch. Chain 1. Skip next stitch) 6 times. 1 treble in last stitch. (9 groups of 3-trebles, plus 1 final treble)

Rows 2–6 Chain 3 (counts as 1 treble). Turn. 1 treble in next chain-space. 1 treble in next stitch. (Chain 1. Skip next stitch. 1 treble in next stitch. 1 treble in next chain-space. 1 treble in next stitch.) 8 times. Chain 1. Skip next stitch. 1 treble in last stitch.

At the end of row 6 swap to shade specified for Block 5.

Colour Block 5

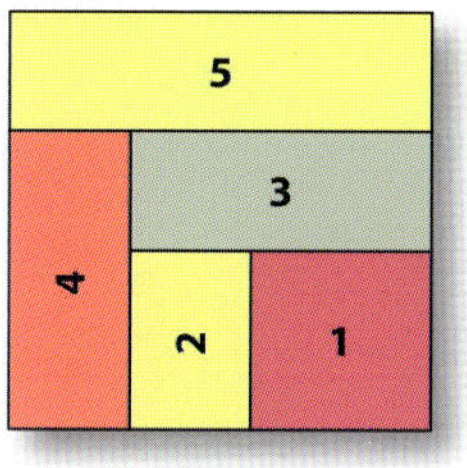

Rotate work and crochet across edges of Blocks 4 and 3 with shade specified for Block 5 as follows:

Row 1 Chain 3 (counts as 1 treble). 1 treble in next edge-space. 1 treble in next row-joint. (Chain 1. 1 treble in next row-joint. 1 treble in next edge-space. 1 treble in next row-joint.) 2 times. Chain 1. *Now work across the top of Block 3.* (1 treble in next stitch. 1 treble in next chain-space. 1 treble in next stitch. Chain 1. Skip next stitch) 9 times. 1 treble in last stitch. (12 groups of 3-trebles, plus 1 final treble)

Rows 2–6 Chain 3 (counts as 1 treble). Turn. 1 treble in next chain-space. 1 treble in next stitch. (Chain 1. Skip next stitch. 1 treble in next stitch. 1 treble in next chain-space. 1 treble in next stitch.) 11 times. Chain 1. Skip next stitch. 1 treble in last stitch.

At the end of row 6 swap to shade specified for Block 6 (if you intend to use the yarn-tails to sew up, leave a suitably long starting yarn-tail.)

Border Block 6

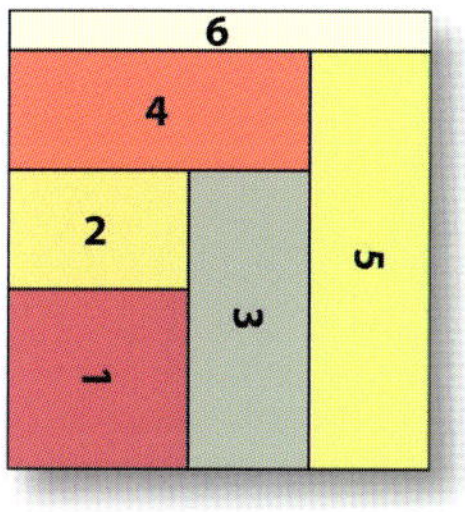

(The border blocks are only two rows deep.) *Rotate work and crochet across edges of Blocks 5 and 4 with shade specified for border as follows:*

Row 1 Chain 3 (counts as 1 treble). 1 treble in next edge-space. 1 treble in next row-joint. (Chain 1. 1 treble in next row-joint. 1 treble in next edge-space. 1 treble in next row-joint.) 2 times. Chain 1. *Now work across the top of Block 4.* (1 treble in next stitch. 1 treble in next chain-space. 1 treble in next stitch. Chain 1. Skip next stitch) 9 times. 1 treble in last stitch. (12 groups of 3-trebles, plus 1 final treble)

Row 2 Chain 3 (counts as 1 treble). Turn. 1 treble in next chain-space. 1 treble in next stitch. (Chain 1. Skip next stitch. 1 treble in next stitch. 1 treble in next chain-space. 1 treble in next stitch.) 11 times. Chain 1. Skip next stitch. 1 treble in last stitch.

Border Block 7

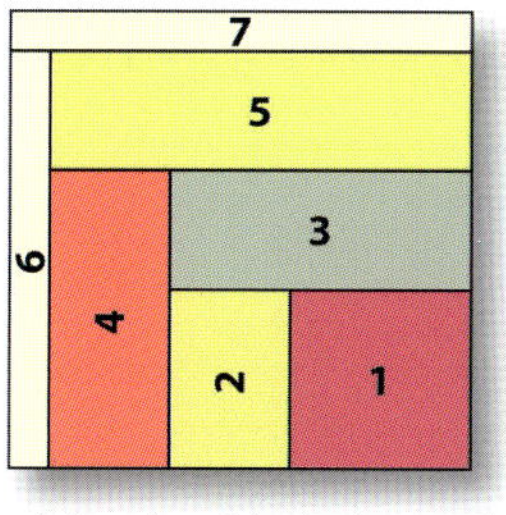

The second border block is worked in the same shade as the previous narrow border. Rotate work and crochet across edges of Block 6 and Block 5 as follows:

Row 1 Chain 3 (counts as 1 treble). 1 treble in next edge-space. 1 treble in next row-joint. Chain 1. *Now work across the top of Block 5.* (1 treble in next stitch. 1 treble in next chain-space. 1 treble in next stitch. Chain 1. Skip next stitch) 12 times. 1 treble in last stitch. (13 groups of 3-trebles, plus 1 final treble)

Row 2 Chain 3 (counts as 1 treble). Turn. 1 treble in next chain-space. 1 treble in next stitch. (Chain 1. Skip next stitch. 1 treble in next stitch. 1 treble in next chain-space. 1 treble in next stitch.) 12 times. Chain 1. Skip next stitch. 1 treble in last stitch.

Fasten off. (If you intend to use the yarn-tails to sew up, leave a suitably long yarn-tail before cutting.)

Log Cabin Corner Useful Information

Sewing up tips

Start by sewing the Log Cabin Corner sections into a strip. Then sew the strips of sections together.

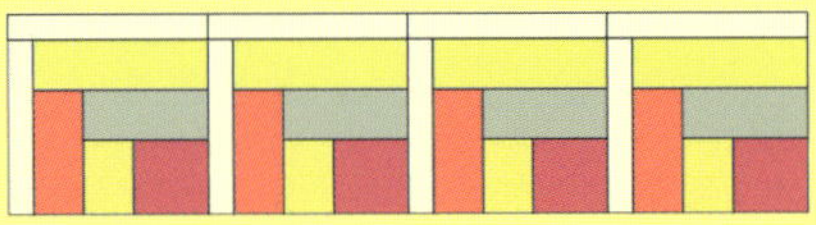

Above *Four sections are sewn into a strip.*

The sections can be sewn together using either the extra long yarn-tails from Blocks 6 & 7, or separate lengths of yarn.

Weaving stitch (see page 9) was used to sew the photographed throw, but you can use another method, or even crochet the squares together using the joining border method on pages 42–43. Ideally use the same shade yarn that was used for crocheting border Blocks 6 and 7.

With short lengths of yarn, loosely tie the chain-spaces of Border Block 6 to the corresponding turning chains along the side edge of the neighbouring section. Remove these ties as the sewing progresses.

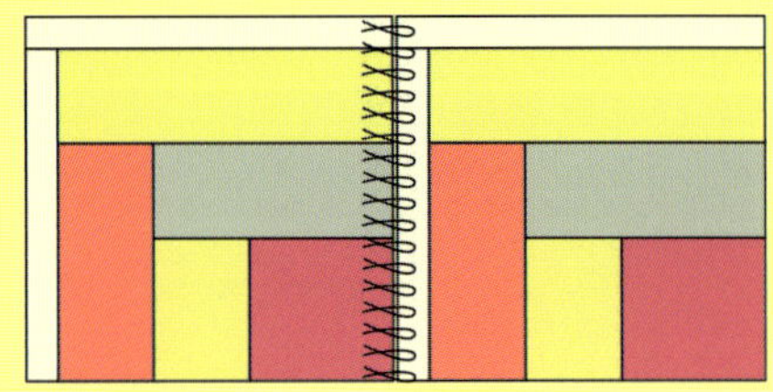

Right *Loosely tie the sections together before sewing.*

Edging

Once all the sections have been sewn together, and with the right side facing, work two rows of the log cabin stitch pattern down the unbordered side edge, then work two rows across the unbordered bottom edge, using the same shade yarn as for Border Blocks 6&7.

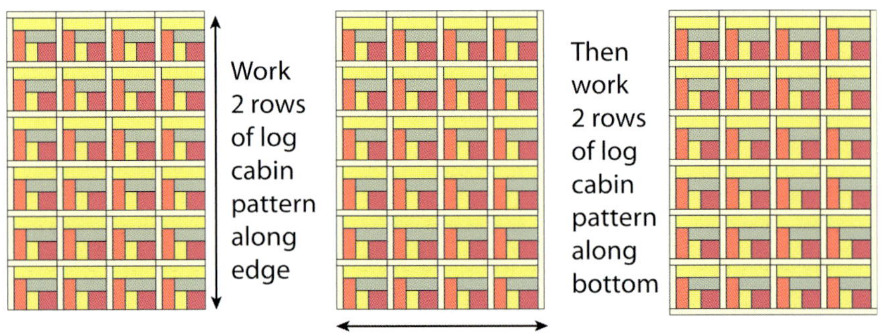

Omitting border block 7

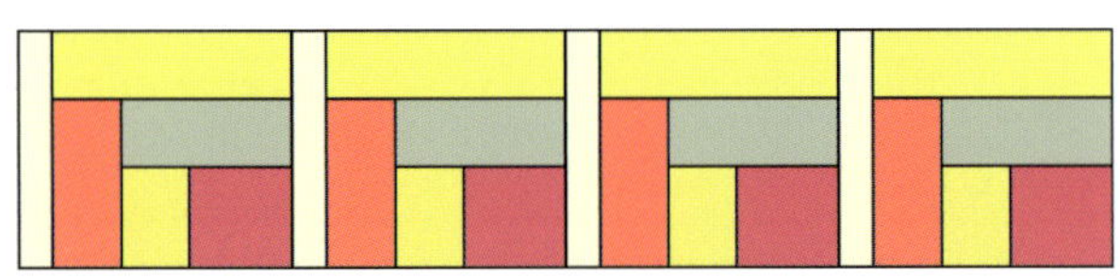

Right *Border Block 7 can be omitted until you have sewn together a strip of sections.*

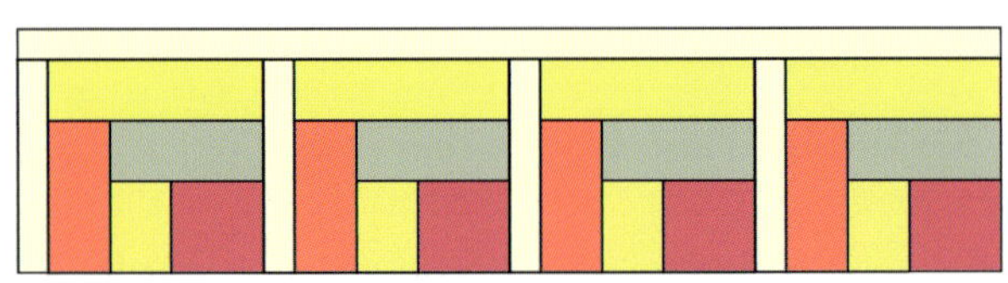

Right *Once you have sewn together a strip of sections, work two rows of the log cabin stitch pattern across the whole length of the strip. Pay particular attention to keeping to the pattern across the joins.*

Calculating yarn quantities

Use this table to estimate how much yarn you will need for your own Log Cabin Corner designs. These weights (based on an acrylic yarn) are ***approximate*** *only, but offer an idea of the* ***proportions*** *required for each shade.*

	1 Section	*4 Sections*	*9 Sections*	*12 Sections*	*24 Sections*
Block 1	*8.5 g*	*34 g*	*77 g*	*102 g*	*204 g*
Block 2	*5 g*	*20 g*	*45 g*	*60 g*	*120 g*
Block 3	*6.5 g*	*26 g*	*59 g*	*78 g*	*156 g*
Block 4	*6.5 g*	*26 g*	*59 g*	*78 g*	*156 g*
Block 5	*8.5 g*	*34 g*	*77 g*	*102 g*	*204 g*
Blocks 6&7	*5 g*	*20 g*	*45 g*	*60 g*	*120 g*
Total	***40 g***	***160 g***	***362 g***	***480 g***	***960 g***

Adding colour blocks

Adding extra pairs of colour blocks to a Log Cabin Corner section is a great way to adapt the size of the design, especially if you're not keen on sewing.

TIP The number of the stitch pattern's 3-treble groups will increase by 3 on the second of each pair of colour blocks.

Below *With an average double knitting yarn, each additional pair of colour blocks will increase the overall size of a Log Cabin Corner section by approximately 7 cm each way.*

5 colour block section measures 30 x 30 cm

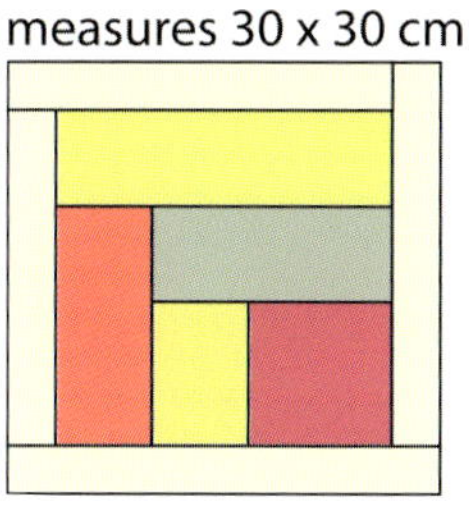

7 colour block section measures 37 x 37 cm

9 colour block section measures 44 x 44 cm

Varying the shades

The position of the shades can vary from section to section.

Above *Five shades are arranged differently in each section.*

Below *The shades vary apart from Colour Block 3.*

Yarn Stash Project

Log Cabin Corner sections are a great way of using up a yarn stash because only small amounts of yarn are needed for each block.

Right *A multi-colour Log Cabin Corner yarn stash design.*

Below *Approximate weight of average double knitting yarn required for each Log Cabin Corner section.*

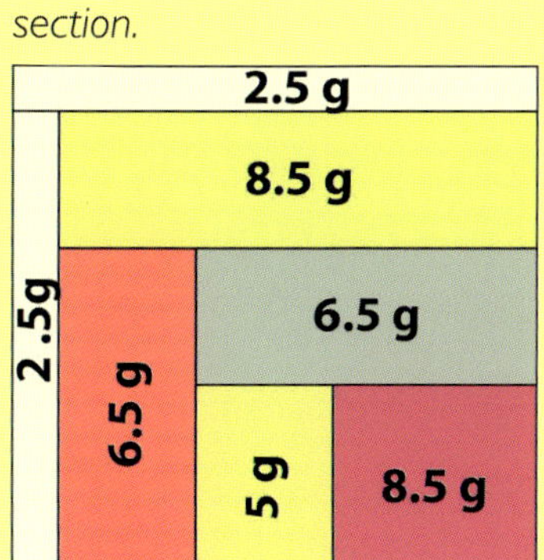

An accurate pair of kitchen scales can help you estimate how much yarn you will need for your own Log Cabin Corner designs. The amounts given (left) are approximate for average double-knitting yarn to make a single section, and together with the table on the facing page, will give you a rough idea of how far your yarn will go.

Log Cabin Corner Colour Combinations

Below *Four Log Cabin Corner colour combinations using Stylecraft Life DK Composition: 75% acrylic, 25% wool. Yardage: 298 metres {326 yards} (approximately)*

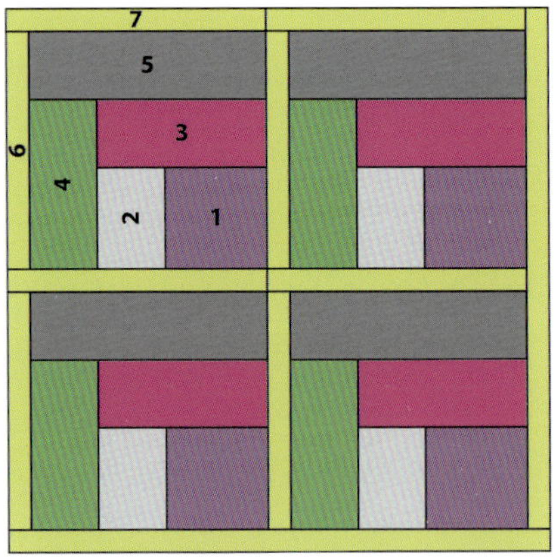

- 1 *Heather (2309)*
- 2 *Silver Grey (2341)*
- 3 *Fuchsia (2344)*
- 4 *Fern (2311)*
- 5 *Pebble Nepp (2327)*
- 6&7 *Zing (2356)*

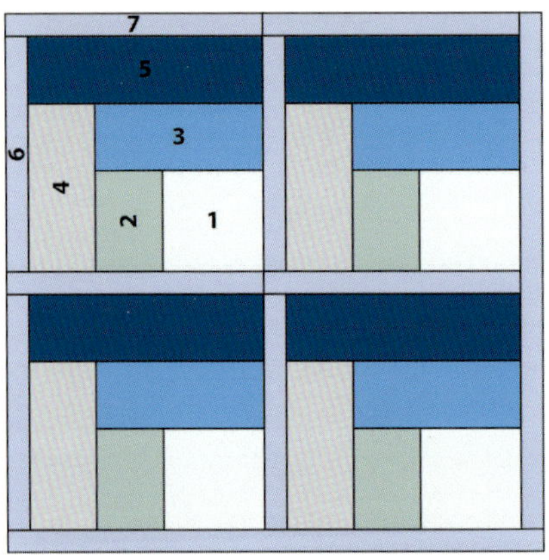

- 1 *Cream (2305)*
- 2 *Mint (2342)*
- 3 *Aqua (2357)*
- 4 *Silver Grey (2341)*
- 5 *Denim Nepp (2368)*
- 6&7 *Ice Blue (2414)*

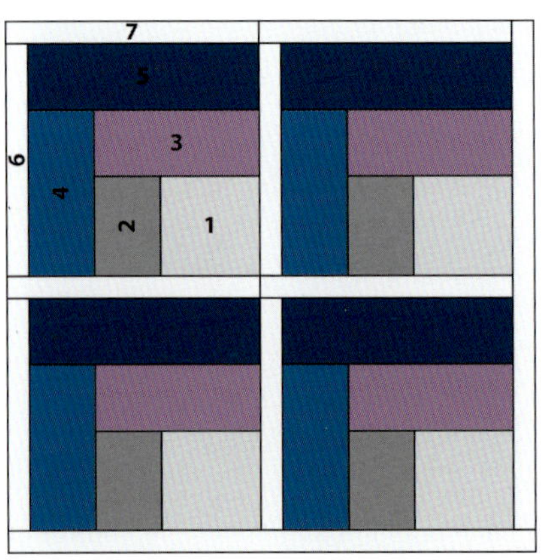

- 1 *Silver Grey (2341)*
- 2 *Pebble Nepp (2327)*
- 3 *Heather (2309)*
- 4 *Denim Nepp (2368)*
- 5 *Blue Haze (2346)*
- 6&7 *Natural Nepp (2325)*

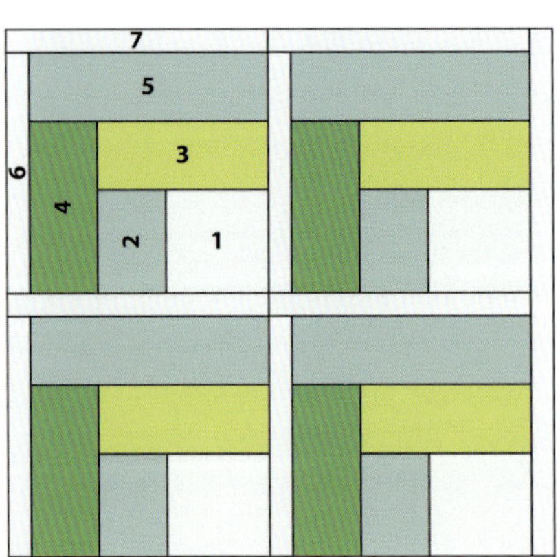

- 1 *Cream (2305)*
- 2 *Mint (2342)*
- 3 *Zing (2356)*
- 4 *Fern (2311)*
- 5 *Mint (2342)*
- 6&7 *Natural Nepp (2325)*

Log Cabin Crochet

Below *Four Log Cabin Corner colour combinations using WYS Ayre Valley Essential DK. Composition: 75% wool, 25% nylon. Yardage: 230 metres {250 yards} (approximately)*

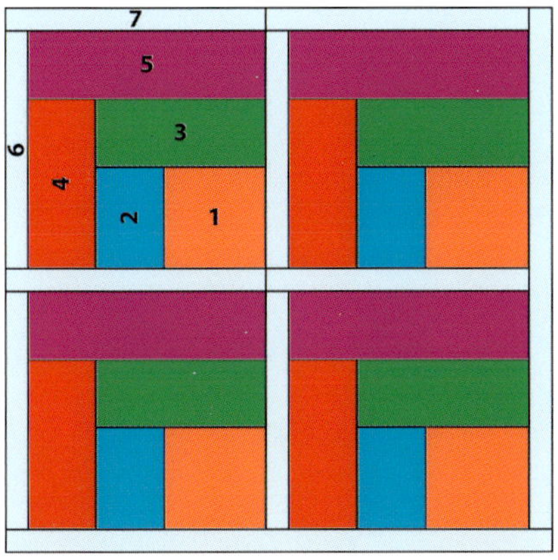

- 1 *Orange (278)*
- 2 *Turquoise (612)*
- 3 *Emerald (394)*
- 4 *Red (549)*
- 5 *Purple (753)*
- 6&7 *Light Turquoise (602)*

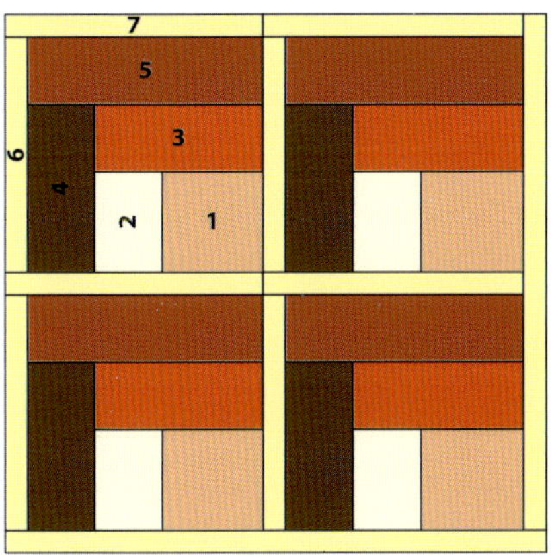

- 1 *Beige (615)*
- 2 *Cream (010)*
- 3 *Burnt Orange (606)*
- 4 *Brown (653)*
- 5 *Nutmeg (630)*
- 6&7 *Cornflower (603)*

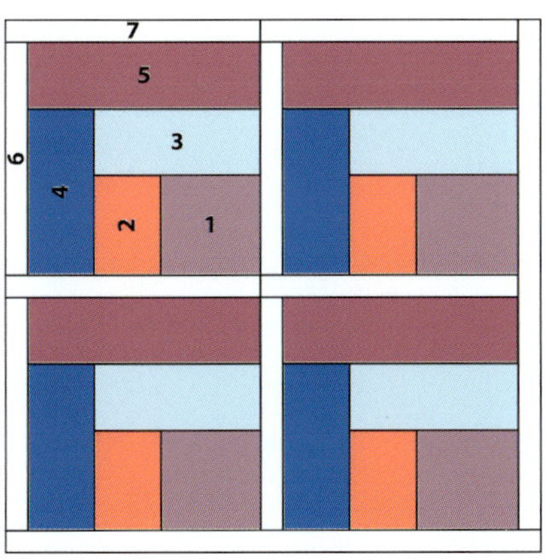

- 1 *Slate (610)*
- 2 *Rose (607)*
- 3 *Light Turquoise (602)*
- 4 *Turquoise (612)*
- 5 *Penny Royal (530)*
- 6&7 *Cloud (601)*

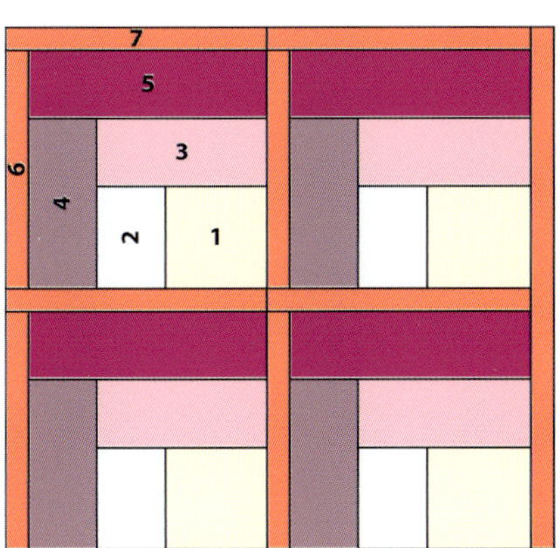

- 1 *Cream (010)*
- 2 *Cloud (601)*
- 3 *Pink (522)*
- 4 *Slate (610)*
- 5 *Purple (753)*
- 6&7 *Rose (607)*

The designs for these crocheted Pioneer Quilts are based on traditional North American sewn patchwork quilts, and they are made in a similar way, too. Sixteen small granny squares are sewn together into manageable sized "blocks". The blocks are then crocheted or sewn together to make the finished quilt.

Pioneer Quilting can be a labour of love for one person, or a group endeavour by a family or whole community; making this a very versatile and cosy craft technique.

Pioneer Quilt

How to Crochet a Pioneer Quilt

1 Choose a design

There are full instructions for the two designs photographed in this book. ***The Stars & Windmills Pioneer Quilt*** (photographed on the previous page) starts on page 40, and the ***Pioneer Sampler Quilt*** (photographed on the front cover) can be found on page 52.

Alternatively, you can design your own Pioneer Quilt using the block and layout library on pages 46–51.

The "Triangles" block (above) and the Rotating Triangles layout design (right) are from the Block and Layout Library on pages 46–51.

2 Choose a colour scheme

The block library has been carefully designed for colour schemes involving light, medium and dark tones. Any colours can be used within a block, but try and stick to light, medium and dark tones.

There are seven colour scheme alternatives for the Stars & Windmill Pioneer Quilt on pages 44–45. These colour schemes can also be used with your own designs.

A stash of left-over yarn could be used to make a truly multi-coloured design, like the Pioneer Sampler Quilt photographed on the cover which uses 17 different shades.

Below *Different colours (purple, blue and yellow) are mixed within a block, while maintaining the light, medium and dark tones.*

Above *The tones of these blue and green shades are too similar, which causes the design to get lost.*

3 Two types of crocheted square

Each quilt block is made from 16 crocheted squares.

There are two types of square:

- ***single-colour squares, and***
- ***double-colour squares***

Instructions for both types of square are on pages 38–39.

Single-colour square

Double-colour square

4 Reading a quilt block chart

The block library on pages 46–48 tells you how many squares of each type and colour to make.

For example for a Polaris Star block you will need:

- 4 single-colour squares in a medium-shade,
- 8 double-colour squares in a medium/light-shade
- 4 double-colour squares in a dark/light-shade.

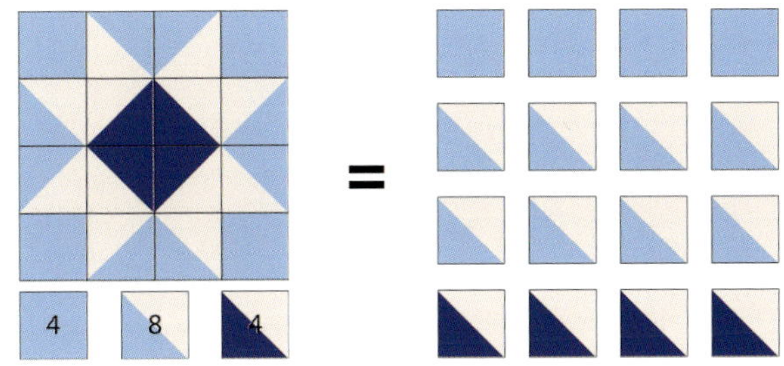

5 Sewing squares together to make a block

An awful lot of sewing is involved in these quilts! The Polaris Star block, for example, will produce a total of 56 yarn-tails.

You could use a separate piece of yarn for the sewing, but since there are so many yarn-tails, it makes sense to use these, so remember to leave a suitably long yarn-tail at the end of each square (leave two long yarn-tails for a double-colour square).

The Pioneer Quilts photographed in this book were sewn together with either running or weaving stitch on the reverse side (see pages 8–9) but it is recommended that you experiment with these and other sewing techniques to find your ideal method.

A *Arrange the squares, according to the block layout diagram.*

B *Sew rows of four squares together first, using the yarn-tails if possible. Do not fasten off the yarn-tails yet.*

C *Then sew the rows together. Again, use the yarn-tails where possible.*

D *Before fastening off, use a yarn-tail to close up the gaps where four squares meet. Sew the yarn-tail in and out of each of the eight corner chain stitches, picking up one thread only. (This can be done either before or after sewing the final seam of the four squares.)*

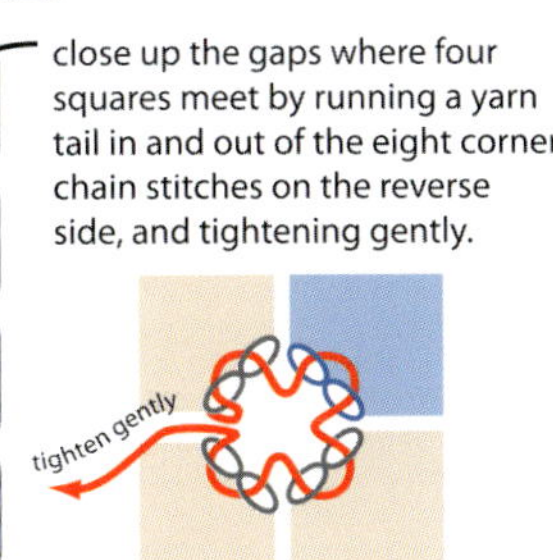

6 Sew or crochet the blocks together

Once the quilt blocks are complete they can be sewn or crocheted together. The quilts photographed in this book were crocheted together using the border method shown on pages 42–43.

Two types of square

Single-colour square

The single-colour square is made with three rounds of a traditional granny square. *The side facing you as you work is the right side*

Foundation chain Chain 5. Join with a slip-stitch to form a ring.

1st round Chain 3 (counts as 1 treble). 2 trebles in ring. (Chain 2. 3 trebles in ring) 3 times. Join with a half-treble to 3rd chain of first 3 chain.

2nd round Chain 3 (counts as 1 treble). 2 trebles in same space. Chain 1. *(3 trebles. Chain 2. 3trebles) in next chain-space. Chain 1.* Repeat from * to * 2 more times. 3 trebles in next space. Join with a half-treble to 3rd chain of first 3 chain.

3rd round Chain 3 (counts as 1 treble). 2 trebles in same space. Chain 1. *3 trebles in next chain-space. Chain 1. (3 trebles. Chain 2. 3 trebles) in next chain-space. Chain 1.* Repeat from * to * 2 more times. 3 trebles in next chain-space. Chain 1. 3 trebles in next chain-space. Chain 2. Join with a slip-stitch to 3rd chain of first 3 chain. *Fasten off, leaving a suitably long yarn-tail for sewing the squares together.*

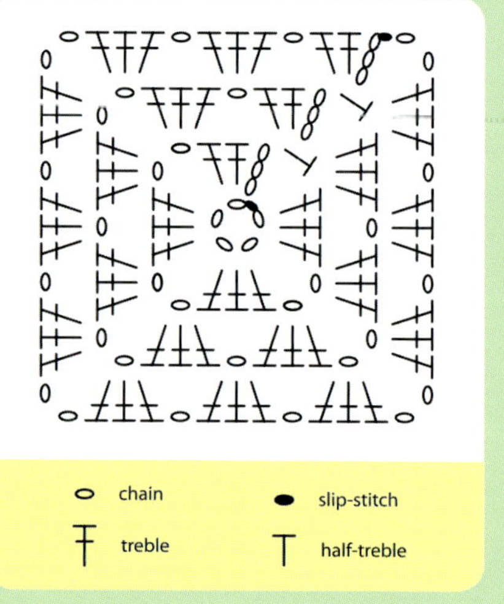

Above *A symbol chart for a single-colour square.*

Double-colour square

The double-colour square looks like a granny square divided diagonally into two colours.

To achieve the colour division, there are two technical differences to its single-colour counterpart:

- ***halfway through each round the yarns are swapped, and***
- ***the direction of crochet changes at the beginning of the 2nd and 3rd rounds.***

TIP Practice making some double-colour squares with left-over scraps of yarn. Once you can achieve an even tension you are ready to begin your quilt.

Far left *A symbol chart for a double-colour square.*

Left-handed

A *The light yarn has been released and one chain has been worked with the dark yarn.*

B *The completed 1st round.*

1st round

(The side facing you as you work the 1st round is the right side.)

Foundation chain With the light yarn chain 5. Join with a slip-stitch to form a ring.

Light half Chain 3 (counts as 1 treble). 2 treble in ring. Chain 2. 3 treble in ring. Chain 1. Release light yarn.

Dark half Pick up dark yarn and chain 1 (**A**). (3 treble. Chain 2. 3 treble) in ring. Join with a half-treble to 3rd chain of first 3 chain (**B**).

TIP Keep the light yarn free because it will be needed again on the next round.

Right-handed

A *The light yarn has been released and one chain has been worked with the dark yarn.*

B *The completed 1st round.*

Left-handed

Halfway through the 2nd round, the dark yarn has been released and one chain has been made with the light yarn.

The completed 2nd round

The completed light half of the 3rd round.

The finished double colour square

2nd round

Dark half *Continue with dark yarn.* Chain 3 (counts as 1 treble). ***Now turn and continue by working around the dark half of the previous round:*** 2 treble in same space. Chain 1. (3 treble. Chain 2. 3 treble) in next space. Chain 1. 3 treble in next space. Chain 1. *Release dark yarn.*

Light half Pick up light yarn and, leaving a small length of yarn the same height as a treble stitch, chain 1 (**C**). 3 treble in same space. Chain 1. (3 treble. Chain 2. 3 treble) in next space. Chain 1. 3 treble in next space. Join with a half-treble to 3rd chain of first 3 chain (**D**).

3rd round

Light half *Continue with light yarn.* Chain 3 (counts as 1 treble). ***Now turn and continue by working around the light half of the previous round:*** 2 treble in same space. Chain 1. 3 treble in next space. Chain 1. (3 treble. Chain 2. 3 treble) in next space. (Chain 1. 3 treble in next space) twice. Chain 1 (**E**).

Cut light yarn, leaving a suitably long yarn-tail for sewing the squares together.

Dark half Pick up dark yarn and, leaving a small length of yarn the same height as a treble stitch, chain 1. 3 treble in same space. Chain 1. 3 treble in next space. Chain 1. (3 treble. Chain 2. 3 treble) in next space. (Chain 1. 3 treble in next space) twice. Chain 2. Join with a slip-stitch to 3rd chain of first 3 chain. *Fasten off dark yarn, leaving a suitably long yarn-tail for sewing the squares together.*

TIP The starting yarn-tails can be darned in, but leave the two ending yarn-tails for sewing the squares together into the quilt block later.

Right-handed

Halfway through the 2nd round, the dark yarn has been released and one chain has been made with the light yarn.

The completed 2nd round

The completed light half of the 3rd round.

The finished double colour square

Stars & Windmills Pioneer Quilt

This large Pioneer Quilt is made from 20 quilt blocks and not only involves a lot of crochet but a lot of sewing up, too! So you might consider joining forces with other crocheters and turn this into a group project.

There are alternative colour schemes for this quilt on pages 44–45.

Materials

Yarn Sirdar Country Style DK

Composition 40% Nylon, 30% Wool, 30% Acrylic

Yardage 155 metres (170 yards) approximately

Shades

- 13 x 50g Antique White (0644) {light tone} (this includes 2 x 50g balls for crocheting the blocks together plus a single round of edging)
- 9 x 50g Blue Blush (0643) {medium tone}
- 3 x 50g Duchess (0623) {dark tone}

Hook 4.00 mm

Tension Each square measures approximately 8 x 8 cm (3.25 x 3.25")
Each 4 x 4 block measures approximately 31 x 31 cm (12 x 12")

Finished size
130 x 165 cm (52 x 65")

TIP Each 50g ball of the yarn specified will make *approximately* 15 single-colour squares. Two 50g balls will make *approximately* 30 double-colour squares.

Instructions

*Familiarise yourself with **all** the information on pages 36–39 before starting this lengthy project.*
Crochet 16 squares for each block shown below and sew them together.
Once you have made all the blocks, you can either sew or crochet them together with the light tone yarn. The border technique for crocheting the blocks together is shown on pages 42–43, but you can use any suitable method.
One or more additional rounds of (chain 1, 1 double-crochet) can be added as an edging in the light tone yarn if required (refer to the Log Cabin Central symbol chart on page 23 if necessary).

Polaris star (make 4)

Eastern star (make 2)

Friendship star (make 2)

Windmill (make 2)

Aircraft (make 2)

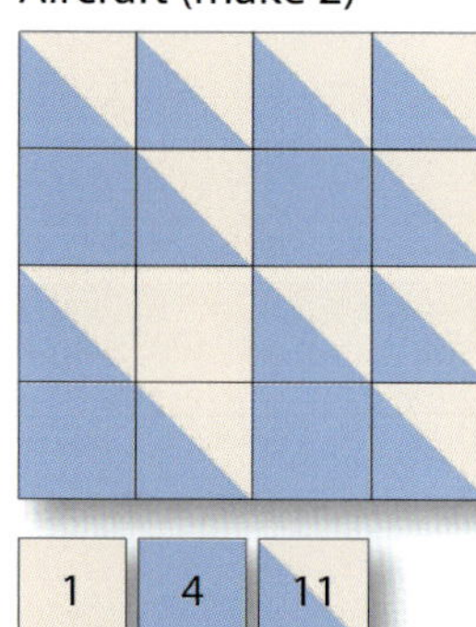

Forest tracks (make 2)

Dutch puzzle (make 2)

Texas star reversed (make 2)

Lucky star (make 2)

Key

Stars & Windmills Pioneer Quilt Block Layout Chart

Below *This chart shows the placement of the 20 quilt blocks required for the Stars & Windmills Pioneer Quilt. The quilt is photographed at the start of this chapter.*

Joining — Border Method

Overview

Block 1

Block 1 is bordered by a round of (Chain 1. 1 double-crochet).

Left *A simplified diagram of the border around Block 1 (the actual border has many more stitches).*

Block 2 — Join on one side

Block 2 is joined to Block 1 along one side: the basic border is worked around the first three sides of Block 2. On the fourth side (the joining side), replace the chain-stitches with slip-stitches. The slip-stitches are worked into the corresponding chain-spaces on Block 1.

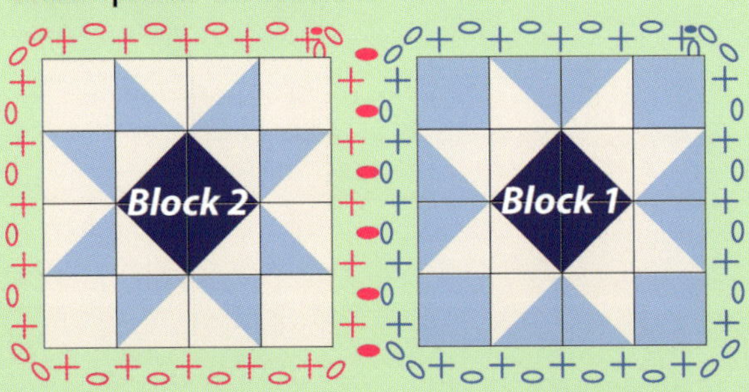

Block 3 — Join on one side

Block 3 is also joined to Block 1 along one side.

Block 4 — Join on two sides

Block 4 is joined to the other blocks along two sides: the basic border is worked around the first two sides of Block 4. The third side is slip-stitched to Block 3. After the last slip-stitch into the Block 3 corner-space, omit the corner-space of Block 1, but make a single chain instead. Then slip-stitch the fourth side to Block 2 as usual.

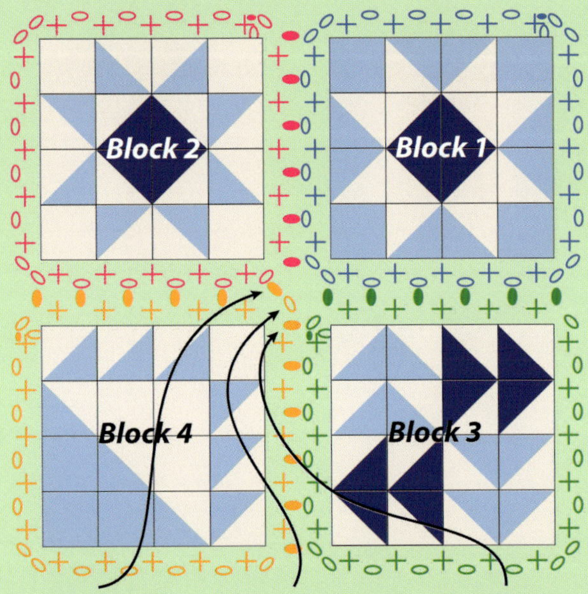

3 Slip-stitch into corner-space of Block 2

2 Omit corner-space of Block 1 and chain 1 instead

1 Slip-stitch into corner-space of Block 3

***Left-handed crocheters** may find it easier to refer to this diagram.*

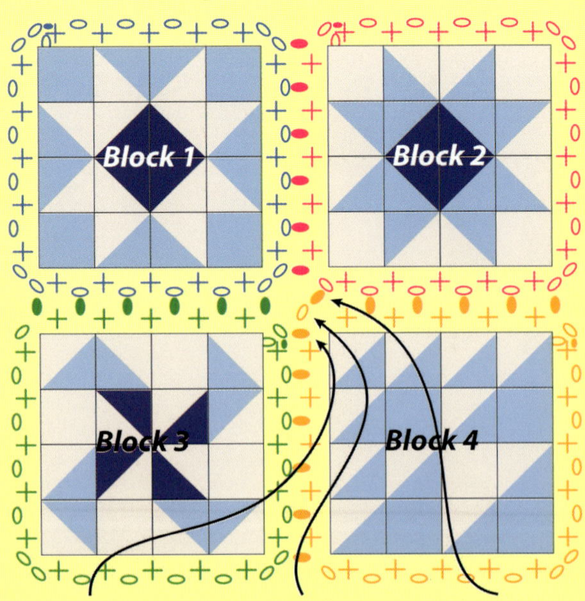

1 Slip-stitch into corner-space of Block 3

2 Omit corner-space of Block 1 and chain 1 instead

3 Slip-stitch into corner-space of Block 2

Instructions

Block 1

With right side facing join yarn to corner chain-space with a slip-stitch. Chain 1. 1 double-crochet in same chain-space. §◊*Chain 1. Skip next stitch. 1 double-crochet in next stitch. Chain 1. Skip next stitch. 1 double-crochet in next chain-space.* Repeat from * to * two more times. Chain 1. 1 double-crochet in next square's corner-space.◊ Repeat from ◊ to ◊ two more times. Then repeat from * to * three more times. (Chain 2. 1 double-crochet) in same corner-space.§. Repeat from § to § three more times. Replace final double-crochet with a slip-stitch into first double-crochet. Fasten off.

Block 2 (one-sided join)

First three sides

Repeat the instructions for Block 1 up to and including the first double-crochet in the third corner space.

Joining side (fourth side)

With both right sides facing up, place Blocks 1 & 2 next to each other on a flat surface.

(When working the slip-stitches, keep the yarn to the back of the work, and insert the hook into the relevant chain-space from front to back.)

Chain 1. Slip-stitch into a Block 1 corner-space. 1 double-crochet in same Block 2 corner-space. ◊*Slip-stitch into next Block 1 chain-space. Skip next Block 2 stitch. 1 double-crochet in next Block 2 stitch. Slip-stitch into next Block 1 chain-space. Skip next Block 2 stitch. 1 double-crochet in next Block 2 chain-space.* Repeat from * to * 2 more times. Slip-stitch into next Block 1 chain-space. 1 double-crochet in next Block 2 square's corner-space.◊ Repeat from ◊ to ◊ three more times. Slip-stitch into Block 1 corner-space. Chain 1.Δ Slip-stitch into first double-crochet. Fasten off.

Block 3 (one-sided join)

Repeat the instructions for Block 2 (substituting the phase "Block 2" with "Block 3").

Block 4 (two-sided join)

First two sides

Repeat the instructions for Block 1 up to and including the first double-crochet in the second corner space.

Third side

Join the third side of Block 4 to Block 3 by following the "Joining side" instructions for Block 2 up to Δ symbol (substituting relevant block numbers).

Fourth side

Omit Block 1 corner-space *(ie, the corner-space diametrically opposite).* Slip-stitch into Block 2 corner-space. 1 double-crochet in same Block 4 corner-space. Repeat Block 2 instructions from ◊ to ◊ four times *(substituting relevant block numbers).* Slip-stitch into Block 2 corner-space.Chain 1.Slip-stitch into first double-crochet. Fasten off.

Above *Symbol chart showing Block 1 border.*

TIP The joining border method can also be used to join individual squares. The border can be the same colour as the square (in which case work the border before fastening off). This technique can also be used on blocks of crochet, as illustrated on page 72 in the geo-filet chapter.

Pioneer Quilt Colour Combinations

Here are some colour choices for the Stars & Windmills Pioneer Quilt. It's always a good idea to experiment with a yarn first before committing to buying the full amount because some yarns are easier to work with than others. Bear in mind, as well, that colours may look very different when viewed in daylight compared to a photograph or shade card.

TIP The yarns used for all these colour combinations are sold in 100g balls. The Stars & Windmills Pioneer Quilt pattern on page 40 uses 50g balls of yarn, so you would only need approximately half as many 100g balls to complete the quilt. See page 53 for more advice` on calculating yarn quantities.

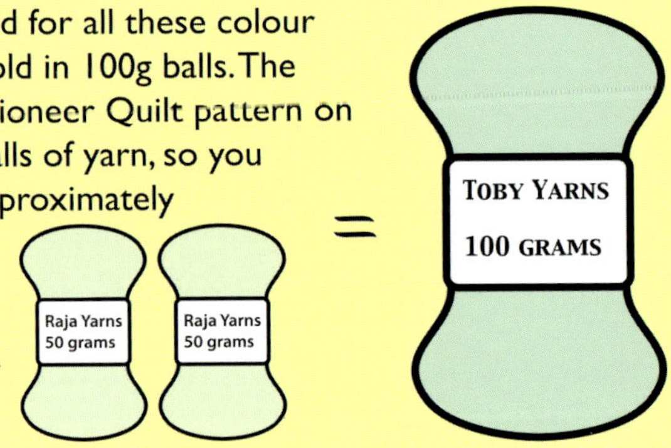

***Yarn** Stylecraft Life DK*
***Composition** 75% acrylic, 25% wool*
***Yardage** 298 metres (326 yards) approximately*
Shades
- *Ice Blue (2414) {light}*
- *Aqua (2357) {medium}*
- *Teal (2416) {dark}*

***Yarn** King Cole Panache DK*
***Composition** 50% wool, 50% acrylic*
***Yardage** 312 metres (341 yards) approximately*
Shades
- *Biscuit (2068) {light}*
- *Oatmeal (2061) {medium}*
- *Chestnut (2064) {dark}*

***Yarn** King Cole Panache DK*
***Composition** 50% wool, 50% acrylic*
***Yardage** 312 metres (341 yards) approximately*
Shades
- *Biscuit (2068) {light}*
- *Dusty Pink (2066) {medium}*
- *Heather (2063) {dark}*

Pioneer Quilt

Yarn *Stylecraft Life DK*
Composition *75% acrylic, 25% wool*
Yardage *298 metres (326 yards) approximately*
Shades

- *Silver Grey (2341) {light}*
- *Heather (2309) {medium}*
- *Cranberry (2319) {dark}*

Yarn *WYS Essential DK*
Composition *75% wool, 25% nylon*
Yardage *230 metres (252 yards) approximately*
Shades

- *Cream (010) {light}*
- *Light turquoise (602) {medium}*
- *Denim (160) {dark}*

Yarn *WYS Essential DK*
Composition *75% wool, 25% nylon*
Yardage *230 metres (252 yards) approximately*
Shades

- *Cornflour (603) {light}*
- *Cardamom (351) {medium}*
- *Mid green (619) {dark}*

Yarn *Stylecraft Life DK*
Composition *75% acrylic, 25% wool*
Yardage *298 metres (326 yards) approximately*
Shades

- *Daffodil (2394) {light}*
- *Copper (2312) {medium}*
- *Chocolate Nepp (2326) {dark}*

Pioneer Quilt Block & Layout Library

1 Polaris star

2 Evening hands

3 Lone star

4 Eastern star

5 Lucky star

6 Friendship star

7 Odd fellows cross

8 Constellation

9 Dutch puzzle

10 Windmill

11 Crossroads

12 Merry-go-round

13 Weather vane

14 Susannah

15 Ribbons

16 Pinwheels

Pioneer Quilt

17 Hovering birds

18 Flock

19 Aircraft

20 Crosses & Losses

21 Four patch

22 Road to Oklahoma

23 Old Tippacanoe

24 Next door neighbour

25 North star

26 North star reversed

27 Eight point star

28 Eight point star reversed

29 Texas star

30 Texas star reversed

31 Pieced Star

32 Spinner

Pioneer Quilt Block & Layout Library

33 Yankee puzzle

34 X-Quartet

35 World's Fair

36 Hourglass

37 Forest tracks

38 Waves of the sea

39 Bear paw

40 Brown goose

41 Windblown square

42 All around the world

43 Hannah

44 Pinwheel

45 Fox and geese

46 Aircraft

47 Birds in flight

48 Triangles

Single Block Layouts

Single blocks can be used as an overall design.

Lone Star block (3)

Windmill block (10)

X-Quartet block (34)

Rotated Block Layouts

Crosses and Losses (20)

Waves of the sea (38)

Triangles (48)

Hovering birds (17)

Forest tracks (37)

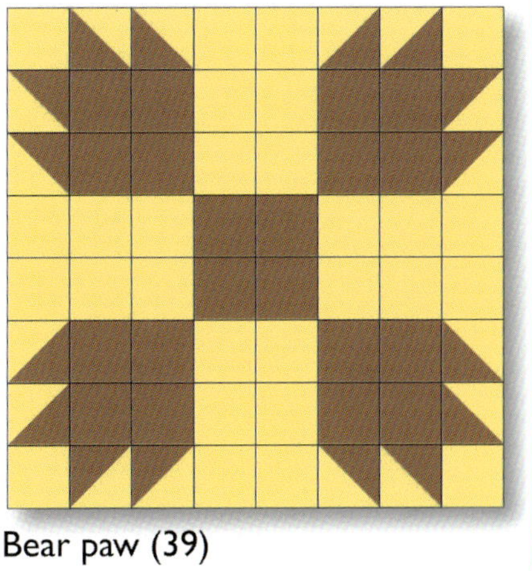

Bear paw (39)

Pioneer Quilt Block & Layout Library

Two colour layout

Right: *The simplicity of a two colour design can be extremely effective.*

4 x Bear paw (39)
4 x Texas star reversed (30)
4 x Birds in flight (47)
4 x Windblown square (41)
2 x All around the world (42)
2 x Brown goose (40)

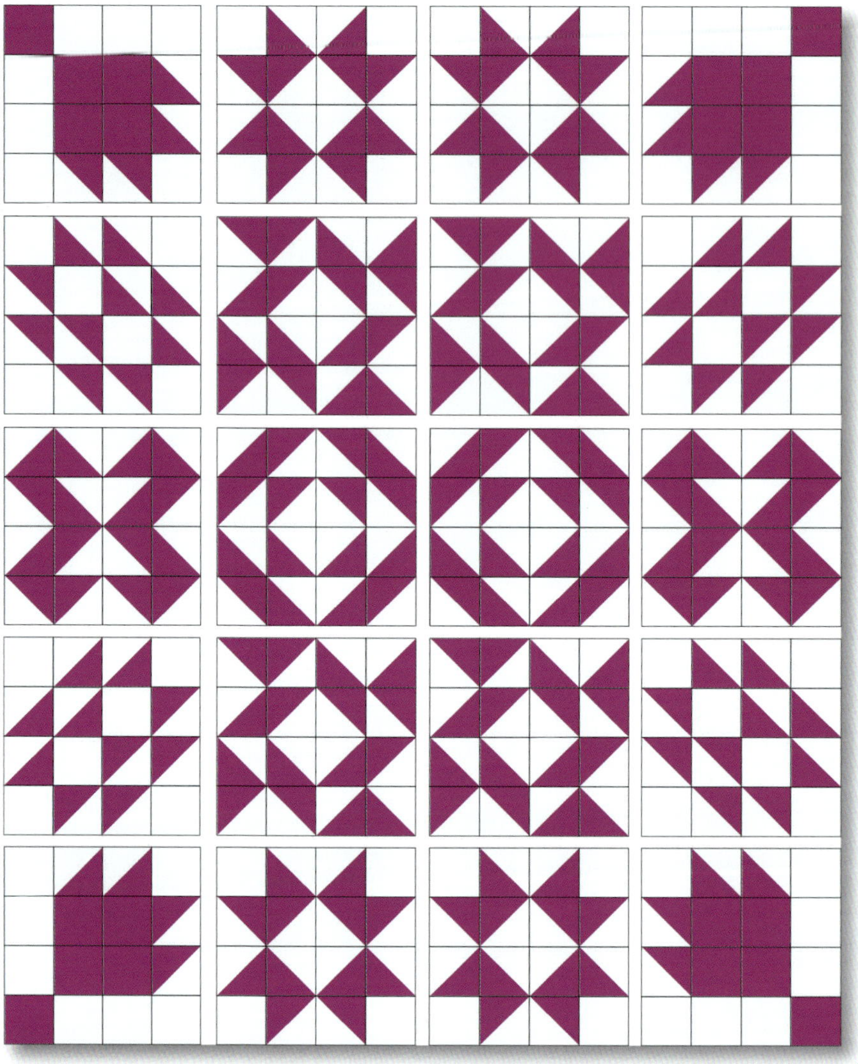

12 block layouts

A 12 block layout Pioneer Quilt make with double-knitting yarn would measure 100 x 134 cm.

Left *A 12 block layout in two colours.*
4 x Bear paw (39)
2 x Texas star reversed (30)
4 x Birds in flight (47)
2 x Windblown square (41)

Right *A 12 block three colour layout.*
4 x Lucky star (5)
2 x Constellation (8)
4 x Pieced star (31)
2 x Pinwheel (44)

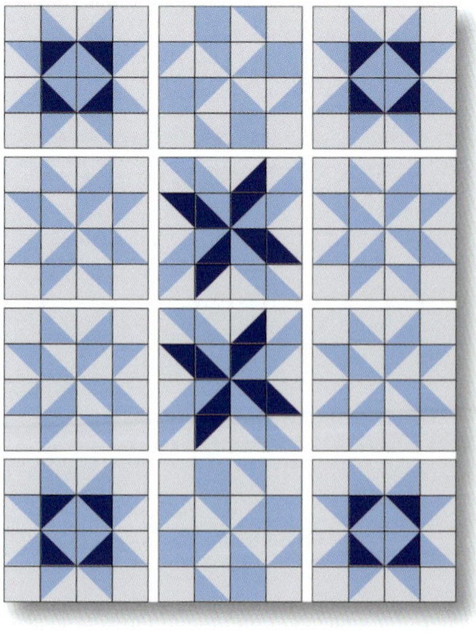

Border layouts

Blocks can be separated by strips of single-colour squares

Above *Four different stars (26, 27, 29 and 30) are bordered with 144 single-colour squares (20 purple, and 124 light blue).*

Above *Twelve Friendship star (6) blocks are bordered with 144 single-colour squares (6 orange and 138 beige).*

Multi-colour layouts

Simple designs work well with multi-colours.

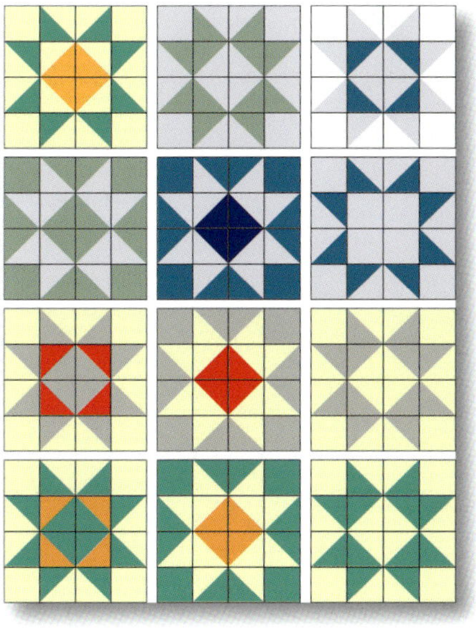

Left: *A mixture of different stars in contrasting and complementary colours.*

4 x Texas star (29)
1 x Friendship star (6)
1 x Eight point star (27)
3 x Lucky star (5)
3 x Polaris star (1)

Right: *The three stars in this design are given bright accents on a neutral background.*

4 x Eight point star reversed (28)
2 x North star reversed (26)
6 x Texas star reversed (30)

Pioneer Sampler Quilt

The yarn and layout for the Pioneer Sampler Quilt photographed on the front cover is given here. Your quilt doesn't have to slavishly follow this design, of course, or use this yarn; see the facing page for some adaptation ideas.

Instructions

Familiarise yourself with ***all*** *the information on pages 36–39 before starting. Crochet 16 squares for each block shown below and sew them together. Once you have made all the blocks, sew or crochet them together with Antique White yarn. Crochet the blocks together with the border technique shown on pages 42–43 (or use your own method). Add one or more additional rounds of (chain 1, 1 double-crochet) in Antique White if required (refer to the symbol chart on page 23 if necessary).*

Block 1 (Lucky Star)

389 Smokey Stone
644 Antique White
649 Vintage Rose
651 Winter Garden

Block 2 (Lone Star)

644 Antique White
649 Vintage Rose
650 Willow

Block 3 (Lucky Star)

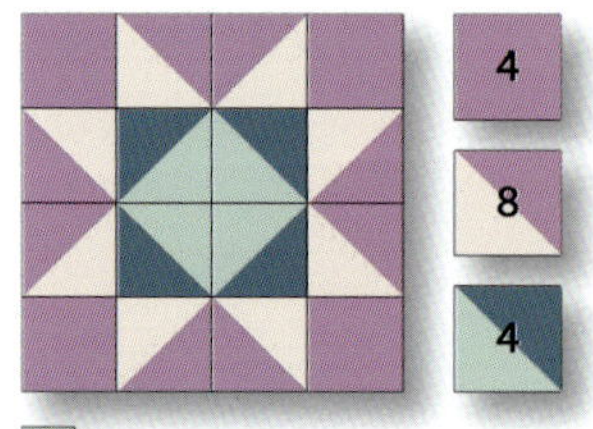

389 Smokey Stone
470 Smokey Green
644 Antique White
651 Winter Garden

Block 4 (Eastern Star)

643 Blue Blush
644 Antique White
623 Duchess

Block 5 (Pieced Star)

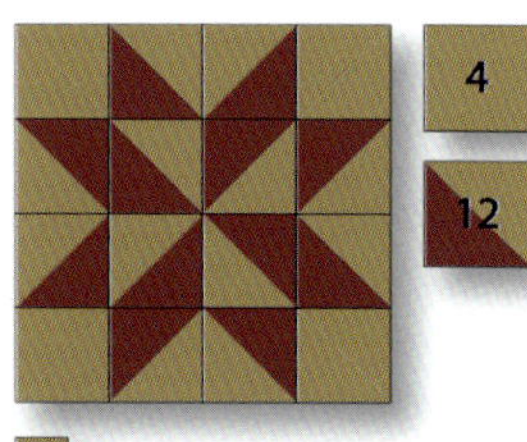

409 Naturelle
642 Spiced Plum

Block 6 (Eastern Star)

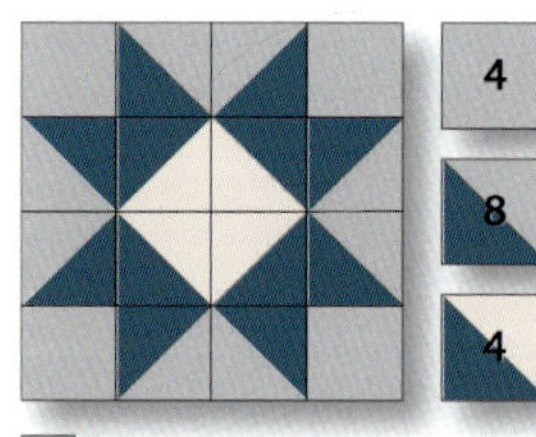

434 Silver Cloud
633 Teal
644 Antique White

Block 7 (Constellation)

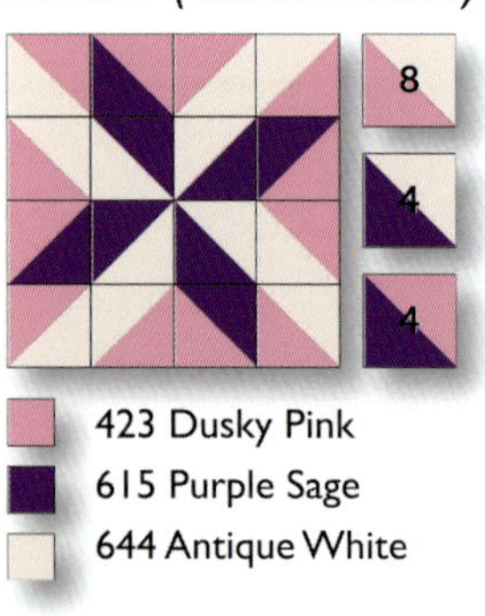

423 Dusky Pink
615 Purple Sage
644 Antique White

Block 8 (Friendship Star)

402 Cherry
643 Blue Blush
644 Antique White

Block 9 (Constellation)

441 Light Navy
643 Blue Blush
644 Antique White

Block 10 (Friendship Star)

389 Smokey Stone
418 Garnet
643 Blue Blush
644 Antique White

Block 11 (Lone Star)

633 Teal
644 Antique White
650 Willow

Block 12 (Friendship Star)

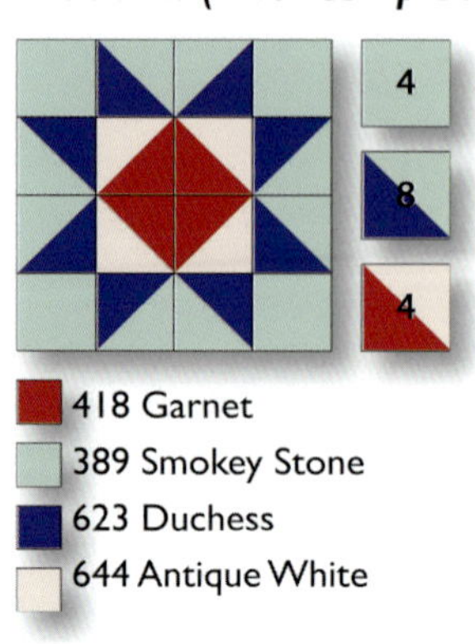

418 Garnet
389 Smokey Stone
623 Duchess
644 Antique White

Sampler Quilt Adaptations

Materials

***Yarn** Sirdar Country Style DK*
***Composition** 40% Nylon, 30% Wool, 30% Acrylic*

***Yardage** 155 metres (170 yards) approximately*

Shades

- *1 x 50g Cherry (402)*
- *1 x 50g Naturelle (409)*
- *1 x 50g Garnet (418)*
- *1 x 50g Dusky Pink (423)*
- *1 x 50g Silver Cloud (434)*
- *1 x 50g Light Navy (441)*
- *1 x 50g Smokey Green (470)*
- *1 x 50g Purple Sage (615)*
- *1 x 50g Duchess (623)*
- *1 x 50g Teal (633)*
- *1 x 50g Spiced Plum (642)*
- *1 x 50g Vintage Rose (649)*
- *1 x 50g Willow (650)*
- *1 x 50g Winter Garden (651)*
- *2 x 50g Smokey Stone (389)*
- *2 x 50g Blue Blush (643)*
- *6 x 50g Antique White (644) (this includes 2 x 50g balls for crocheting the blocks together and approximately four rounds of edging)*

***Hook** 4.00 mm*
***Tension** Each square measures approximately 8 x 8 cm (3.25 x 3.25")*
Each 4 x 4 block measures approximately 31 x 31 cm (12 x 12")

***Finished size** 100 x 134 cm (40 x 53")*

Traditionally, patchwork quilts were a way of using up remnants of fabric. The same principle can be applied to a crocheted quilt, of course, by using a stash of left-over yarn.

To help you gauge how far your yarn will stretch, as it were, here is a rough guide to calculating how many squares you can make from 50g balls of double knitting yarn.

1 x 50 grams = approximately 15 single colour squares

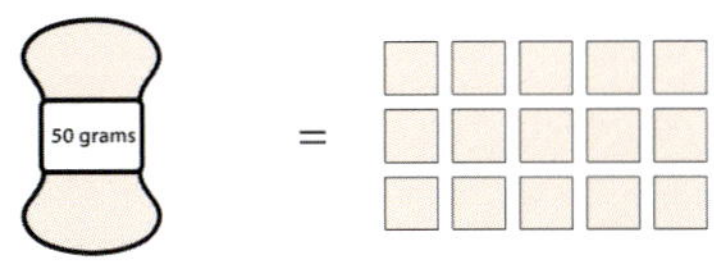

2 x 50 grams = approximately 30 double colour squares

If you would prefer not to purchase a lot of different shades, you could just select one or two blocks or colour schemes from the Pioneer Sampler Quilt.

***Above left** Only blocks 1 and 2 are used in this design.*

***Above right** Only the shades from block 9 (light navy, blue blush and antique white) are used in this design.*

***Left** Block 7 (Constellation) is worked with the three of the shades from block 1 (smokey stone, antique white and vintage rose).*

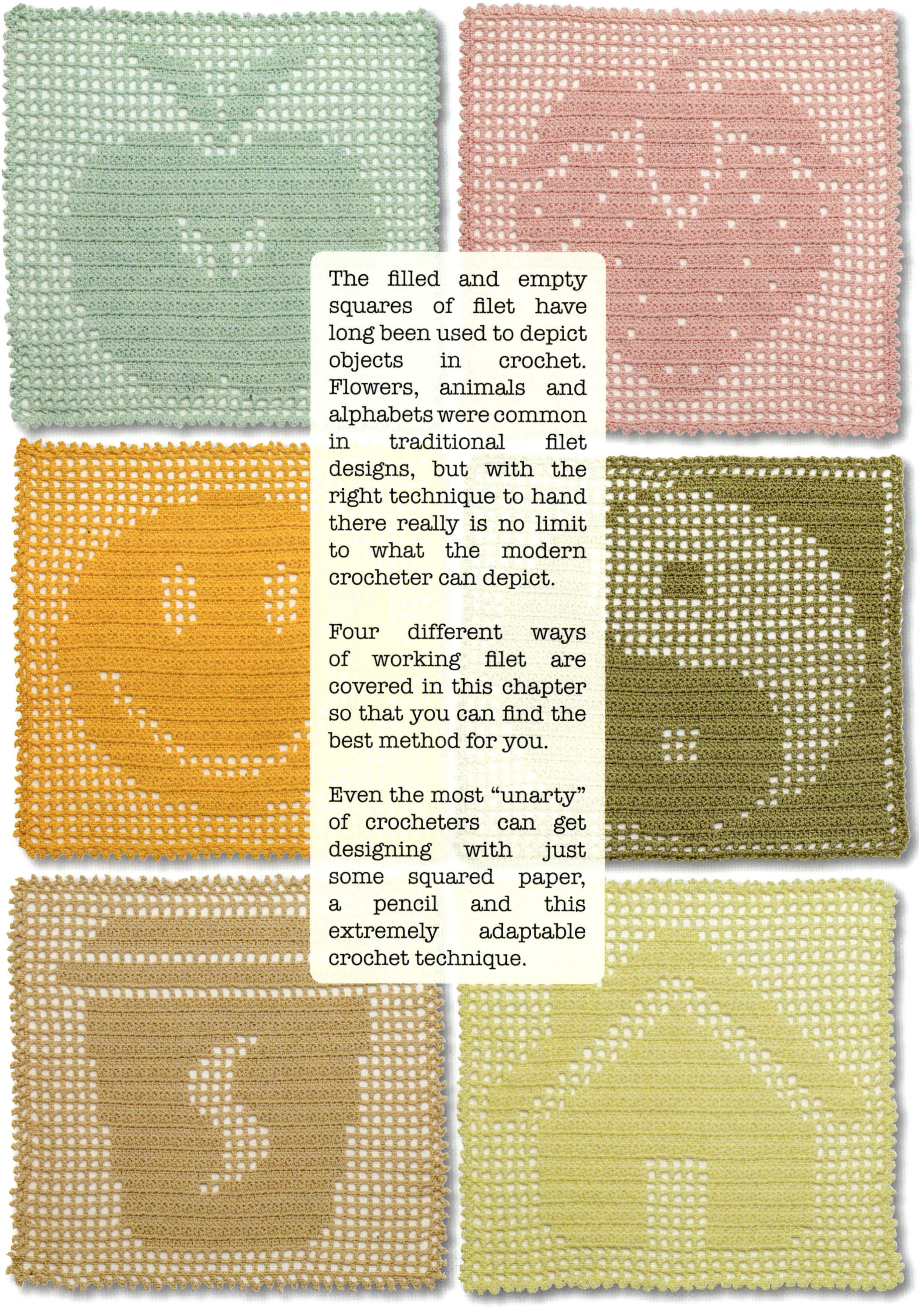

The filled and empty squares of filet have long been used to depict objects in crochet. Flowers, animals and alphabets were common in traditional filet designs, but with the right technique to hand there really is no limit to what the modern crocheter can depict.

Four different ways of working filet are covered in this chapter so that you can find the best method for you.

Even the most "unarty" of crocheters can get designing with just some squared paper, a pencil and this extremely adaptable crochet technique.

Geo-Filet
Crochet

What is filet crochet?

Filet is a traditional style of crochet characterised by designs of filled and empty squares. In crochet terminology these squares are called "blocks and spaces". There are various methods of filet crochet. This chapter shows you three traditional filet methods, as well as a new variation which uses a "geo-treble" stitch.

TIP On a chart each block can be seen separately, but in the finished piece, areas of blocks merge together.

Above *A filet chart of a fleur-de-lis design showing blocks and spaces.*

Above *The fleur-de-lis has been crocheted with the geo-fill method using Adriafil Uno A Ritorto 5 and a 1.50 mm hook.*

Four filet crochet methods

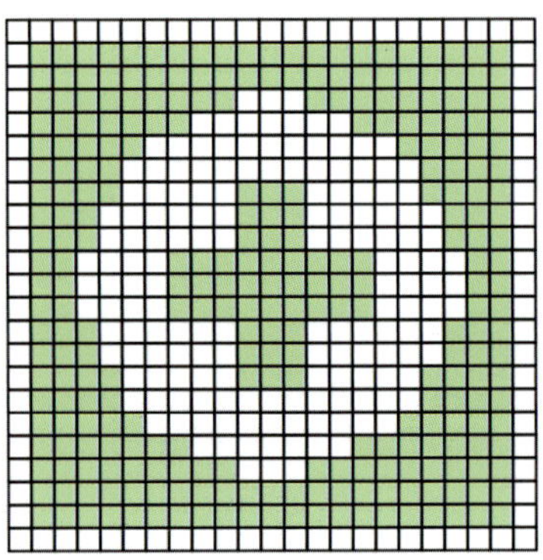

In order to achieve a finished piece of filet crochet that closely resembles the proportions of the original design, the crocheted blocks and spaces need to be as square and as evenly matched in size as possible.

Because stitch height, width and density varies with each crocheter, this chapter describes four different ways to create filet blocks and spaces.

Compare the four samples shown here and then try each of the methods to find which you prefer by following the step-by-step exercises on page 58–62.

1 Single-Fill

In the single-fill sample, the crocheter has achieved well proportioned blocks and spaces, but the spaces are not distinctive.

2 Double-Fill

In the double-fill sample, the crocheter manages to emphasise the spaces, but they are wider than they are tall.

3 Extended-Fill

In the extended-fill sample, the crocheter has made the spaces stand out, and the blocks and spaces well proportioned, but the design is distorted because the blocks are slightly wider than the spaces.

4 Geo-Fill

The crocheter has achieved the best result with the geo-fill method. The spaces are well defined, and the blocks and spaces well proportioned.

What type of yarn?

In keeping with tradition, the filet designs in this chapter have been made with a special yarn known as "crochet thread" or "crochet cotton". Crochet thread is usually 100% cotton and is often labelled "mercerized." This means the thread has undergone a special treatment giving it strength and lustre.

Crochet thread is available in thicknesses from the fineness of sewing thread through to the thickness of standard 4 ply yarn. Some crochet thread will be numbered, for example, No 3, No 5 or No 8. The higher the number, the thinner the thread. Other crochet thread will just suggest a hook size. The suggested hook size, together with the metreage per 100g will give you an indication as to whether it would be a good substitute for the crochet thread used in this chapter. See also page 73 for more information about suitable yarn for filet crochet.

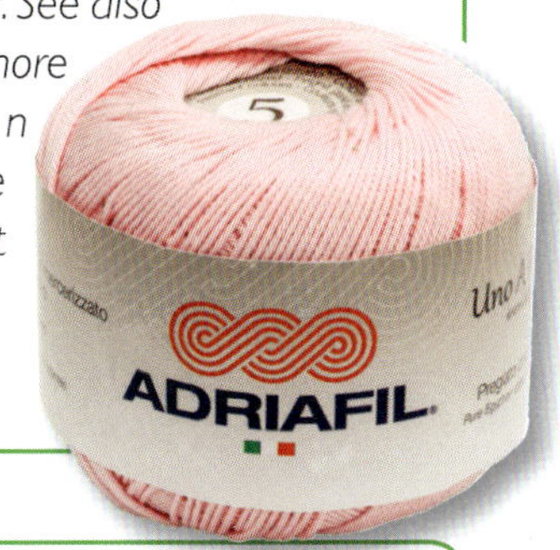

What type of hook?

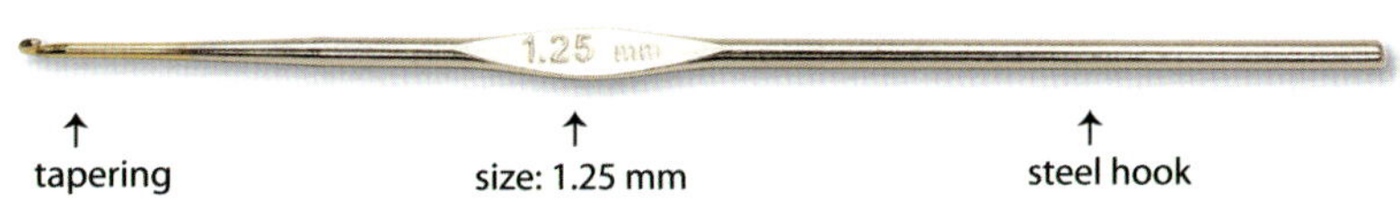

Crochet thread needs a correspondingly small hook. Hooks between 1.00–2.00 mm in size are generally made from steel and usually have a tapered shaft. It takes practice to be able to slide the loops up the tapered shaft by the same distance each time in order to create even stitches. The tapering is useful if, for example, a foundation chain needs to be slightly larger or smaller than an average chain. Keep the loops close to the hook for small chains, or keep the loops nearer the fingerplate for larger chains.

The chart below shows a range of popular crochet threads and their suggested hook sizes:

Name of Thread	**DMC Petra No 8**	**Adriafil Uno A Ritorto Mako 8**	**DMC Cébélia**	**Adriafil Uno A Ritorto Mako 5**	**DMC Petra No 5**	**DMC Petra No 3**
Size of Ball	100 g	50 g	50 g	50 g	100 g	100 g
Recommended Hook Size	1–1.25 mm	1.25 mm	1.50 mm	1.50–1.75 mm	1.75–2.00 mm	2.50 mm
Metres per 100 g	800 m	620 m	520 m	400 m	400 m	280 m

Which method?

The four different filet methods are shown in more detail on pages 58–62.

Try each method before deciding which one suits your personal style of crocheting. You do not necessarily have to achieve well proportioned blocks and spaces, just use the method which suits you best. You might even wish to use different methods for different projects, but remember to be consistent within in each project.

Filet charts

The simplicity of filet allows designs to be conveyed effectively by block and space charts rather than by crochet symbol charts or written instructions.

Right *The design is more evident in the filet chart than in the symbol chart.*

Filet chart

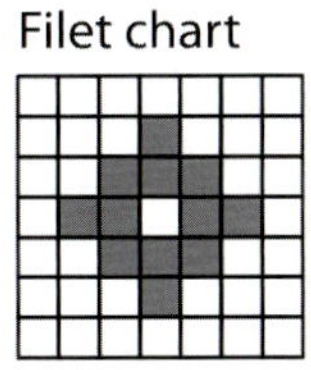

Symbol chart

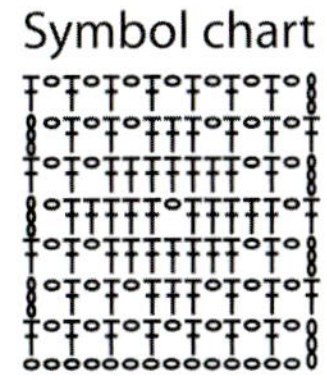

The exercises on the following pages use the filet design on the left to introduce you to each of the different filet methods, and to help you learn to read filet charts. Symbol charts and written instructions are given for each of the different methods as well.

1. Single-Fill Filet Method

Read through this page, then attempt the sample. If you get stuck, there are written instructions for the first four rows.

(On the illustrations below, the lines of the filet chart have been thickened so that the symbol chart can be superimposed over it.)

Filet chart

Symbol chart

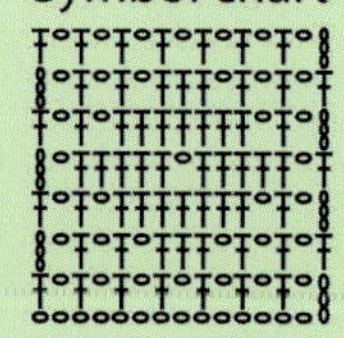

Calculating chains (when the design starts with a space)

- To work out how many chains to crochet for a foundation chain in the single-fill method, multiply the number of squares in the first row by 2, then add 4, for example:
  (7 squares x 2) = 14.
  14 + 4 = chain 18.
- The first treble is worked into the 6th chain from the hook.

Foundation chain

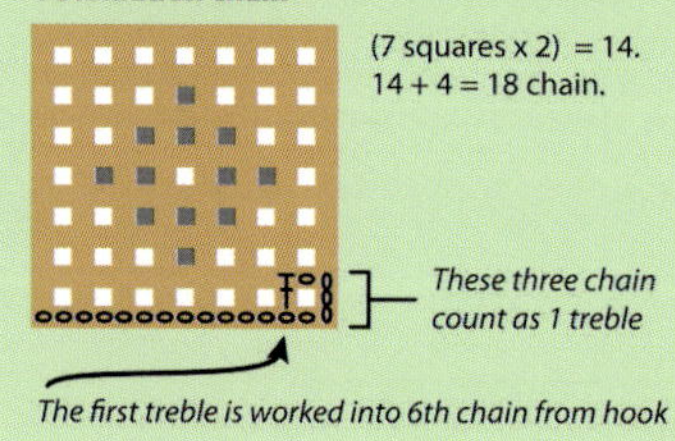

Grid stitches and filet spaces

- The vertical lines on a filet chart represent a single stitch. Think of these vertical lines as "grid stitches"; they help maintain the grid-like structure of filet crochet. In the single-fill method grid stitches are trebles.
- In the single-fill method, a "space" (or empty square) on the filet chart means that there is one chain between the grid stitches.

Row 1

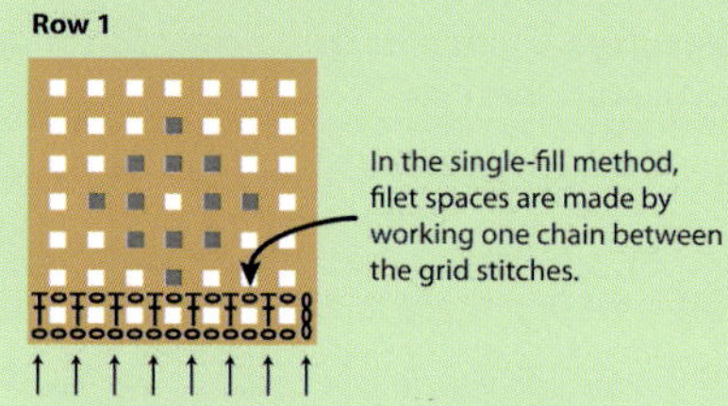

Each vertical line represents one grid stitch. Trebles are used in the single-fill method.

Filet blocks

- In the single-fill method, a "block" (or filled square) on the filet chart means that there is one treble between the grid stitches. ***Where a block is directly over a space, work the treble into the chain-space.***

Row 2

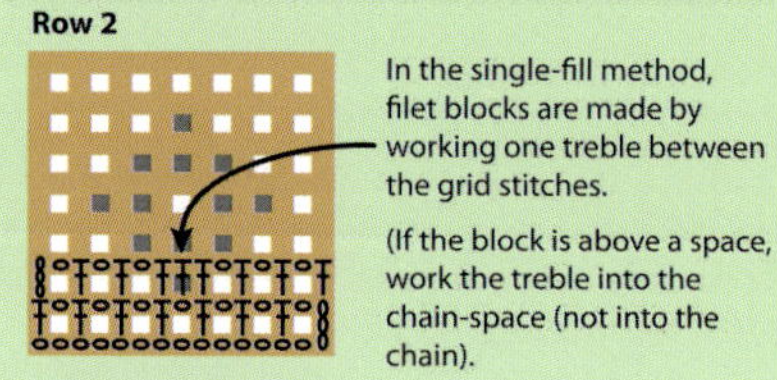

Calculating stitches (single-fill)

- To work out how many trebles to crochet between chain-spaces when working multiple blocks, multiply the number of blocks by 2, then add 1 (see examples, right).

Completed sample

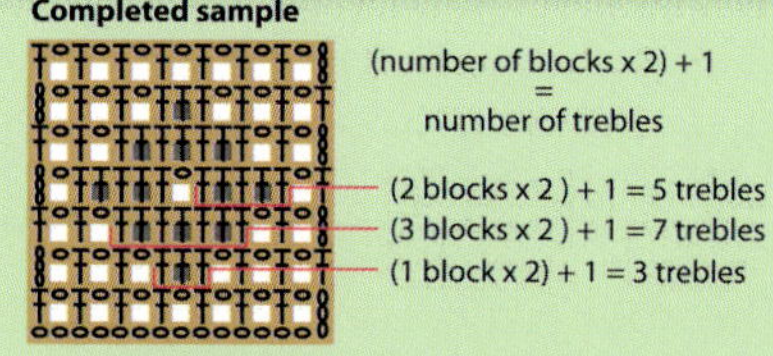

Written instructions (rows 1–4)

Foundation chain Chain 18.

Row 1 1 treble in 6th chain from hook. (Chain 1. Skip next chain. 1 treble in next chain) 6 times. (7 chain-spaces)

Row 2 Chain 4 (counts as 1 treble and 1 chain-space). Turn. Skip next chain-space. 1 treble in next stitch. *(Chain 1. Skip next chain-space. 1 treble in next stitch.)* twice. 1 treble in next chain-space. 1 treble in next stitch. Repeat from * to * 3 times.

Row 3 Chain 4 (counts as 1 treble and 1 chain-space). Turn. Skip next chain-space. 1 treble in next stitch. Chain 1. Skip next chain-space. 1 treble in next stitch. 1 treble in next chain-space. 1 treble in each of next 3 stitches. 1 treble in next chain-space. 1 treble in next stitch. (Chain 1. Skip next chain-space. 1 treble in next stitch) twice.

Row 4 Chain 4 (counts as 1 treble and 1 chain-space). Turn. Skip next chain-space. 1 treble in next stitch. 1 treble in next chain-space. 1 treble in each of next 3 stitches. Chain 1. Skip next stitch. 1 treble in each of next 3 stitches. 1 treble in next chain-space. 1 treble in next stitch. Chain 1. Skip next chain-space. 1 treble in next stitch.

2. Double-Fill Filet Method

Read through this page, then attempt the sample. If you get stuck, there are written instructions for the first four rows.

(On the illustrations below, the lines of the filet chart have been thickened, and the squares elongated, so that the symbol chart can be superimposed over it.)

Filet chart

Symbol chart

Calculating chains (when the design starts with a space)

- To work out how many chains to crochet for the foundation chain in the double-fill method, multiply the number of squares in the first row by 3, then add 5, for example:

  (7 squares x 3) = 21.

  21 + 5 = chain 26.

- The first treble is worked into the 8th chain from the hook.

Foundation chain

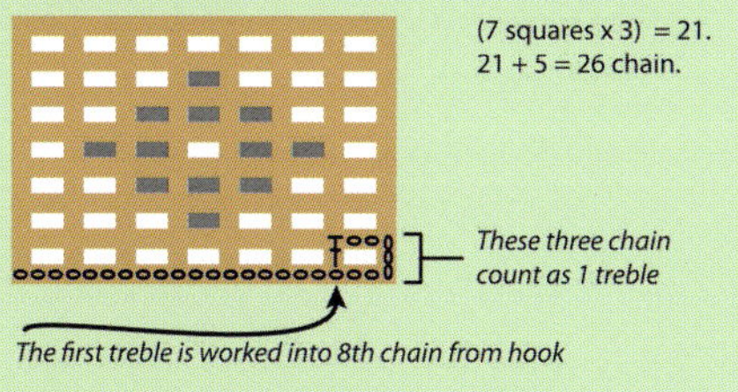

Grid stitches and filet spaces

- The vertical lines on a filet chart represent a single stitch. Think of these vertical lines as "grid stitches"; they help maintain the grid-like structure of filet crochet. In the double-fill method grid stitches are trebles.
- In the double-fill method, a "space" (or empty square) on the filet chart means that there are two chains between the grid stitches.

Row 1

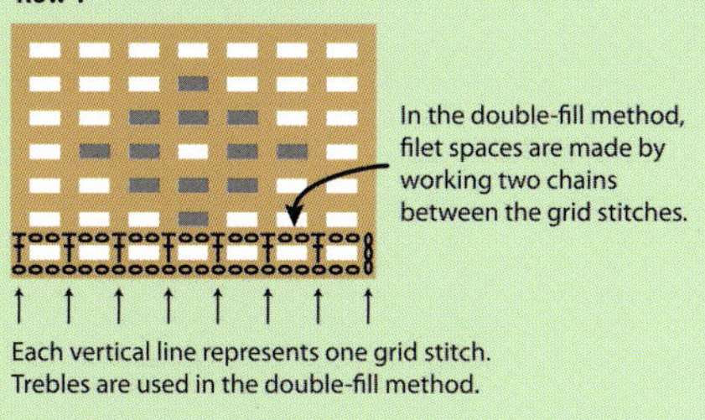

Filet blocks

- In the double-fill method, a "block" (or filled square) on the filet chart means that there are two trebles between the grid stitches. ***Where a block is directly over a space, work the trebles into the chain-space.***

Row 2

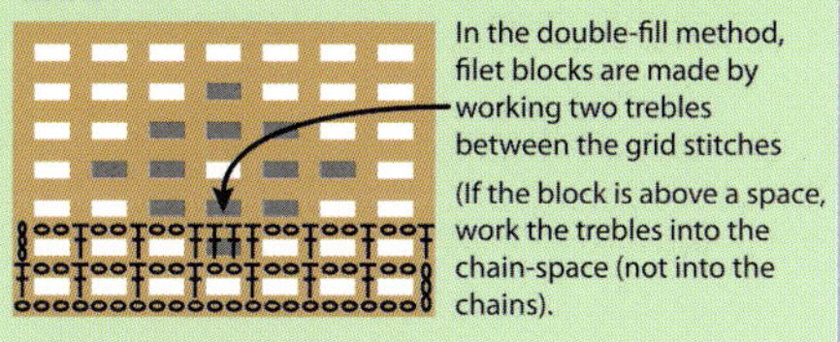

Calculating stitches (double-fill)

- To work out how many trebles to crochet between chain-spaces when working multiple blocks, multiply the number of blocks by 3, then add 1 (see examples, right).

Completed sample

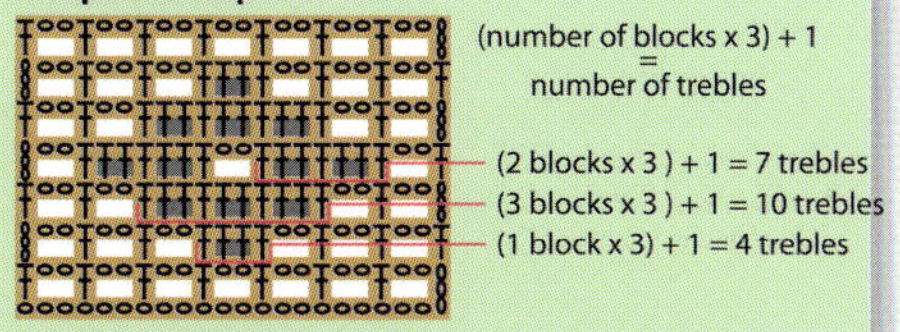

Written instructions (rows 1–4)

Foundation chain Chain 26.

Row 1 1 treble in 8th chain from hook. (Chain 2. Skip next 2 chains. 1 treble in next chain) 6 times. (7 chain-spaces)

Row 2 Chain 5 (counts as 1 treble and 1 2-chain-space). Turn. Skip next chain-space. 1 treble in next stitch. *(Chain 2. Skip next chain-space. 1 treble in next stitch.)* twice. 2 treble in next chain-space. 1 treble in next stitch. Repeat from * to * 3 times.

Row 3 Chain 5 (counts as 1 treble and 1 2-chain-space). Turn. Skip next chain-space. 1 treble in next stitch. Chain 2. Skip next chain-space. 1 treble in next stitch. 2 treble in next chain-space. 1 treble in each of next 4 stitches. 2 treble in next chain-space. 1 treble in next stitch. (Chain 2. Skip next chain-space. 1 treble in next stitch) twice.

Row 4 Chain 5 (counts as 1 treble and 1 2-chain-space). Turn. Skip next chain-space. 1 treble in next stitch. 2 treble in next chain-space. 1 treble in each of next 4 stitches. Chain 2. Skip next 2 stitches. 1 treble in each of next 4 stitches. 2 treble in next chain-space. 1 treble in next stitch. Chain 2. Skip next chain-space. 1 treble in next stitch.

3. Extended-Fill Filet Method

Read through this page, then attempt the sample. If you get stuck, there are written instructions for the first four rows.

Filet chart

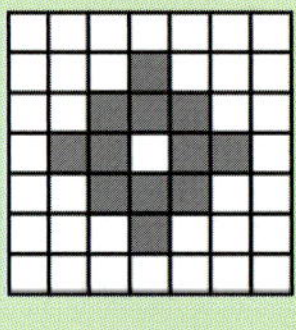

Symbol chart

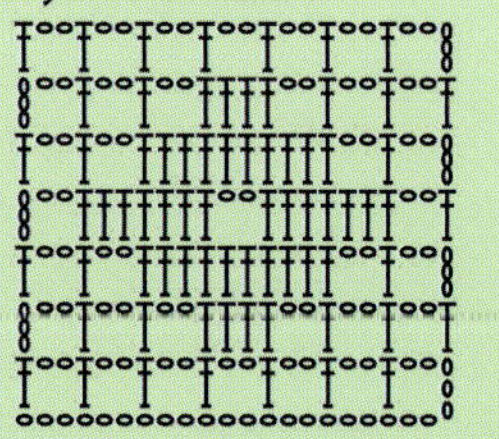

(On the illustrations below, the lines of the filet chart have been thickened, so that the symbol chart can be superimposed over it.)

Ī = extended-treble

(See page 7 for how to crochet an extended-treble.)

Calculating chains (when the design starts with a space)

- To work out how many chains to crochet for the foundation chain in the extended-fill method, multiply the number of squares in the first row by 3, then add 5, for example:

  (7 squares x 3) = 21
  21 + 5 = chain 26

- The first extended-treble is worked into the 8th chain from the hook.

Foundation chain

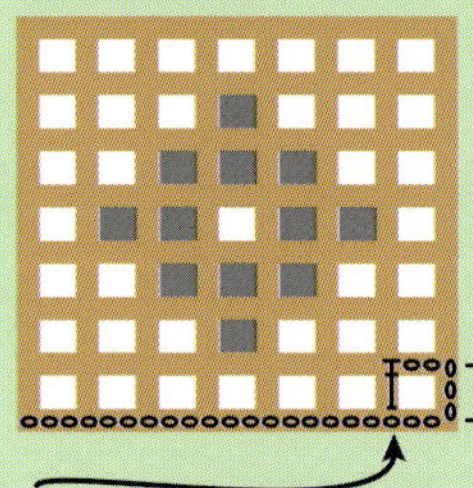

Grid stitches and filet spaces

- The vertical lines on a filet chart represent a single stitch. Think of these vertical lines as "grid stitches"; they help maintain the grid-like structure of filet crochet. In the extended-fill method grid stitches are extended-trebles.
- In the extended-fill method, a "space" (or empty square) on the filet chart means that there are two chains between the grid stitches.

Row 1

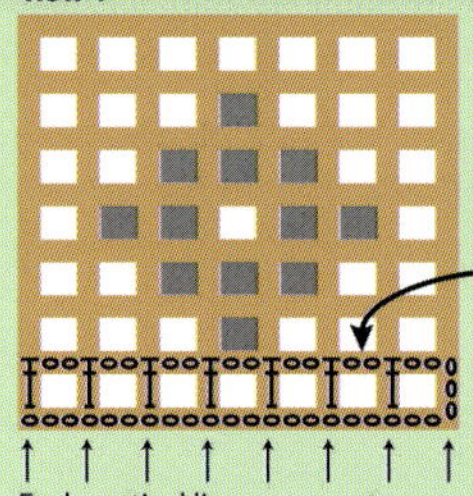

Filet blocks

- In the extended-fill method, a "block" (or filled square) on the filet chart means that there are two extended-trebles between the grid stitches. ***Where a block is directly over a space, work the extended -trebles into the chain-space.***

Row 2

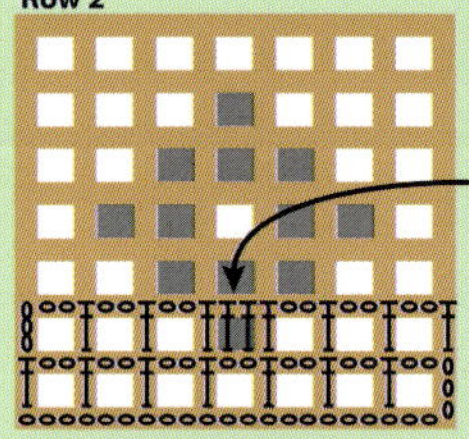

Calculating stitches (extended-fill)

- To work out how many extended-trebles to crochet between chain-spaces when working multiple blocks, multiply the number of blocks by 3, then add 1 (see examples, right).

Completed sample

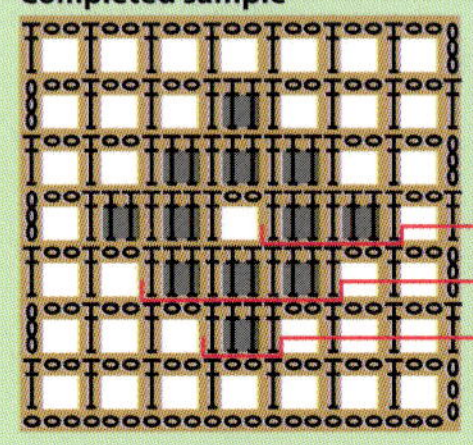

Instructions (rows 1–4)
Abbreviation:
ext-trb = extended-treble.
Foundation chain Chain 26.
Row 1 1 ext-trb in 8th chain from hook. (Chain 2. Skip next 2 chains. 1 ext-trb in next chain) 6 times. (7 chain-spaces)
Row 2 Chain 5 (counts as 1 ext-trb and 1 2-chain-space). Turn. Skip next chain-space. 1 ext-trb in next stitch. *(Chain 2. Skip next chain-space. 1 ext-trb in next stitch.)* twice. 2 ext-trb in next chain-space. 1 ext-trb in next stitch. Repeat from * to * 3 times.
Row 3 Chain 5 (counts as 1 ext-trb and 1 2-chain-space). Turn. Skip next chain-space. 1 ext-trb in next stitch. Chain 2. Skip next chain-space. 1 ext-trb in next stitch. 2 ext-trb in next chain-space. 1 ext-trb in each of next 4 stitches. 2 ext-trb in next chain-space. 1 ext-trb in next stitch. (Chain 2. Skip next chain-space. 1 ext-trb in next stitch) twice.
Row 4 Chain 5 (counts as 1 ext-trb and 1 2-chain-space). Turn. Skip next chain-space. 1 ext-trb in next stitch. 2 ext-trb in next chain-space. 1 ext-trb in each of next 4 stitches. Chain 2. Skip next 2 stitches. 1 ext-trb in each of next 4 stitches. 2 ext-trb in next chain-space. 1 ext-trb in next stitch. Chain 2. Skip next chain-space. 1 treble in next stitch.

4. Geo-Fill Filet Method

Instructions for the geo-treble stitch are on page 62. Read through this page, then attempt the sample. If you get stuck, there are written instructions for the first four rows.

(On the illustrations below, the lines of the filet chart have been thickened, so that the symbol chart can be superimposed over it.)

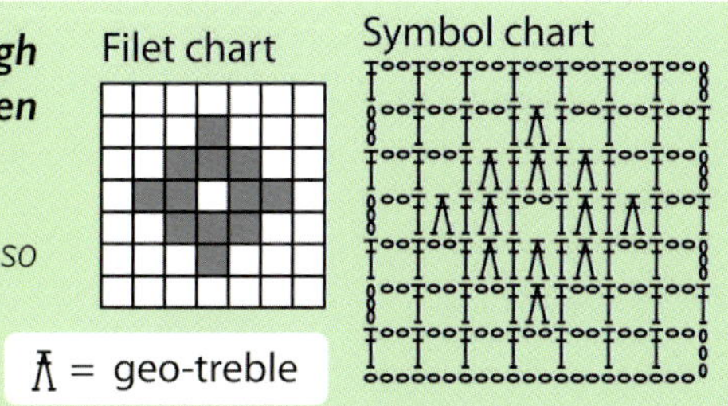

Calculating Chains (when the design starts with a space)

- To work out how many chains to crochet for the foundation chain in the geo-fill method, multiply the number of squares in the first row by 3, then add 5, for example:
  (7 squares x 3) = 21.
  21 + 5 = chain 26.
- The first extended-treble is worked into the 8th chain from the hook.

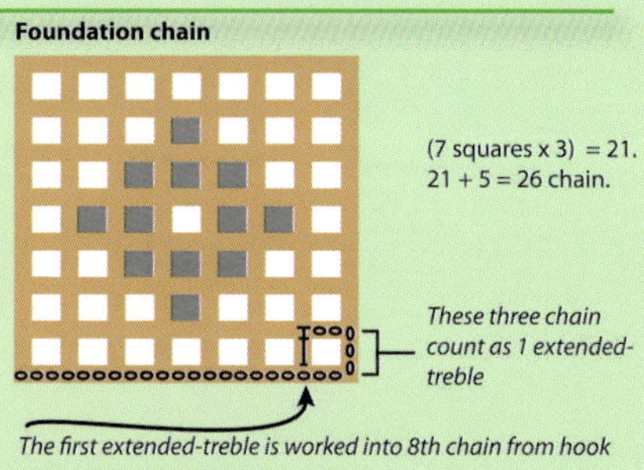

Grid stitches and filet spaces

- The vertical lines on a filet chart represent a single stitch. Think of these vertical lines as "grid stitches"; they help maintain the grid-like structure of filet crochet. In the geo-fill method grid stitches are extended-trebles.
- In the geo-fill method, a "space" (or empty square) on the filet chart means that there are two chains between the grid stitches.

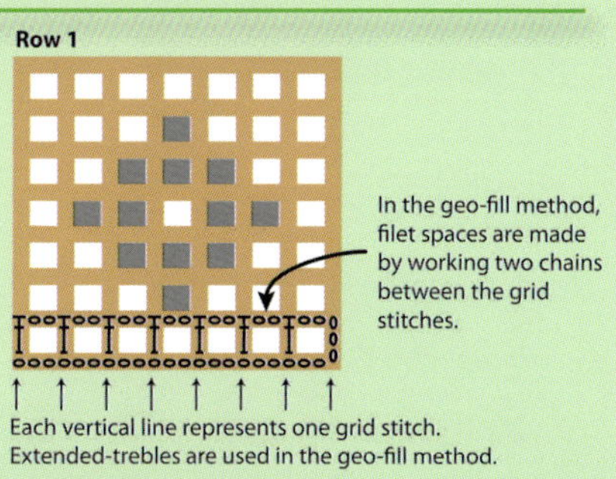

Filet blocks

- In the geo-fill method, a "block" (or filled square) on the filet chart means that there is one geo-treble between the grid stitches (see page 62). ***Where a block is directly over a space, work the geo-trebles into the chain-space.***

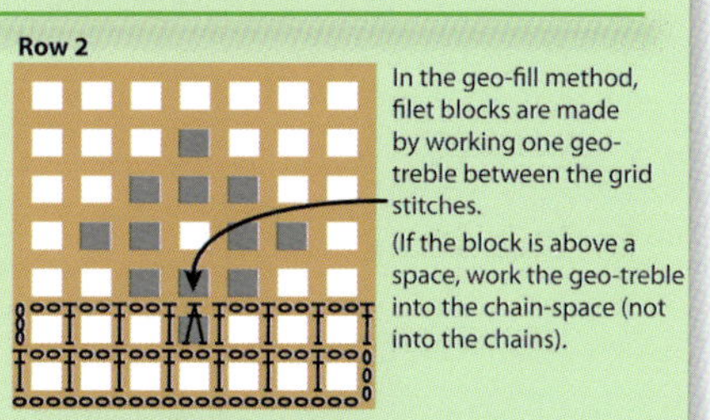

Multiple blocks (geo-fill method)

- When crocheting multiple blocks, work (1 extended-treble. 1 geo-treble) for each block, and finish with 1 extended-treble.

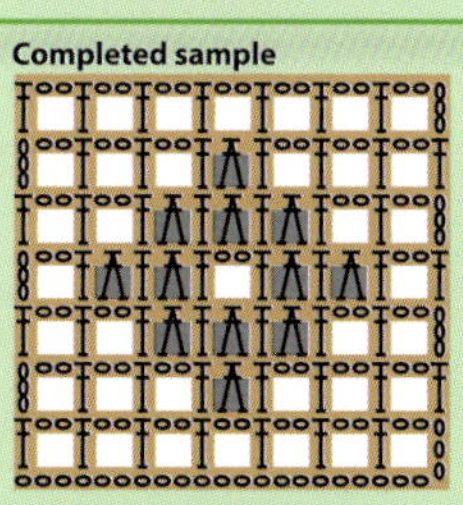

Instructions (rows 1–4)
Abbreviations
ext-trb = extended-treble.
ch-sp = chain-space
Foundation chain Chain 26.
Row 1 1 ext-trb in 8th chain from hook. (Chain 2. Skip next 2 chains. 1 ext-trb in next chain) 6 times. (7 chain-spaces)
Row 2 Chain 5 (counts as 1 ext-trb and 1 2-ch-sp). Turn. Skip next ch-sp. 1 ext-trb in next stitch. *(Chain 2. Skip next ch-sp. 1 ext-trb in next stitch.)* twice. 1 geo-treble in next ch-sp. 1 ext-trb in next stitch. Repeat from * to * 3 times.
Row 3 Chain 5 (counts as 1 ext-trb and 1 2-ch-sp). Turn. Skip next ch-sp. 1 ext-trb in next stitch. Chain 2. Skip next ch-sp. *1 ext-trb in next stitch. 1 geo-treble in next ch-sp. 1 ext-trb in next stitch.* 1 geo-treble in next stitch. Repeat from * to * once. (Chain 2. Skip next ch-sp. 1 ext-trb in next stitch) twice.
Row 4 Chain 5 (counts as 1 ext-trb and 1 2-ch-sp). Turn. Skip next ch-sp. 1 ext-trb in next stitch. 1 geo-treble in next ch-sp. 1 ext-trb in next stitch. 1 geo-treble in next stitch. 1 ext-trb in next stitch. Chain 2. Skip next stitch. 1 ext-trb in next stitch. 1 geo-treble in next stitch. 1 ext-trb in next stitch. 1 geo-treble in next ch-sp. 1 ext-trb in next stitch. Chain 2. Skip next ch-sp. 1 ext-treble in next stitch.

How to Make a Geo-treble

The concept behind the geo-treble is to produce a stitch which is roughly the width of two chains, thereby helping to create evenly proportioned blocks and spaces in filet crochet. Using a geo-treble as a fill stitch also makes counting the number of blocks worked easier compared to other filet methods.

Left-handed

Step 1 Yarn over. Pick up a loop from chain-space or stitch indicated (three loops on hook).

Right-handed

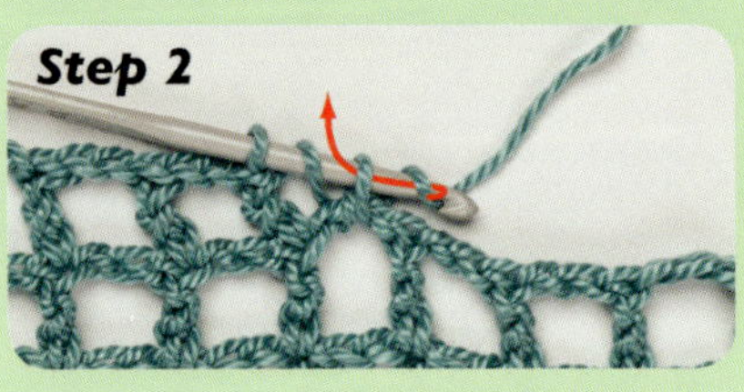

Step 2 Yarn over and draw through one loop (three loops remain on hook).

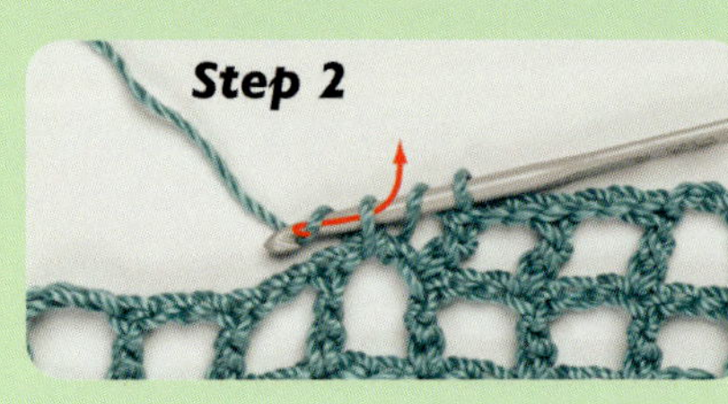

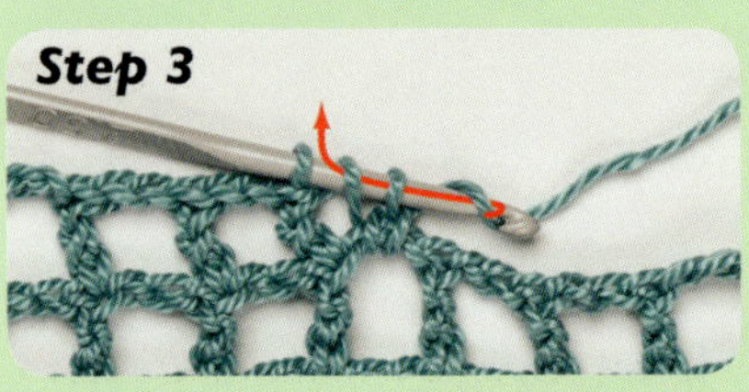

Step 3 Yarn over and draw through two loops (two loops remain on hook).

Step 4 Yarn over. Pick up a loop from same chain-space or stitch (four loops on hook).

Step 5 Yarn over and draw through two loops (3 loops remain on hook).

Step 6 Yarn over and draw through all three loops on hook.

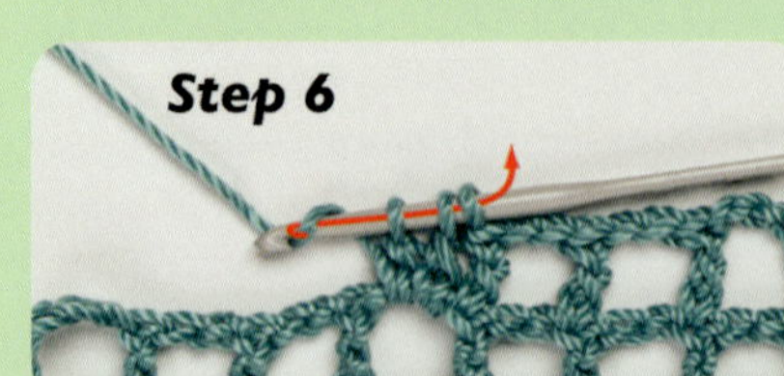

The final illustration shows the completed geo-treble. The width of the geo-treble closely matches the width of a 2-chain-space making it an ideal stitch for "blocks" in filet crochet.

Symmetrical charts

Symmetrical filet charts are easy to follow because the rows can be read in either direction.

When the work is turned at the end of a row, the design in the crochet will still match the design in the chart.

Symmetrical chart

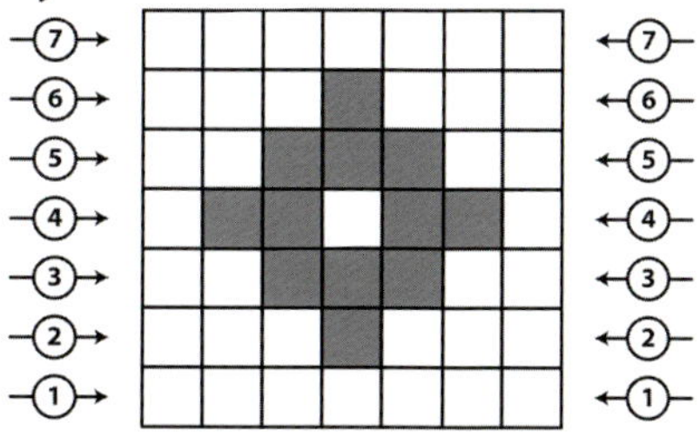

Rows can be read in either direction.

Left-handers *may wish to follow rows in a symmetrical filet chart from left to right because this is the direction in which they crochet.*

Right-handers *may wish to follow rows in a symmetrical filet chart from right to left because this is the direction in which they crochet.*

Asymmetrical charts

Asymmetrical charts are more challenging to follow because on every other row the design in the chart will be a mirror image of the design in the crochet.

One solution is to make a reverse copy of the chart. If the two charts are swapped each row, all rows can be read in the same direction and the design in the chart will always match the design in the crochet.

Asymmetrical chart

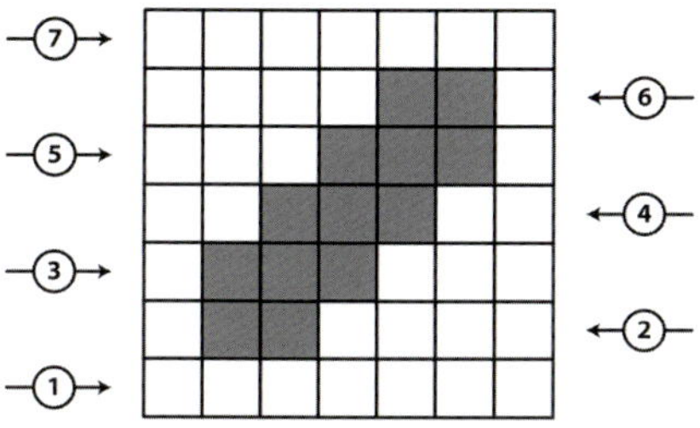

Rows are read in alternate directions

Asymmetrical chart

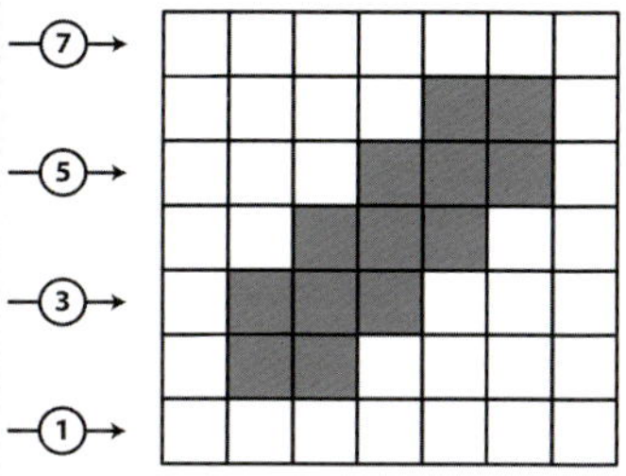

Asymmetrical chart - reverse copy

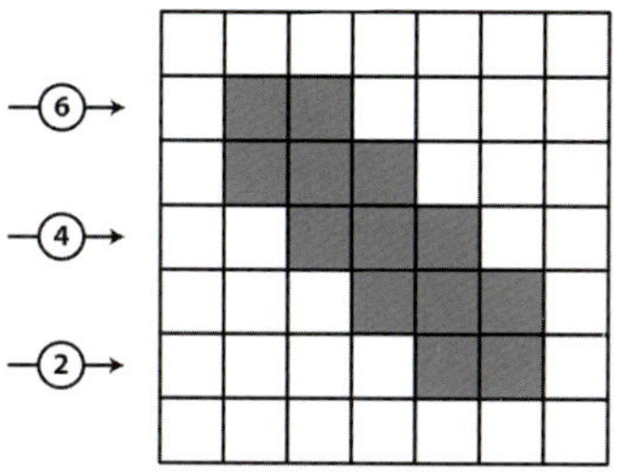

If odd rows are read from one chart, and even rows from the reverse copy, all rows can be read in same direction (left to right is illustrated).

Foundation chains

Foundation chains can be a problem in filet crochet. They can either be too tight or too loose and thus spoil the overall effect. The technique on page 5 can help you achieve the right tension. Achieving the right size foundation chains can make a big difference to a finished project.

TIP If you would like extra practice in your chosen filet method before embarking on a major project, you could try crocheting any of the charts on this page. These small pieces are also ideal for experimenting with the different edgings on page 70–71.

Keeping track

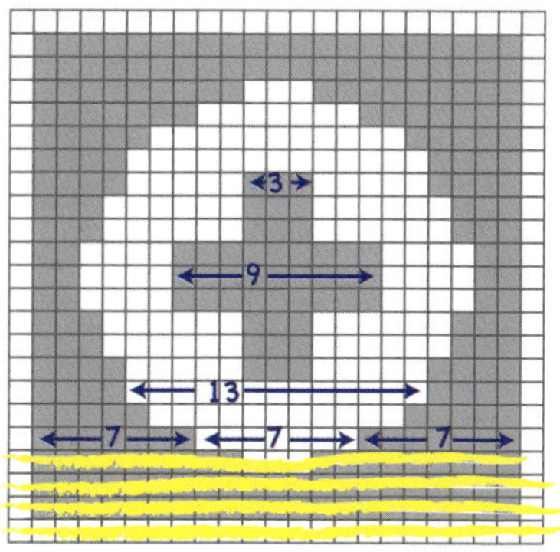

Everyone has their own way of following a pattern. Here are a couple of hints which may help:

- Write how many consecutive blocks/spaces there are on the chart.
- Use a highlighter or pen to mark off each row as it is completed.

Motif Mats

The six motif mats photographed at the start of this chapter were all made with the geo-filet method. There are written instructions for the first row in each method to help you get started.

TIP The Smiley Face, and Apple designs are completely symmetrical so the charts can be read from left to right, or from right to left. The Yin & Yang, Strawberry, Coffee Cup and House designs, have areas which are not symmetrical, so take extra care when reading the chart. See the note on the previous page about following asymmetrical charts.

Materials

Thread *Adriafil Uno A Ritorto 5 (50g)*
Composition *100% mercerised cotton*
Yardage *200 metres (218 yards) approximately*
Hook *1.50 mm*
Finished size *29 x 26 cm (geo-fill method) approximately*

Quantities

- *Single-fill method: 1 x 50g each mat*
- *Double, Extended and Geo-fill methods: 2 x 50g balls each mat (see tip box below)*

Shades

- *Smiley face* — *Saffron (07)*
- *Yin and Yang* — *Light Army Green (79)*
- *Apple* — *Sea Green (08)*
- *Strawberry* — *Pink (03) {light pink}*
- *Coffee cup* — *Ecru (12)*
- *House* — *Baby Light Yellow (05)*

Instructions

Single-fill method

Foundation chain Chain 70.
1st row 1 treble in 6th chain from hook. (Chain 1. Skip 1 chain. 1 treble in next chain) 32 times. (33 chain-spaces)

Double-fill method

Foundation chain Chain 104.
1st row 1 treble in 8th chain from hook. (Chain 2. Skip 2 chains. 1 treble in next chain) 32 times. (33 chain-spaces)

Extended-fill method

Foundation chain Chain 104.
1st row 1 extended-treble in 8th chain from hook. (Chain 2. Skip 2 chains. 1 extended-treble in next chain) 32 times. (33 chain-spaces)

Geo-fill method

Foundation chain Chain 104.
1st row 1 extended-treble in 8th chain from hook. (Chain 2. Skip 2 chains. 1 extended-treble in next chain) 32 times. (33 chain-spaces)

All methods

Rows 2–33 follow the relevant chart.
After the last row, crochet an edging from pages 70–71. Fasten off. Block if required (see page 69).

TIP Although 2 x 50g balls of thread have been specified to make one mat, not all the of the second ball will be needed, so 7 or 8 x 50g balls of the same colour will make all six mats.

Symbol Chart (Row 1)

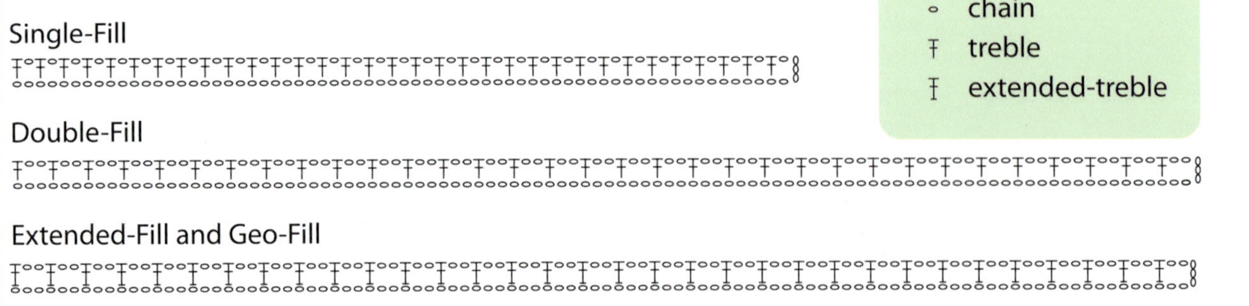

Geo-filet

Smiley Face

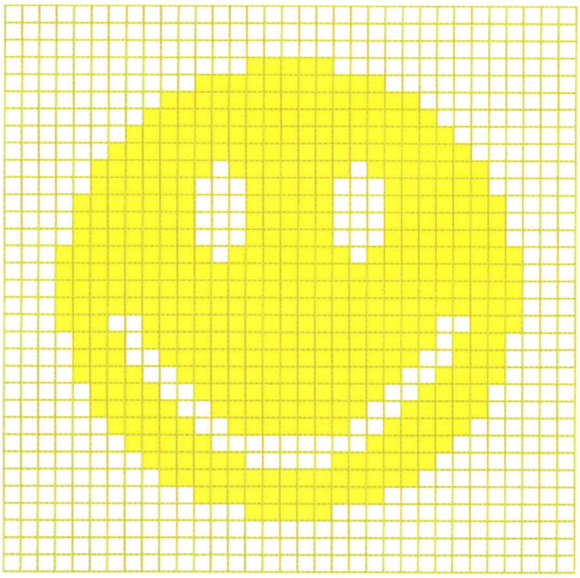

Yin & Yang

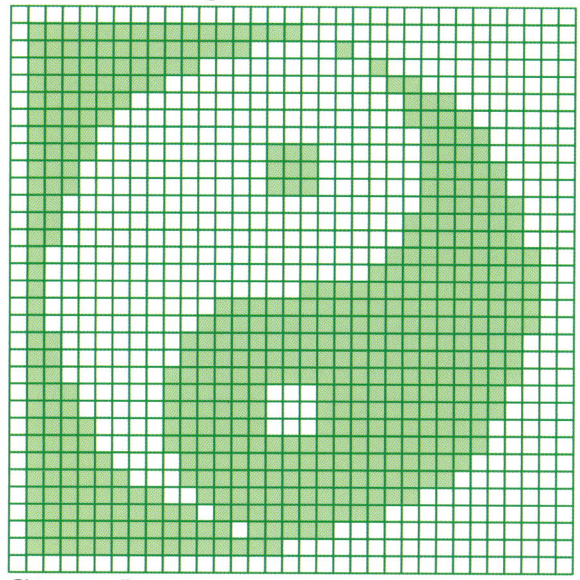

Apple

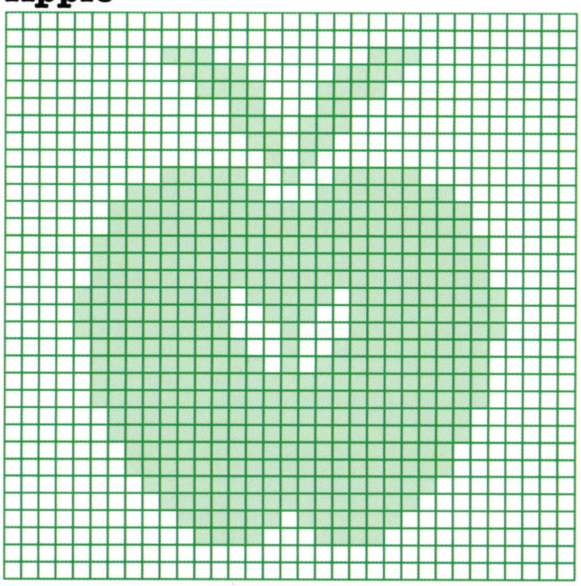

Strawberry

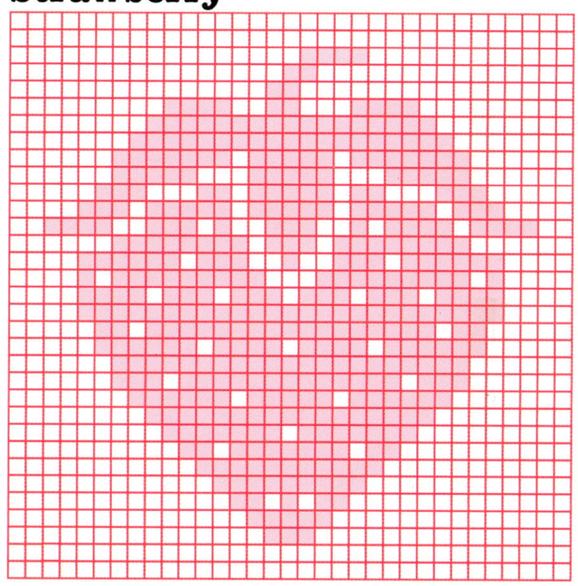

Coffee Cup

House

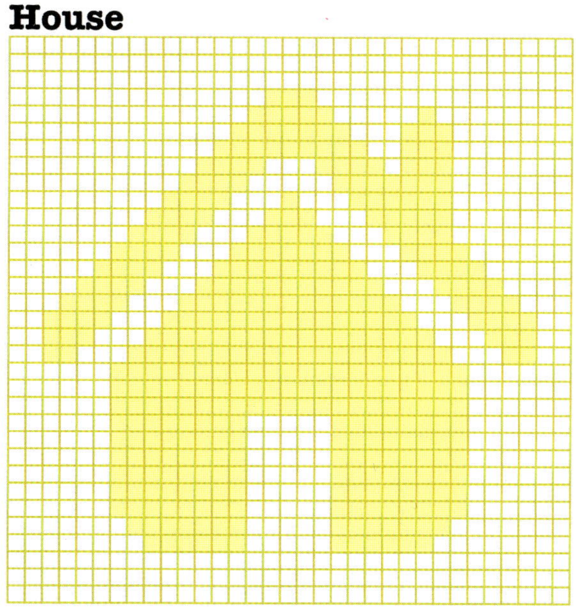

Whimsical Mats

The five whimsical mats photographed on the next three pages were all made with the geo-filet method. There are written instructions for the first and second rows in each method to help you get started.

TIP These designs are all asymmetrical (see page 63). The photos and charts are mirror images to help you follow the design.

Materials

Thread *Adriafil Uno A Ritorto 5 (50g)*
Composition *100% mercerised cotton*
Yardage *200 metres (218 yards) approximately*
Hook *1.50 mm*
Finished size *43 x 30 cm (geo-fill method) approximately*
Quantities *2 x 50g balls each mat (tip box below)*
Shades

- *Empty plate — Turquoise (73)*
- *Dinner time — Light Blue (09)*
- *Apple — Green Yellow (87)*
- *Strawberry — Deep Pink (04)*
- *Burger — Light Army Green (79)*

Instructions

Single-fill method

Foundation chain Chain 98.
Row 1 1 treble in 6th chain from hook. (Chain 1. Skip 1 chain. 1 treble in next chain) 46 times. (47 chain-spaces)
Row 2 Chain 4 (counts as 1 treble and 1 chain-space). Turn. Skip next chain-space. 1 treble in next stitch. (Chain 1. Skip next chain-space. 1 treble in next stitch) 46 times.

Double-fill method

Foundation chain Chain 146.
Row 1 1 treble in 8th chain from hook. (Chain 2. Skip 2 chains. 1 treble in next chain) 46 times. (47 chain-spaces)
Row 2 Chain 5 (counts as 1 treble and 1 2-chain-space). Turn. Skip next chain-space. 1 treble in next stitch. (Chain 2. Skip next chain-space. 1 treble in next stitch) 46 times.

Extended-fill method

Foundation chain Chain 146.
Row 1 1 extended-treble in 8th chain from hook. (Chain 2. Skip 2 chains. 1 extended-treble in next chain) 46 times. (47 chain-spaces)
Row 2 Chain 5 (counts as 1 extended-treble and 1 2-chain-space). Turn. Skip next chain-space. 1 extended-treble in next stitch. (Chain 2. Skip next chain-space. 1 extended-treble in next stitch) 46 times.

TIP About 80g of thread will be needed for each mat (with the geo-fill method), so although 2 x 50g balls of thread have been specified for each mat, only 8 or 9 x 50g balls of thread are needed to make all five mats in the same colour.

Geo-fill method

Foundation chain Chain 146.
Row 1 1 extended-treble in 8th chain from hook. (Chain 2. Skip 2 chains. 1 extended-treble in next chain) 46 times. (47 chain-spaces)
Row 2 Chain 5 (counts as 1 extended-treble and 1 2-chain-space). Turn. Skip next chain-space. 1 extended-treble in next stitch. (Chain 2. Skip next chain-space. 1 extended-treble in next stitch) 46 times.

All methods

Rows 2–37 Follow the relevant chart.
After the last row, crochet an edging from pages 70–71 (Edging No 4 was used in the photographed mats). Fasten off. Block if required (see page 69).

Symbol Chart (Row 1)

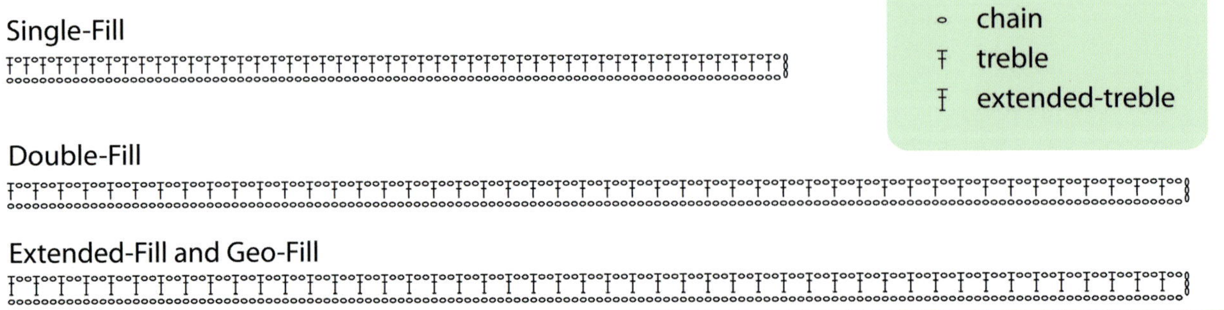

Dinner Time

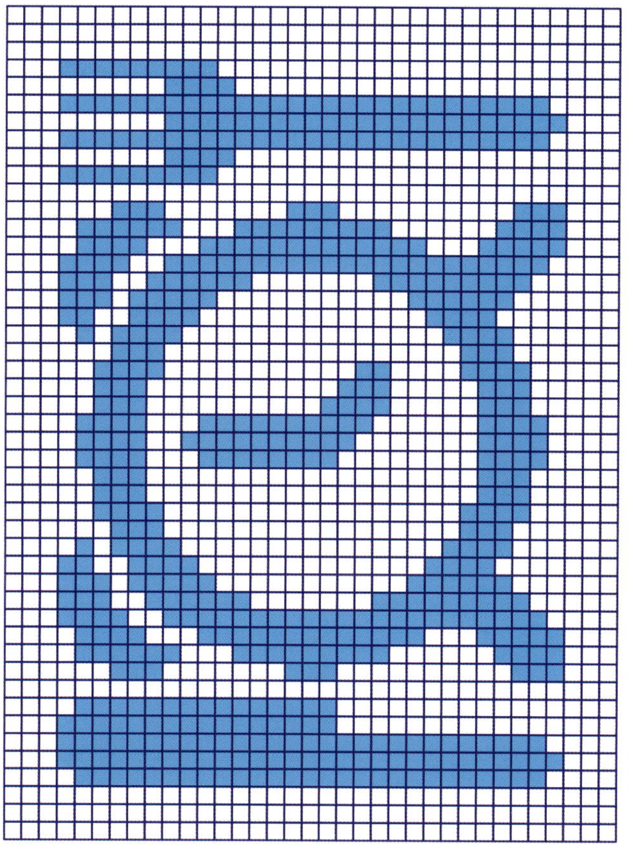

Empty Plate

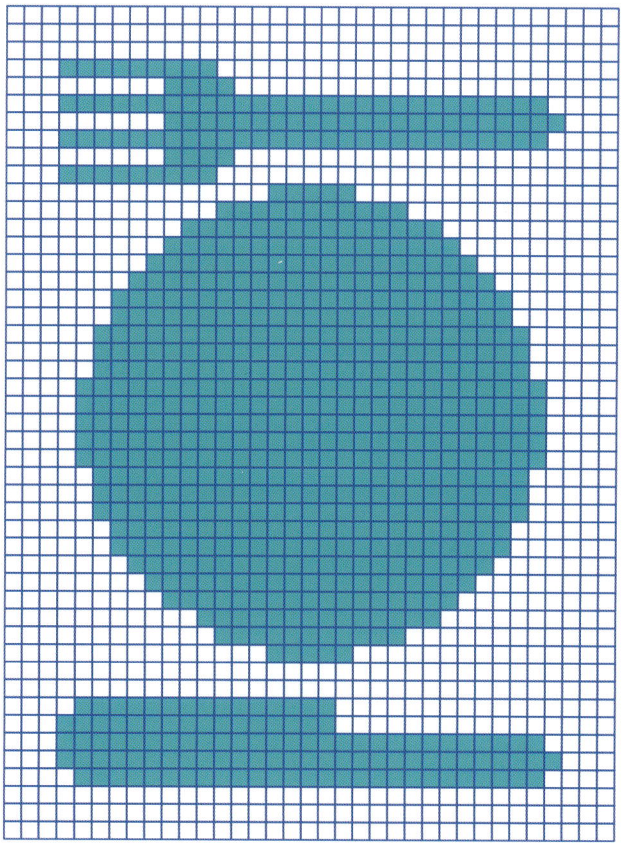

Whimsical Mats – continued

Strawberry

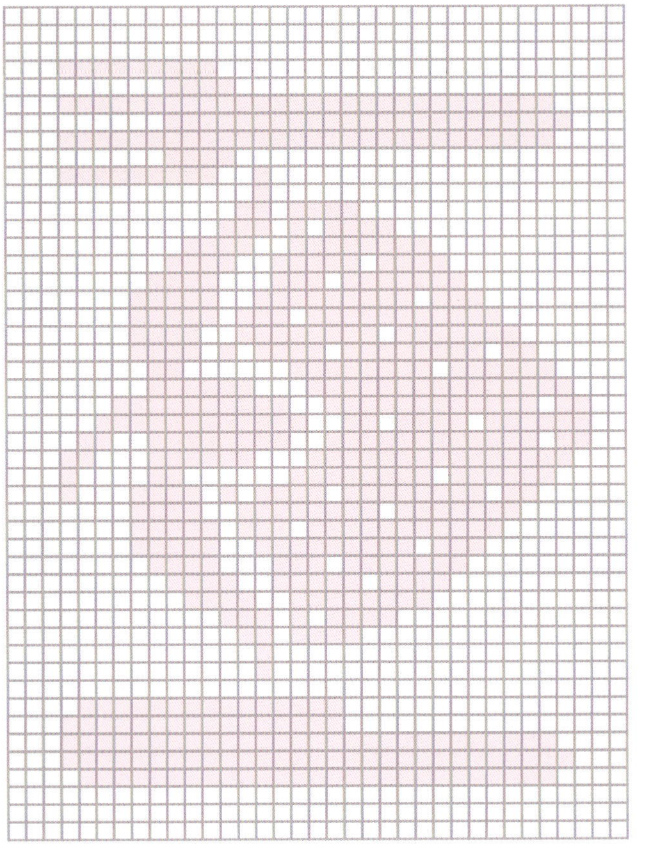

Burger

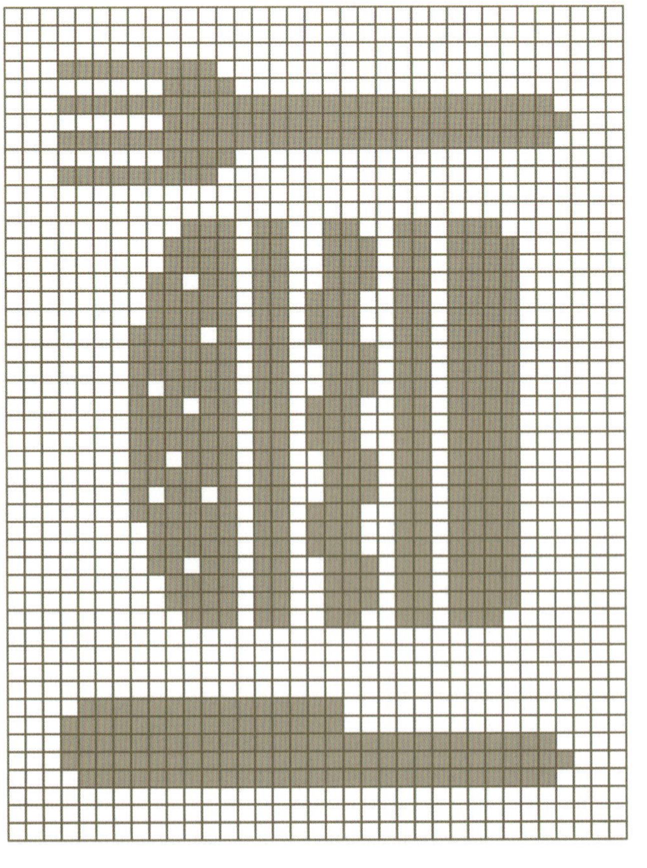

Apple

Blocking

"Blocking" is an optional finishing technique that can give filet crochet a more uniform appearance. Using rust-free dressmaking pins, pin the piece to an ironing board or folded towel, lightly stretching into an even shape as you go. Spritz with room temperature water and leave to dry in a safe place.

Blocking can also help remedy irregularly shaped squares. For instance, if the piece's squares are wider than they are tall, spritz with water first, then gently stretch the piece out top and bottom till you have achieved the required proportions before pinning and leaving to dry.

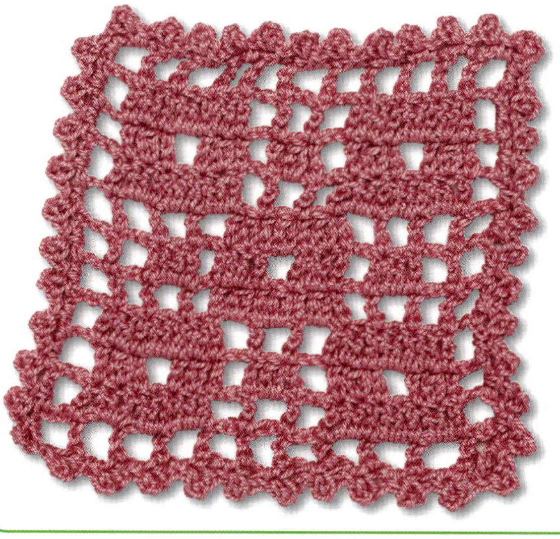

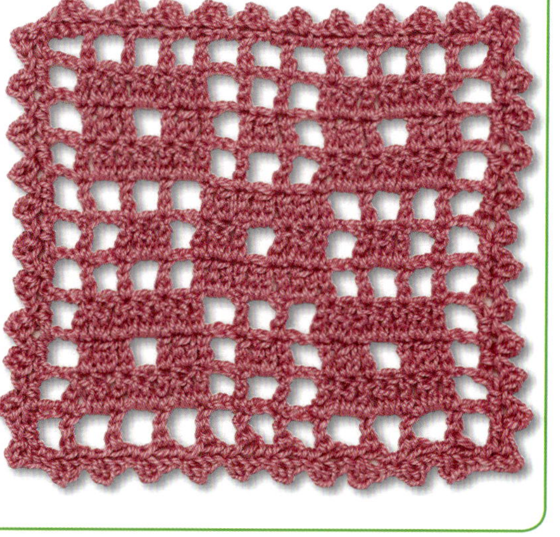

Filet Edgings

These edgings can be used on any of the designs in this chapter, or indeed on any piece of filet crochet that has a border of spaces. You may need to adapt an edging slightly to suit your personal style. Make sure you choose an edging that is appropriate to your particular filet method. Follow the symbol charts in a anti-clockwise direction.

TIP The instructions assume that you will start the edging at a corner-space. Either work the edging after finishing the last row of the item, or, if the thread or yarn has already been fastened off, the join the thread to a corner-space with a slip-stitch.

- ∘ chain
- • slip-stitch
- + double-crochet
- T half-treble

No 1 edging (single fill method)

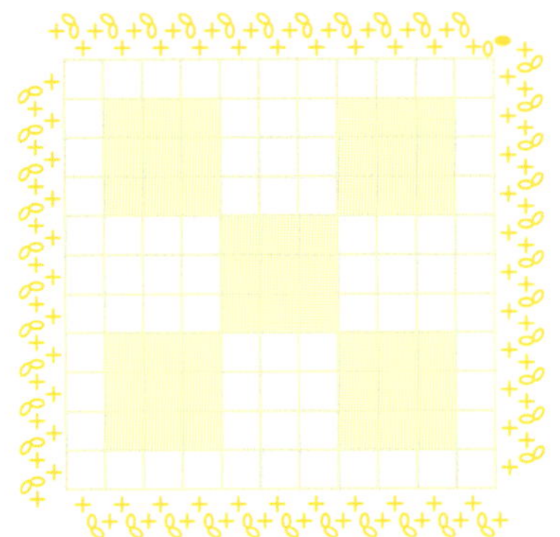

Chain 1. 1 double-crochet in same corner-space. ◊*Chain 2. 1 double-crochet in 2nd chain from hook. 1 double-crochet in next space.* Repeat from * to * up and including next corner-space. Chain 2. 1 double-crochet in 2nd chain from hook. 1 double-crochet in same corner-space.◊ Repeat from ◊ to ◊ two more times. Then repeat from * to * up to and including last corner-space. Chain 2. 1 double-crochet in 2nd chain from hook. Slip-stitch into first double-crochet. Fasten off.

No 2 edging (single fill method)

Chain 3. 1 half-treble in same corner-space. ◊*Chain 1. 1 half-treble in next space.* Repeat from * to * up to and including next corner-space. (Chain 1. 1 half-treble) two more times in same corner-space.◊ Repeat from ◊ to ◊ two more times. Repeat from * to * up to and including last corner-space. Chain 1. Slip-stitch into 2nd of first 3 chain. Fasten off.

No 3 edging (double-fill, extended fill & geo-fill methods)

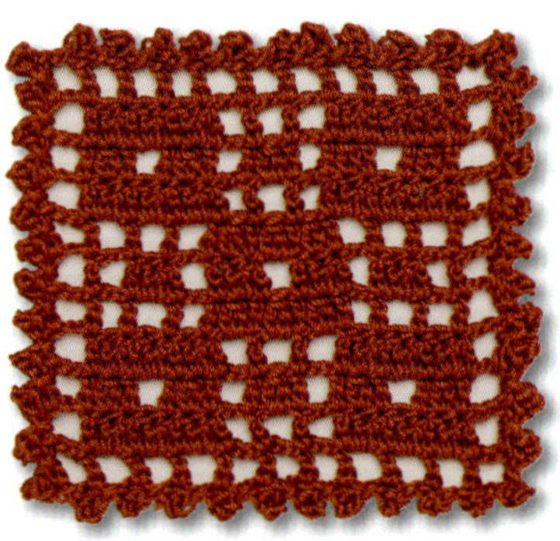

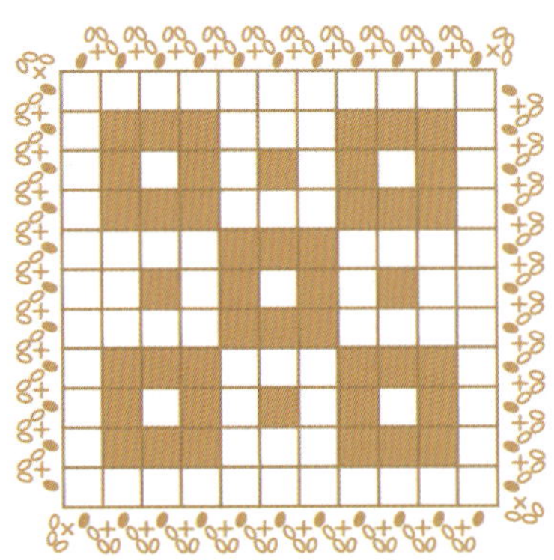

Chain 3. 1 double-crochet in 3rd chain from hook. Slip-stitch into same corner-space. ◊*Chain 3. 1 double-crochet in 3rd chain from hook. Slip-stitch into next space.* Repeat from * to * up to and including next corner-space. Chain 3. 1 double-crochet in 3rd chain from hook. Slip-stitch into same corner-space.◊ Repeat from ◊ to ◊ two more times. Repeat from * to * up to and including last corner-space. Fasten off.

No 4 edging (double-fill, extended fill & geo-fill methods)

Chain 1. 1 double-crochet in same corner-space. ◊*Chain 3. 1 half-treble in 3rd chain from hook. 1 double-crochet in next space.* Repeat from * to * up to and including next corner-space. Chain 3. 1 half-treble in 3rd chain from hook. 1 double-crochet in same corner-space.◊ Repeat from ◊ to ◊ two more times. Repeat from * to * up to and including last corner-space. Chain 3. 1 half-treble in 3rd chain from hook. Slip-stitch into first double-crochet. Fasten off.

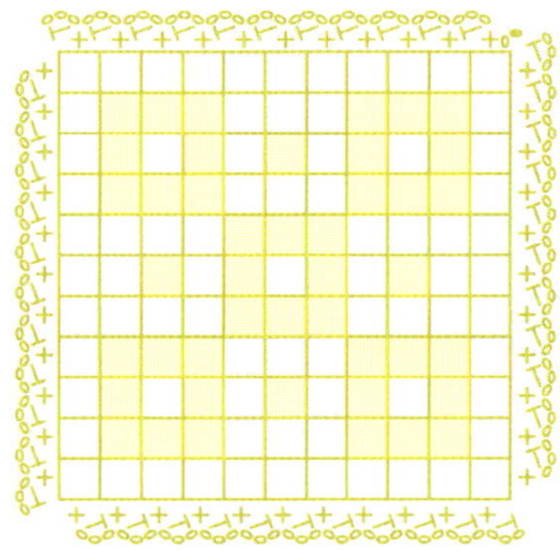

No 5 edging (double-fill, extended fill & geo-fill methods)

Chain 4. 1 half-treble in same corner-space. ◊*Chain 2. 1 half-treble in next space.* Repeat from * to * up to and including next corner-space. (Chain 2. 1 half-treble in same corner-space) twice.◊ Repeat from ◊ to ◊ two more times. Repeat from * to * up to and including last corner-space. Chain 2. Slip-stitch into 2nd of first 4 chain. Fasten off.

No 6 edging (double-fill, extended fill & geo-fill methods)

Chain 4. 1 half-treble in same corner-space. *◊(1 half-treble. Chain 2. 1 half-treble) in next space.* Repeat from * to * up to and including next corner-space. (Chain 2. 1 half-treble. Chain 2. 1 half-treble) in same corner-space.◊ Repeat from ◊ to ◊ two more times. Repeat from * to * up to and including the last corner-space. Chain 2. Slip-stitch into 2nd of first 2 chain. Fasten off.

No 7 edging (double-fill, extended fill & geo-fill methods)

Chain 6. Slip-stitch into 3rd chain from hook. Chain 1. 1 half-treble in same corner-space. ◊*Chain 4. Slip-stitch into 3rd chain from hook. Chain 1. 1 half-treble in next space.* Repeat from * to * up to and including next corner-space. (Chain 4. Slip-stitch into 3rd chain from hook. Chain 1. 1 half-treble) two more times in same corner-space.◊ Repeat from ◊ to ◊ two more times. Repeat from * to * up to and including last corner-space. (Chain 4. Slip-stitch into 3rd chain from hook. Chain 1. Slip-stitch into 2nd of first 4 chain. Fasten off.

Adapting Geo-filet

Create your own designs

Once you can achieve nice evenly balanced blocks and spaces, you can easily create your own designs. Filet techniques lend themselves to large, well defined shapes rather than intricate repeating patterns. Motifs, logos, shapes, letters and numbers are ideal material to incorporate into filet crochet. Simply use squared paper and a pencil to map out your ideas.

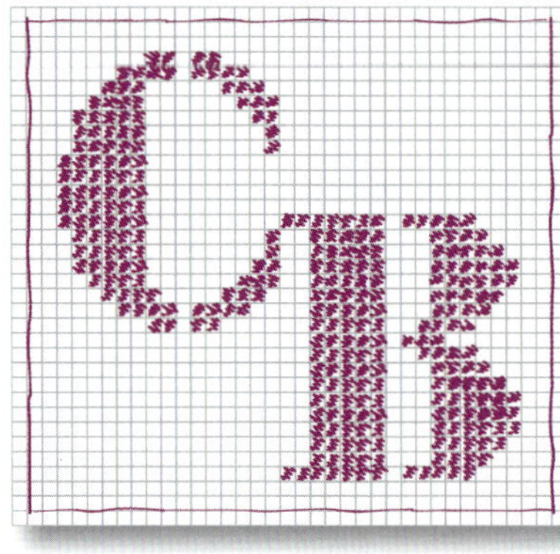

Above *Thread: Adriafil Uno A Ritorto 5 (100% mercerised cotton). Shade: lilac (90). Hook: 1.50 mm.*

Incorporating Colours

Filet crochet tends to be done in a single shade, so if you wish to inject some colour try working "granny square" sized pieces of filet crochet in different colours and join them together using the border method shown on pages 42–43. You may need to experiment with the tension of the joining border, but it is worth doing because this is a very effective way of joining filet that has a border of spaces.

Joining squares of filet crochet in this way also enables you to make larger items that might otherwise be too challenging if they were worked as a single piece.

Thread *DMC Petra No 3*
Composition *100% mercerised cotton*
Shades
A *5608 {peachey orange}*
B *53845 {turquoise}*
C *5742 {bright yellow}*
Hook *2.50 mm*

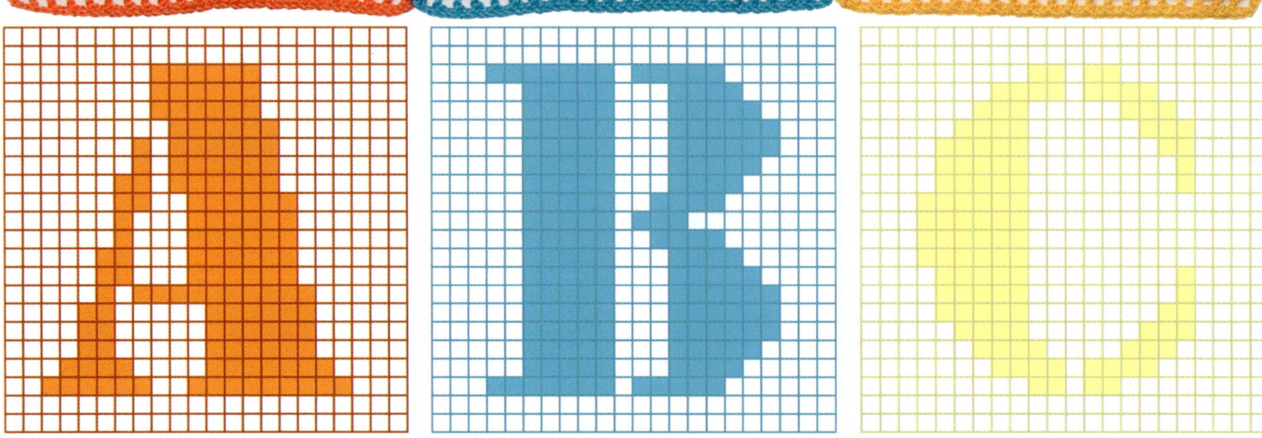

Starting with blocks

You may have noticed that all the designs in this chapter have a border of spaces.

Having spaces (rather than blocks) around the edge of a filet design makes it easier for you to check that there are right number of stitches on row 1. It also makes it easier to add an edging (like the ones on pages 70–71). Choosing designs that have a border of spaces also means you have the option to join pieces of filet together using the joining technique on pages 42–43.

However, if another pattern calls for the design to start with a block you will need to alter the number of foundation chains accordingly.

Right *Use this chart to calculate foundation chains where the design starts with a block.*

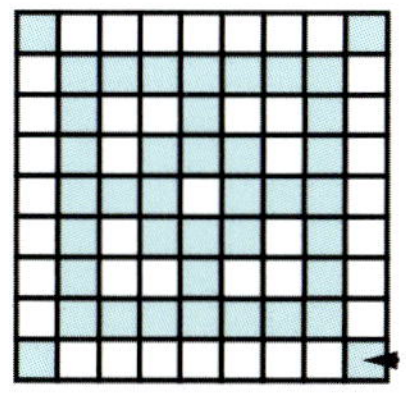

Single-Fill first row starts with a block
(number of squares x 2) + 3 = foundation chain number
eg (9 squares x 2) + 3 = chain 21

First treble is worked into 4th chain from hook
First three chain count as 1 treble

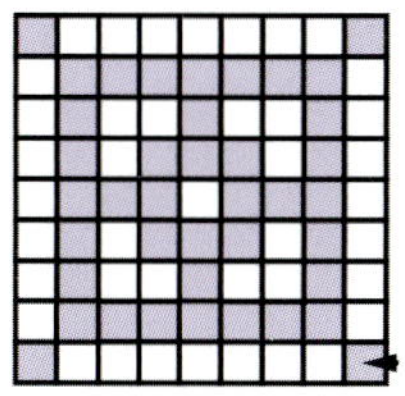

Double-Fill first row starts with a block
(number of squares x 3) + 3 = foundation chain number
eg (9 squares x 3) + 3 = chain 30

First treble is worked into 4th chain from hook
First three chain count as 1 treble

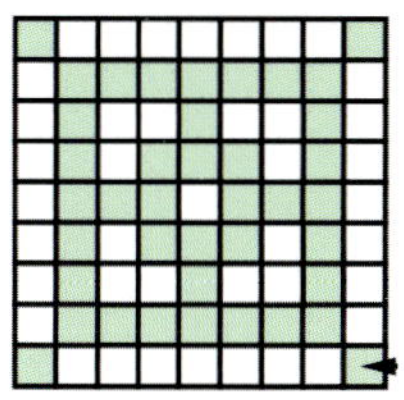

Extended-Fill first row starts with a block
(number of squares x 3) + 4 = foundation chain number
eg (9 squares x 3) + 4 = chain 31

First extended-treble is worked into 5th chain from hook
First four chain count as 1 extended-treble

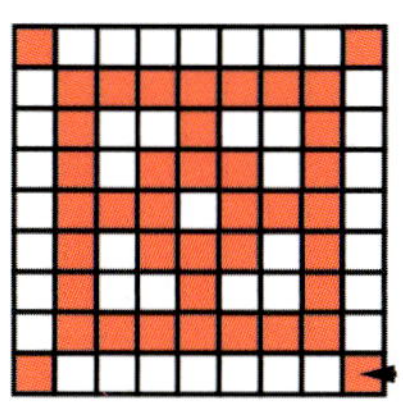

Geo-Fill first row starts with a block
(number of squares x 3) + 4 = foundation chain number
eg (9 squares x 3) + 4 = chain 31

First geo-treble is worked into 5th & 6th chains from hook
First four chain count as 1 extended-treble

Adapting yarns with geo-filet

Filet crochet is generally used for making small decorative items with fine, 100% cotton, crochet thread. If you want to make a larger filet item with double-knit yarn, try using one that is 50% cotton 50% acrylic. (Items made with 100% cotton double knit yarns tend to be somewhat heavy and unwieldy, and the subtlety of filet designs can get lost.) Filet crochet doesn't always translate to a double knit yarn so it is best to experiment first before committing to buying a large amount of yarn.

Thread *Adriafil Uno A Ritorto 5*
Composition *100% mercerised cotton*
Shade *Pink (03)*
Hook *1.50 mm*

21 x 19 cm

Thread *DMC Petra No 3*
Composition *100% mercerised cotton*
Shade *(54463) {light blue}*
Hook *2.50 mm*

24 x 23 cm

Yarn *James C Brett Cotton On (DK)*
Composition *50% cotton 50% acrylic*
Shade *(CO30) {light yellow}*
Hook *4.00 mm*

34 x 30 cm

Add texture to your crochet by working **between** stitches as well as into the top of them.

This chapter has 21 texture rich stitch patterns which can be incorporated into all types of crochet project. Advice is also given on adding stripes along with a helpful technique for minimising yarn-tails.

Once you develop this texture habit, your stitch pattern repertoire will expand and never leave you short of design ideas again!

Texture
Technique

Texture Technique

*In this chapter texture is added through the simple technique of working **between** stitches — both on its own and combined with the standard method of working into the top of the stitch (see panel below). These stitch patterns can be used by themselves or mixed together for added interest (see page 88). An ideal way to try this technique is to make a simple scarf using one or more of the stitch patterns; and, if stripey scarves are your thing, there also are some suggested stripe sequences and a step-by-step exercise in crocheting two-colour stripes.*

If you are unfamiliar with working between stitches, start by reading the green panel below, and then practise the basic treble stitch pattern on the facing page before attempting the more complex stitch patterns.

How to work between stitches

Understanding the term "eyelet"

*This chapter uses two ways of placing stitches: a) **the standard method** of working into the top of a stitch, and b) working in the gap between two stitches which in this chapter is referred to as an **"eyelet"**.*

Stitch symbols with down pointing arrowheads indicate that the stitch should be worked into the eyelet.

Left-handed

a) treble in next stitch

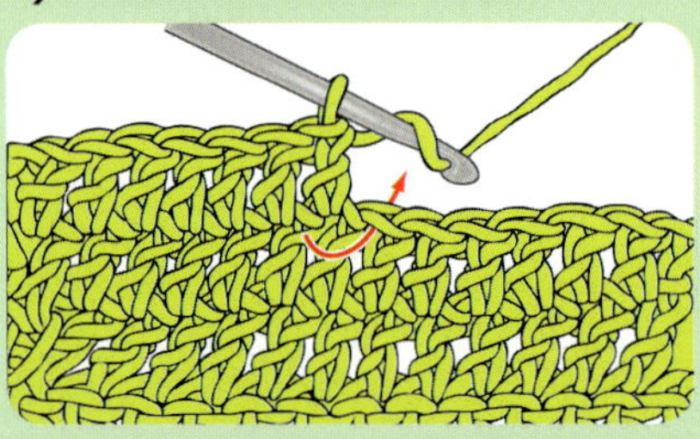

a) "in next stitch" ***means placing a new stitch into the top of the stitch on the row below, ie under the top two threads.***

 = treble in top of stitch

Right-handed

a) treble in next stitch

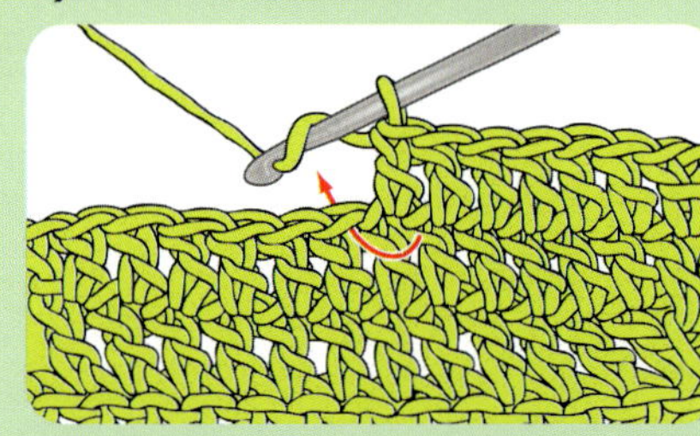

b) treble in next eyelet (left-handed)

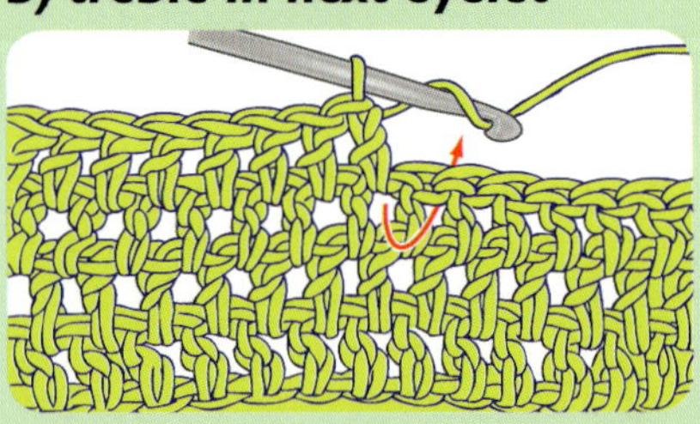

b) "in next eyelet" ***means placing a new stitch in the gap between two stitches in the row below.***

 = treble in eyelet

b) treble in next eyelet (right-handed)

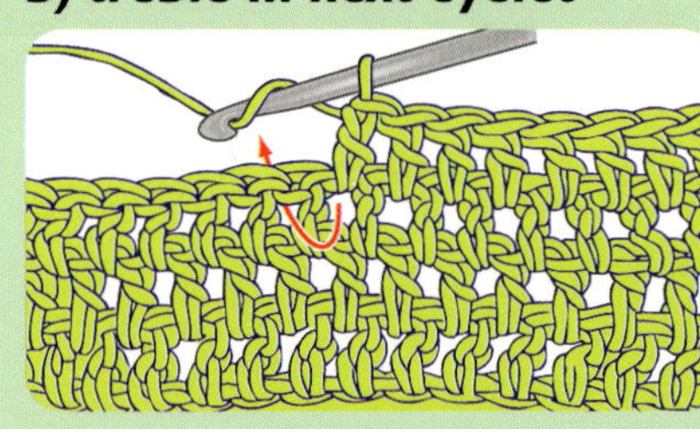

Tips

1 Because working between stitches widens the crochet compared to standard crochet, you will generally need to make the foundation chains larger or looser. And the patterns will generally benefit from a fairly loose tension. If you tend to crochet tightly, experiment with using a larger hook.

2 Until you are confident with a stitch pattern, keep checking you have the correct number of stitches at the end of each row.

3 Like all new techniques, working between stitches does take practice and patience. It might be harder to keep nice straight parallel edges especially where stitches of different heights are used on adjacent rows. The work may also "drift" slightly to one side because of the nature of the technique. The patterns have been carefully written to minimise the drift, but it will still be evident in some of the stitch patterns.

4 Row numbers are given in a circle with an arrow (see below). The arrow indicates the direction in which the row should be read. Coloured rows on the symbol charts indicate which rows are repeated to form the pattern. So, if only one row is coloured, just repeat that row. If two rows are coloured, repeat both rows in order.

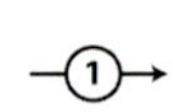 = row number and direction of row

1. basic treble

Foundation chain Chain 22 loosely.

Row 1 1 treble in 4th chain from hook and in each of remaining 18 chains (the first 3 unworked chains count as one stitch). (20 stitches)

Row 2 Chain 2 (counts as one stitch). Turn. (1 treble in each of next 19 eyelets. (20 stitches)

Repeat Row 2 as required.

***Yarn** Sublime Evie (Aran)*
***Shade** Fondant (510)*
***Composition** 94% Cotton 6% Nylon*
***Hook** 5.00 mm*

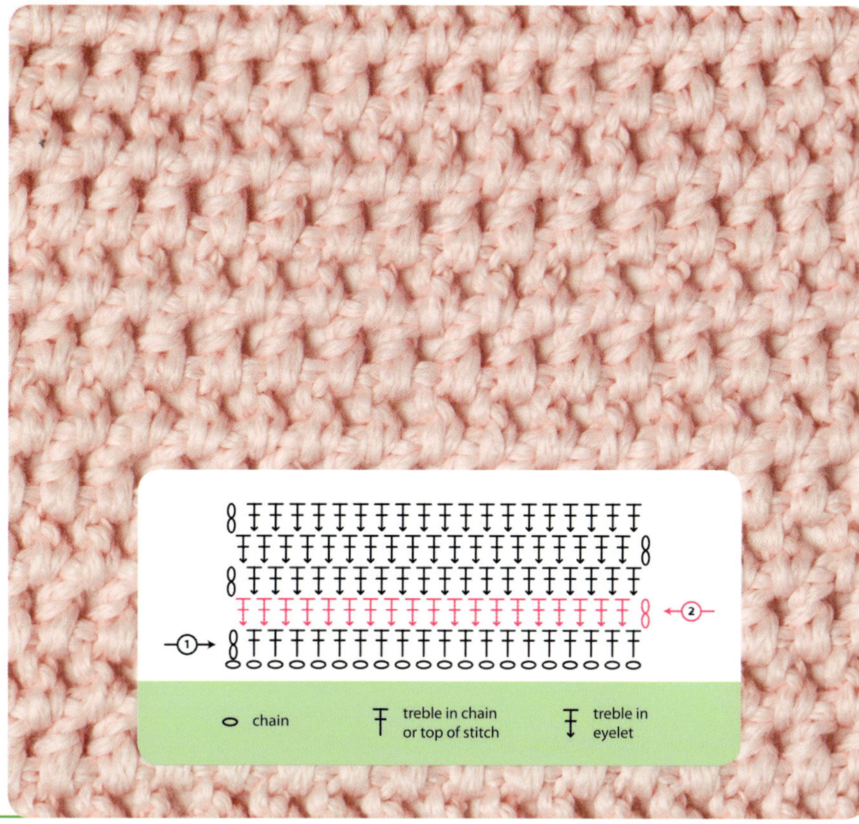

2. treble & double-crochet

Foundation chain Chain 22 loosely.

Row 1 1 treble in 4th chain from hook and in each of remaining 18 chains (the first 3 unworked chains count as one stitch). (20 stitches)

Row 2 Chain 1 (does **not** count as a stitch). Turn. (1 double-crochet in each of next 19 eyelets. (19 stitches)

Row 3 Chain 2 (does **not** count as a stitch). Turn. 1 treble in each of next 19 stitches*.

* **NB** The turning chain does not count as a stitch, so work the first treble of row 3 into the last stitch of row 2.

Repeat Rows 2–3 as required.

***Yarn** Sublime Evie (Aran)*
***Shade** Marisol (511)*
***Composition** 94% Cotton 6% Nylon*
***Hook** 5.00 mm*

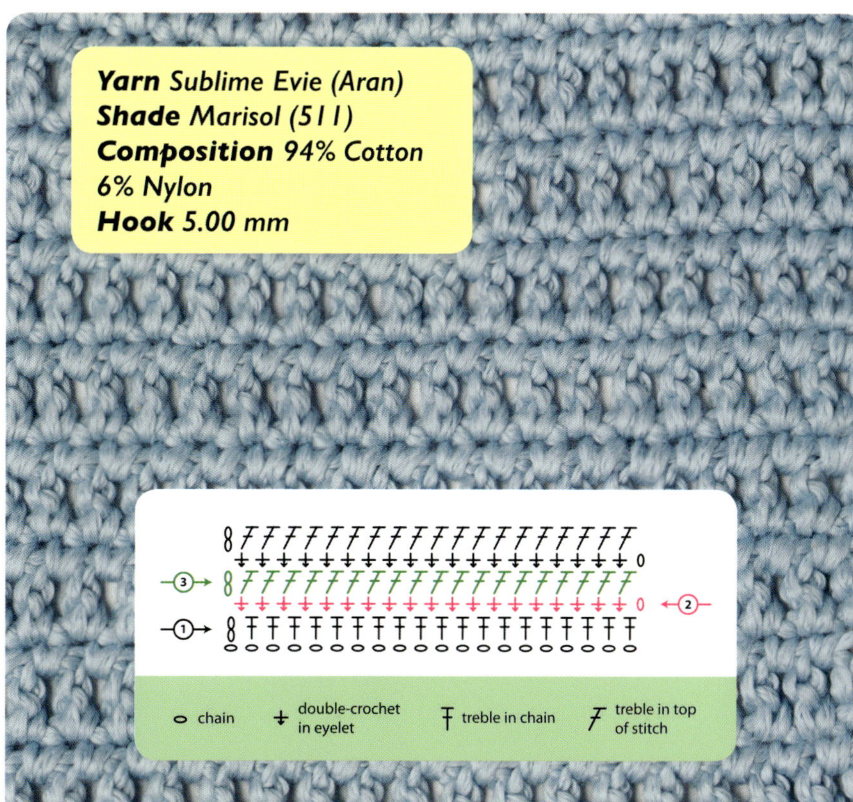

Texture Stitch Pattern Library

3. treble pairs aligned

Foundation chain Chain 22 loosely.
Row 1 1 treble in 4th chain from hook and in each of remaining 18 chains (the first 3 unworked chains count as one stitch). (20 stitches)
Row 2 Chain 2 (counts as 1 stitch). Turn. 1 treble in next eyelet. (Skip next eyelet. 2 treble in next eyelet) 9 times. (20 stitches)
Repeat Row 2 as required.
Final row (optional) Chain 2. Turn. 1 treble in each of the next 19 eyelets. Fasten off.

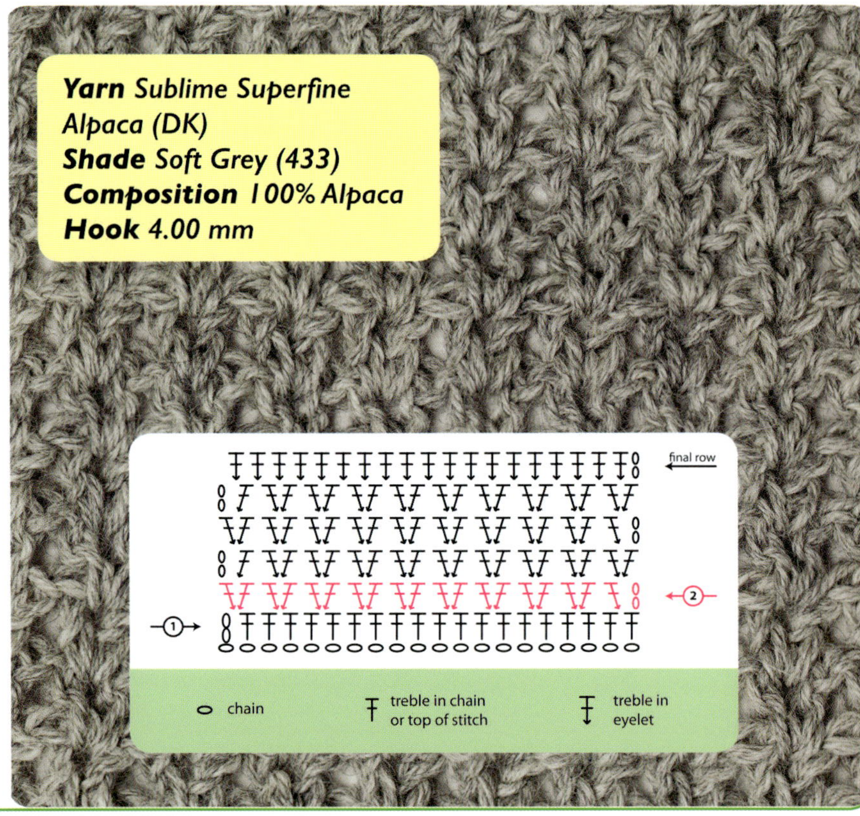

4. treble pairs staggered

Foundation chain Chain 22 loosely.
Row 1 1 treble in 4th chain from hook and in each of remaining 18 chains (the first 3 unworked chains count as one stitch). (20 stitches)
Row 2 Chain 2 (counts as 1 stitch). Turn. 1 treble in next eyelet. (Skip next eyelet. 2 trebles in next eyelet) 9 times. (20 stitches)
Row 3 Chain 2 (counts as 1 stitch). Turn. (Skip next eyelet. 2 trebles in next eyelet) 9 times. 1 treble in last eyelet. (20 stitches)
Repeat rows 2–3 as required.
Final row (optional) Chain 2. Turn. 1 treble in each of the next 19 eyelets. Fasten off.

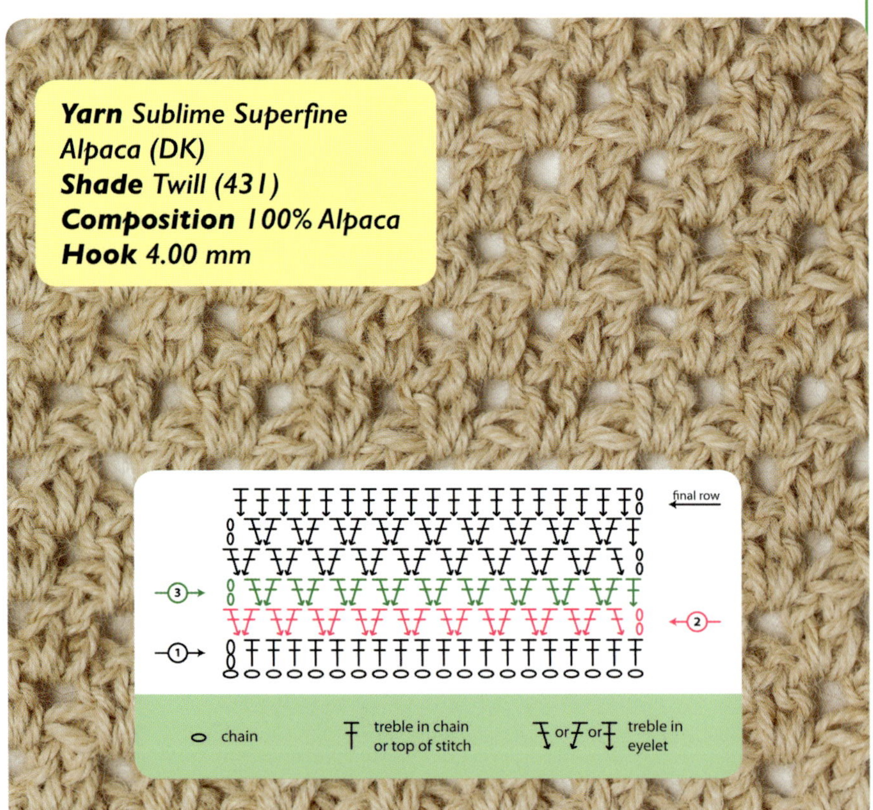

5. treble pairs & chains aligned

Foundation chain Chain 22 loosely.
Row 1 1 treble in 4th chain from hook and in each of remaining 18 chains (the first 3 unworked chains count as one stitch). (20 stitches)
Row 2 Chain 1 (counts as a turning-chain). Turn. 1 double-crochet in next eyelet. (Chain 2. Skip next eyelet. 1 double-crochet in next eyelet.) 9 times. (10 double-crochet, 9 chain-spaces plus turning-chain.)
Row 3 Chain 2 (counts as 1 stitch). Turn. (Skip next stitch. 2 treble in next chain-space) 9 times. Skip next stitch. 1 treble in turning chain. (20 stitches)
Repeat rows 2–3 as required.

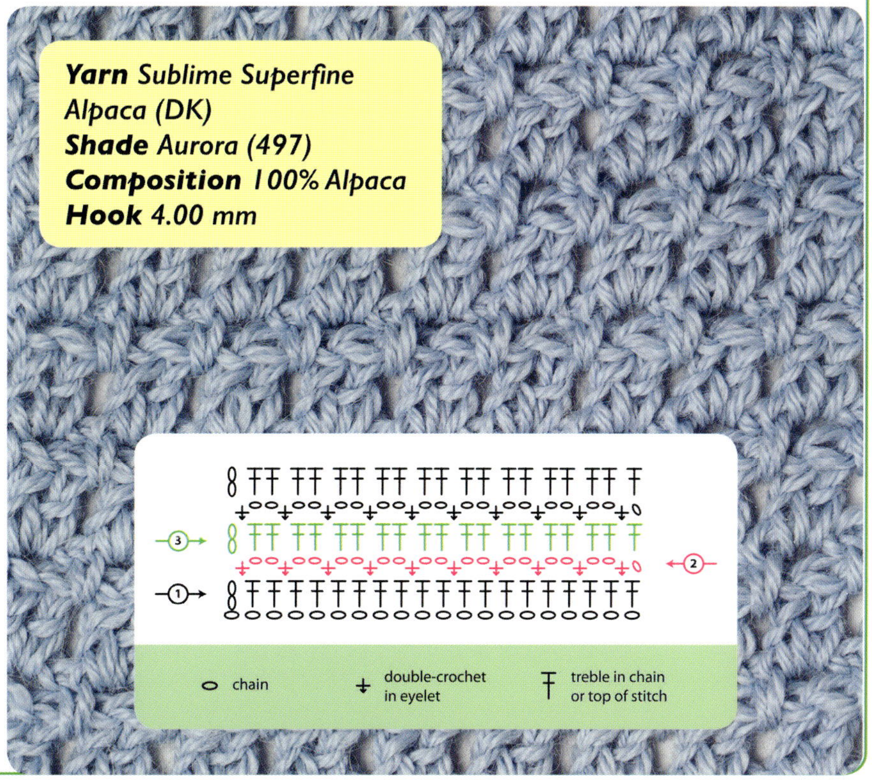

6. treble pairs & chains staggered

Foundation chain Chain 22 loosely.
Row 1 1 treble in 4th chain from hook and in each of remaining 18 chains (the first 3 unworked chains count as one stitch). (20 stitches)
Row 2 Chain 1 (counts as a turning-chain). Turn. 1 double-crochet in next eyelet. (Chain 2. Skip next eyelet. 1 double-crochet in next eyelet.) 9 times. (10 double-crochet, 9 chain-spaces plus turning-chain.)
Row 3 Chain 2 (counts as 1 stitch). Turn. (Skip next stitch. 2 treble in next chain-space) 9 times. Skip next stitch. 1 treble in turning chain. (20 stitches)
Row 4 Chain 2 (counts as 1 chain-space). Skip next eyelet. 1 double-crochet in next eyelet. (Chain 2. Skip next eyelet. 1 double-crochet in next eyelet) 8 times. Chain 1. 1 double-crochet in last eyelet.
Row 5 Chain 2 (counts as 1 treble). 1 treble in next chain-space. (Skip next stitch. 2 treble in next chain-space) 9 times.
Repeat rows 2–5 as required.

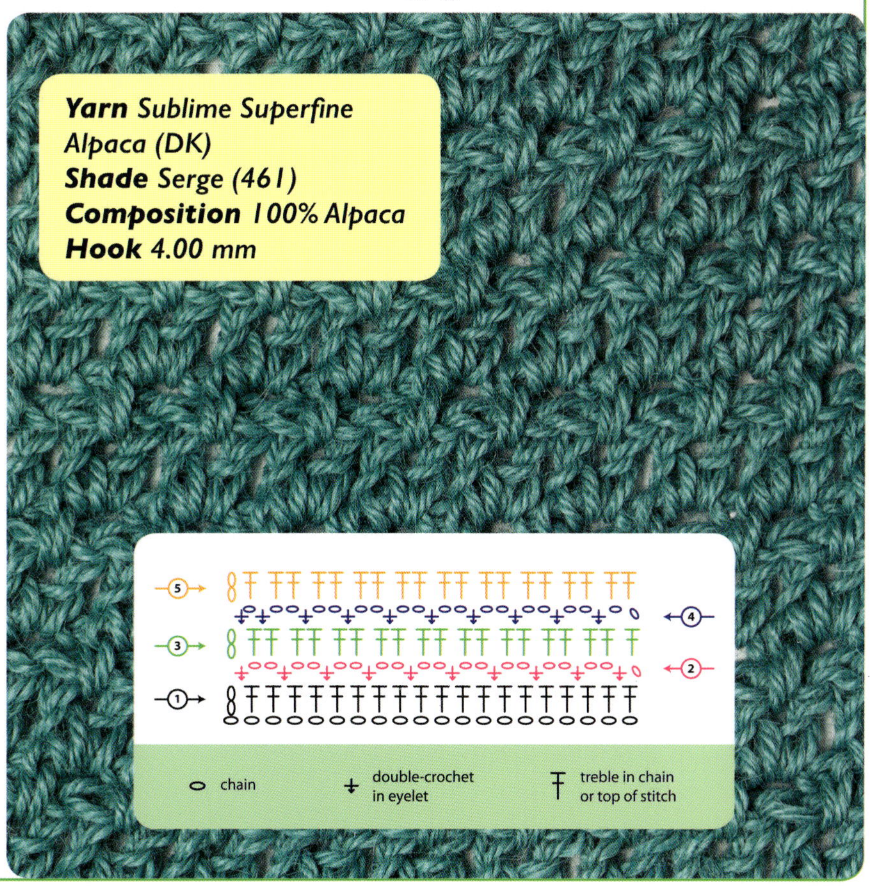

7. trebles & single chains

Foundation chain Chain 22 loosely.
Row 1 1 treble in 4th chain from hook and in each of remaining 18 chains (the first 3 unworked chains count as one stitch). (20 stitches)
Row 2 Chain 2 (counts as one chain-space). Turn. 1 double-crochet in next eyelet. (Chain 1. 1 double-crochet in next eyelet) 18 times. (19 double-crochet. 19 chain-spaces.)
Row 3 Chain 2 (counts as 1 treble). Turn. 1 treble in each of next 18 chain-spaces. 1 ***half-treble*** in last chain-space. (20 stitches)

Repeat rows 2–3 as required.

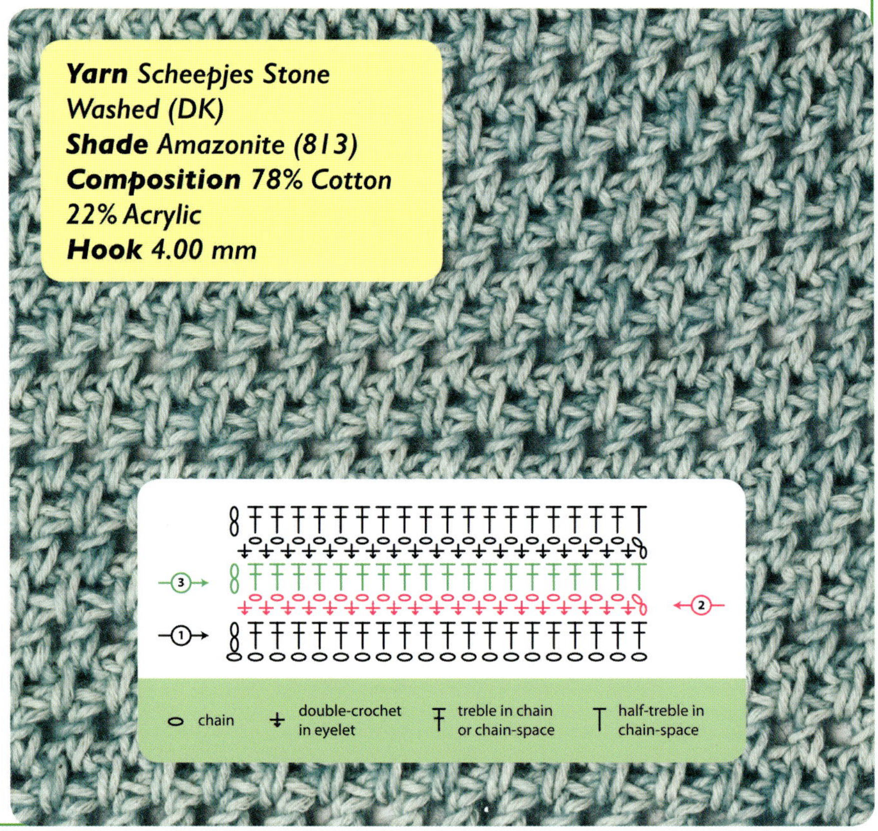

8. trebles & two chains

Foundation chain Chain 22 loosely.
Row 1 1 treble in 4th chain from hook and in each of remaining 18 chains (the first 3 unworked chains count as one stitch). (20 stitches)
Row 2 Chain 2 (counts as one chain-space). Turn. 1 double-crochet in next eyelet. (Chain 2. 1 double-crochet in next eyelet) 18 times. (19 double-crochet. 19 chain-spaces.)
Row 3 Chain 3 (counts as 1 treble). Turn. 1 treble in each of next 19 chain-spaces. (20 stitches)

Repeat rows 2–3 as required.

For another variation, the 2-chain-space of row 2 can be replaced with a 3-chain-space.

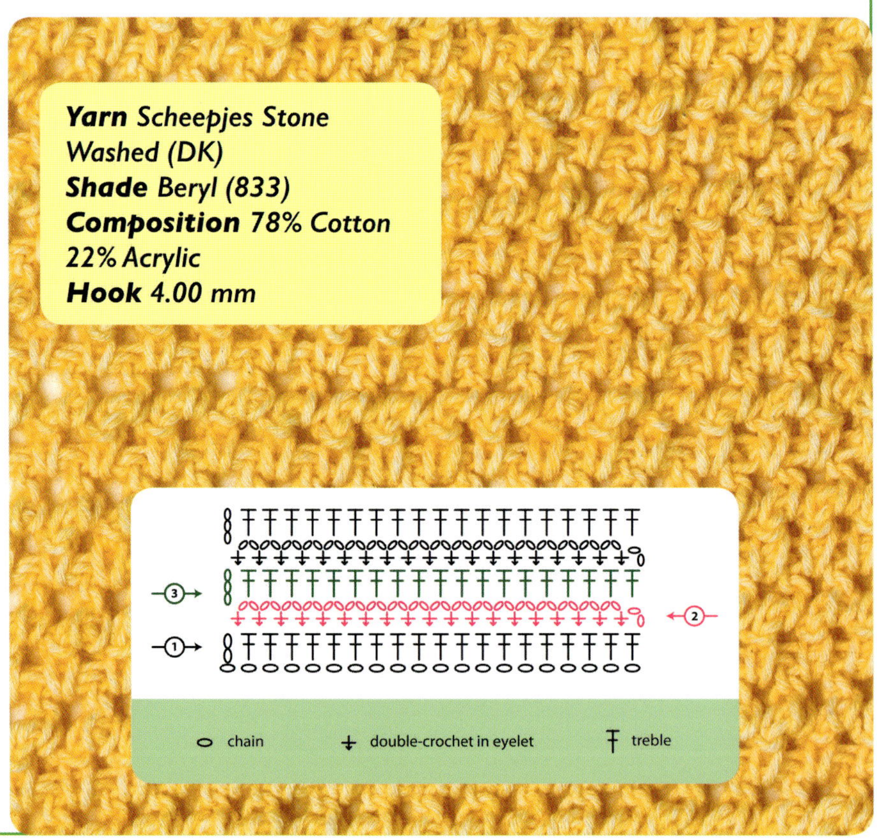

9. double-treble & half-treble

Double-treble: *Yarn over twice. Pick up a loop from stitch indicated (four loops on hook). (Yarn over and draw through two loops) 3 times.*

Foundation chain Chain 23 loosely.

Row 1 1 treble in 4th chain from hook and in each of remaining 19 chains (the first 3 unworked chains count as one stitch). (21 stitches)

Row 2 Chain 2 (does **not** count as a stitch). Turn. (1 half-treble in each of next 20 eyelets. (20 stitches)

Row 3 Chain 3 (does **not** count as a stitch so work the first double-treble of this row into the last stitch of the previous row). Turn. 1 double-treble in each of next 20 stitches.

Rows 4–5 Repeat rows 2–3.

Row 6 Chain 2. Turn. Skip next eyelet. 1 half-treble in each of next 19 eyelets. 1 additional half-treble in last eyelet. (20 stitches)

Row 7 Repeat row 3.

Repeat Rows 2–7 as required..

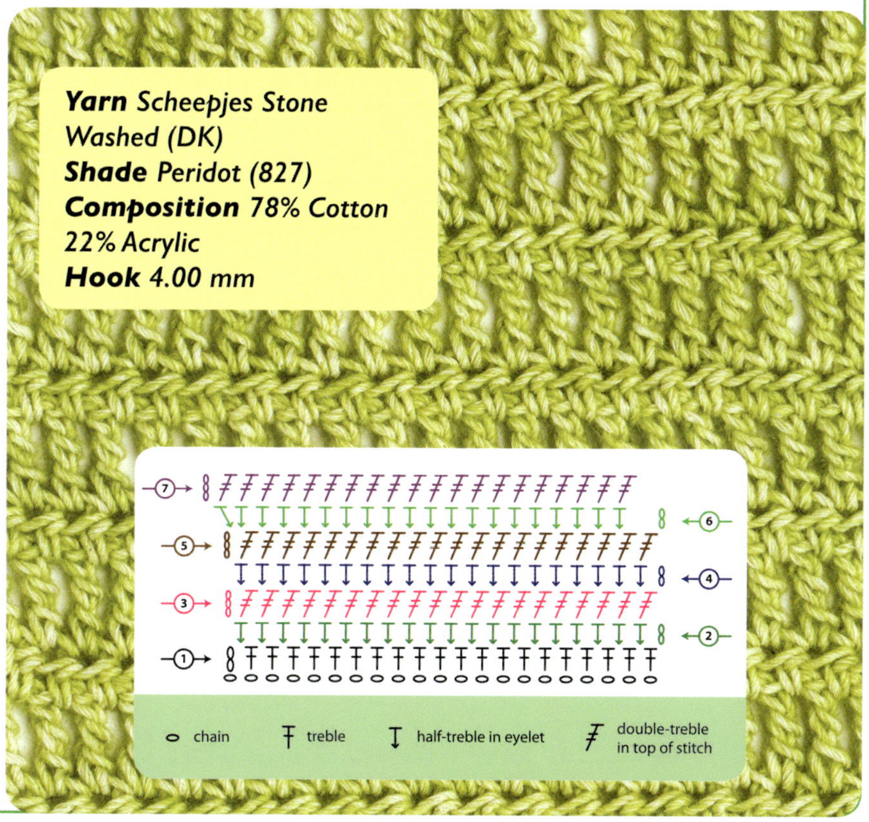

10. treble & extended-dc

Extended-double-crochet: *Pick up a loop in eyelet indicated (2 loops on hook). Yarn over and draw through 1 loop. Yarn over and draw through remaining 2 loops.*

Foundation chain Chain 22 loosely.

Row 1 1 treble in 4th chain from hook and in each of remaining 18 chains (the first 3 unworked chains count as one stitch). (20 stitches)

Row 2 Chain 1 (does **not** count as a stitch). Turn. 1 extended-double-crochet in each of the 19 eyelets. (19 stitches)

Row 3 Chain 2 (does **not** count as a stitch). Turn. 1 treble in each of next 19 stitches. (19 stitches)

Row 4 Repeat row 2.

Row 5 Chain 2 (does **not** count as a stitch). Turn. Skip first stitch. 1 treble in each of next 18 stitches. 1 additional treble in last stitch. (19 stitches)

Repeat Rows 2–5 as required.

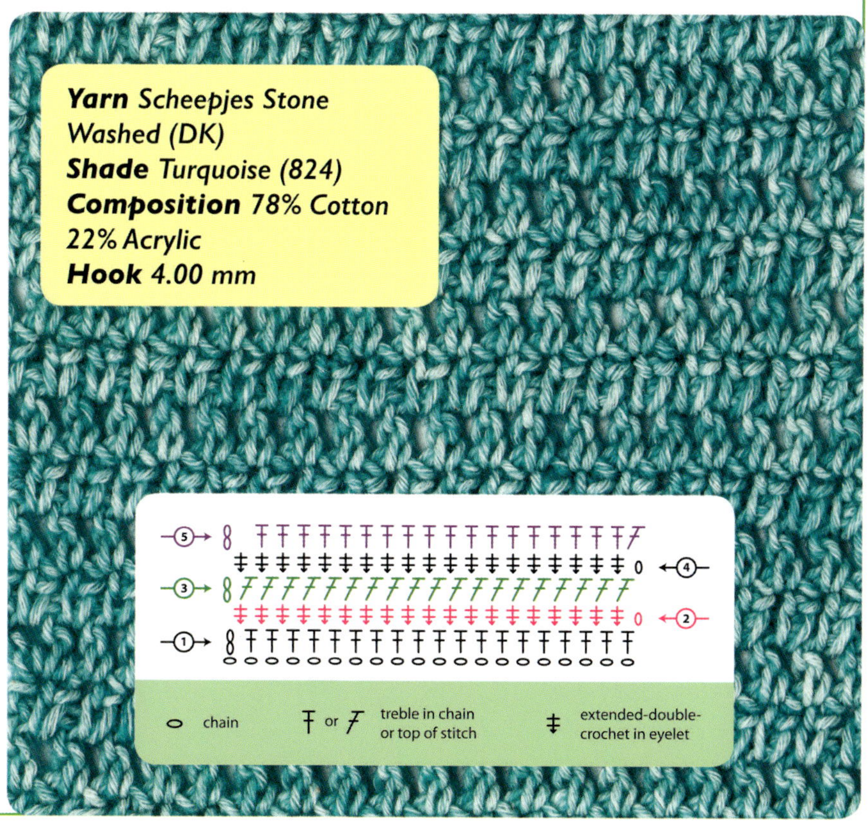

Texture Stitch Pattern Library

11. criss cross row

Foundation chain Chain 22 loosely.

Row 1 1 treble in 4th chain from hook and in each of remaining 18 chains (the first 3 unworked chains count as one stitch). (20 stitches)

Row 2 Chain 2 (counts as one stitch). Turn. (Skip next eyelet. 1 treble in next eyelet. 1 treble in previous eyelet) 9 times. 1 treble in last eyelet. (20 stitches)

Row 3 Chain 2 (counts as 1 stitch). Turn. 1 treble in each of next 19 eyelets. (20 stitches)

Repeat Rows 2–3 as required.

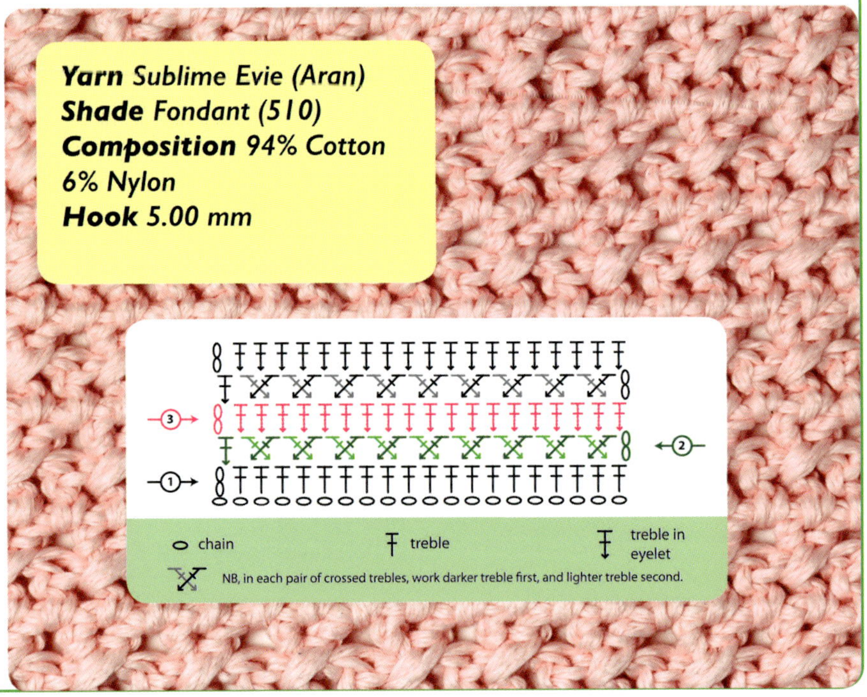

12. small popcorn rows

***Small popcorn:** Yarn over. Pick up loop in eyelet specified. Yarn over and draw through two loops on hook. Yarn over. Pick up loop in same eyelet. Yarn over and draw through two loops on hook. Yarn over and draw through remaining three loops on hook.*

Foundation chain Chain 22 very loosely.

Row 1 1 treble in 4th chain from hook and in each of remaining 18 chains (the first 3 unworked chains count as one stitch). (20 stitches)

Row 2 Chain 3 (counts as 1 treble and 1 chain-space). Turn. (1 small popcorn in next eyelet. Chain 1) 18 times. 1 treble in last eyelet. (18 small popcorn and 1 treble at each end)

Row 3 Chain 3 (counts as 1 treble). Turn. 1 treble in next chain-space. (Skip next popcorn. 1 treble in next chain-space.) 18 times. (20 stitches)

Repeat rows 2–3 as required.

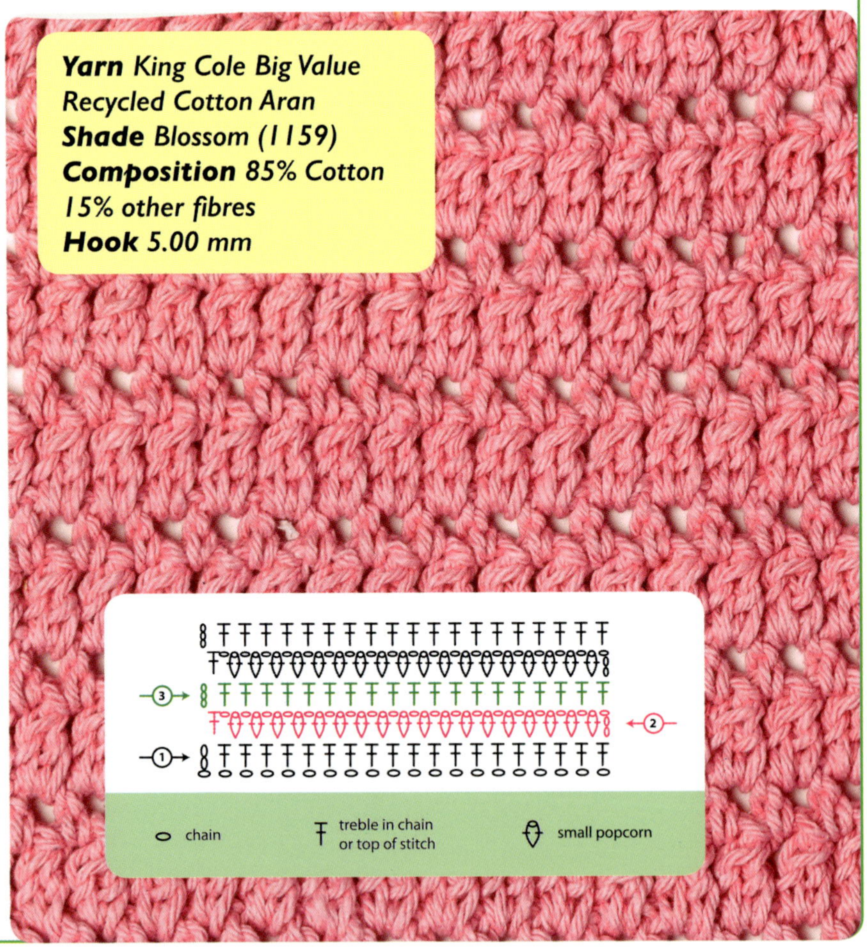

13. woven criss cross

Foundation chain Chain 22 loosely.

Row 1 1 treble in 4th chain from hook and in each of remaining 18 chains (the first 3 unworked chains count as one stitch). (20 stitches)

Row 2 Chain 2 (counts as one stitch). Turn. (Skip next eyelet. 1 treble in next eyelet. 1 treble in previous eyelet) 9 times. 1 treble in last eyelet. (20 stitches)

Repeat Row 2 as required.

Final row (optional) Chain 2. Turn. 1 treble in each eyelet to end. (20 stitches) *Fasten off.*

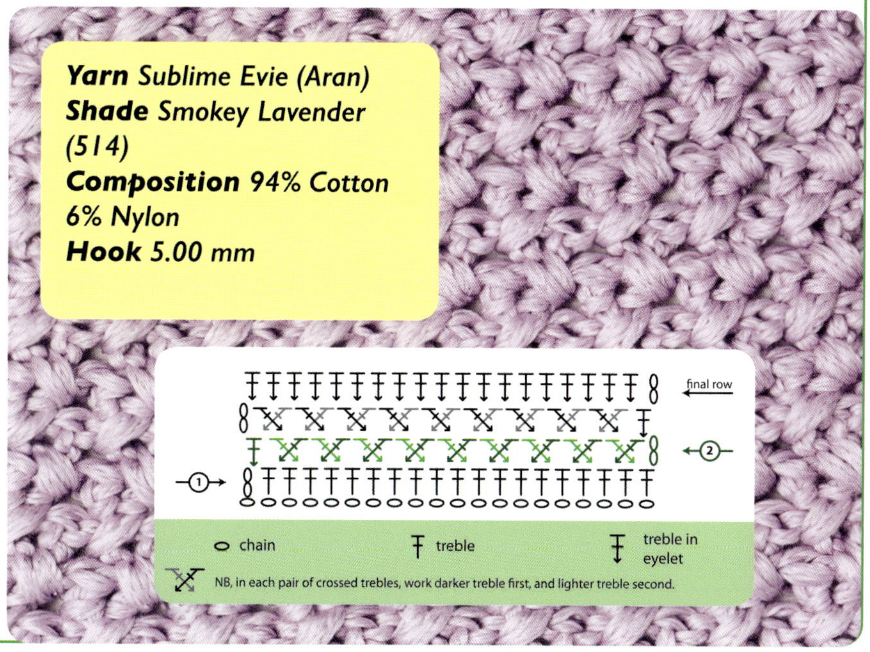

14. large popcorn staggered

Large popcorn: *Yarn over. Pick up loop in eyelet specified. Yarn over and draw through two loops on hook (2 loops remain on hook). *Yarn over. Pick up loop in same eyelet. Yarn over and draw through two loops on hook.* Repeat from * to * once. Yarn over and draw through all four loops on hook.*

Foundation chain Chain 22 loosely.

Row 1 1 treble in 4th chain from hook and in each of remaining 18 chains (the first 3 unworked chains count as one stitch). (20 stitches)

Row 2 Chain 3 (counts as 1 treble and 1 chain-space). Turn. (Skip next eyelet. 1 large popcorn in next eyelet. Chain 1) 9 times. 1 treble in last eyelet. (9 large popcorn and 1 treble at each end)

Row 3 Chain 2 (counts as 1 stitch). Turn. 1 treble in next chain-space. (Skip next popcorn. 2 treble in next chain-space) 9 times. (20 stitches)

Row 4 Chain 2 (counts as 1 treble). Turn. 1 treble in next eyelet. (Chain 1. Skip next eyelet. 1 popcorn in next eyelet) 8 times. Chain 1. Skip next eyelet. 2 treble in last eyelet. (8 large popcorn and 2 treble at each end.

Row 5 Chain 2 (counts as 1 treble). (Skip next stitch. 2 treble in next chain space) 9 times. 1 treble in last eyelet. (20 trebles)

Repeat rows 2–5 as required.

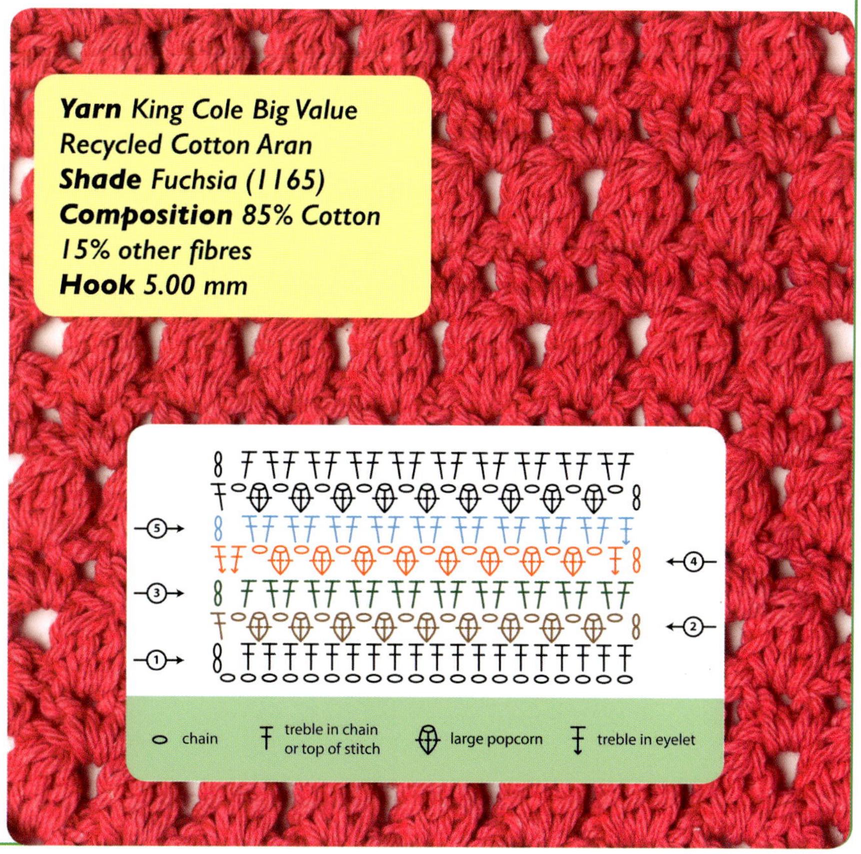

Texture Stitch Pattern Library

15. treble-bobble

Treble-bobble: *1 treble in eyelet or chain-space indicated. 1 half-treble around the post of the treble just worked.*

Foundation chain Chain 22 loosely.

Row 1 1 treble in 4th chain from hook and in each of remaining 18 chains (the first 3 unworked chains count as one stitch). (20 stitches)

Row 2 Chain 2 (counts as one treble). Turn. 1 treble-bobble in first eyelet. (Chain 1. Skip next eyelet. 1 treble-bobble in next eyelet) 8 times. Chain 1. Skip next eyelet. 1 treble in last eyelet. (9 treble-bobbles and 1 treble at each end)

Row 3 Chain 2 (counts as one treble). Turn. (Skip next stitch. 1 treble-bobble in next chain-space. Chain 1) 9 times. Skip next stitch. 1 treble in last eyelet.

Repeat row 3 as required.

Final row (optional) Chain 2 (counts as 1 stitch). Turn. 1 treble in next chain-space. (Skip next stitch. 2 treble in next chain-space) 8 times. Skip next stitch. 2 treble in last eyelet. (20 stitches) *Fasten off.*

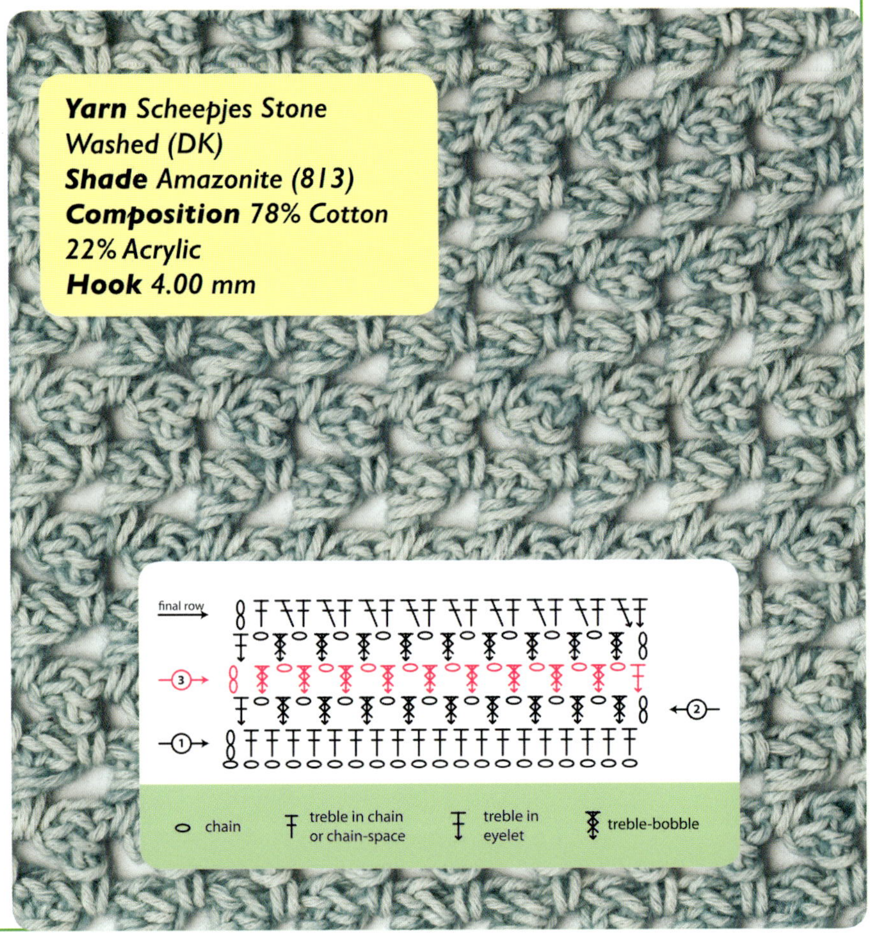

16. treble grid

Foundation chain Chain 22 very loosely.

Row 1 1 treble in 4th chain from hook and in each of remaining 18 chains (the first 3 unworked chains count as one stitch). (20 stitches)

Row 2 Chain 2 (counts as one stitch). Turn. (1 double-crochet in next eyelet. 1 double-crochet in next stitch.) 19 times. (39 stitches)

Row 3 Chain 3 (counts as 1 stitch). Turn. (Skip next stitch. 1 treble in next stitch) 19 times. (20 stitches)

Repeat Rows 2–3 as required.

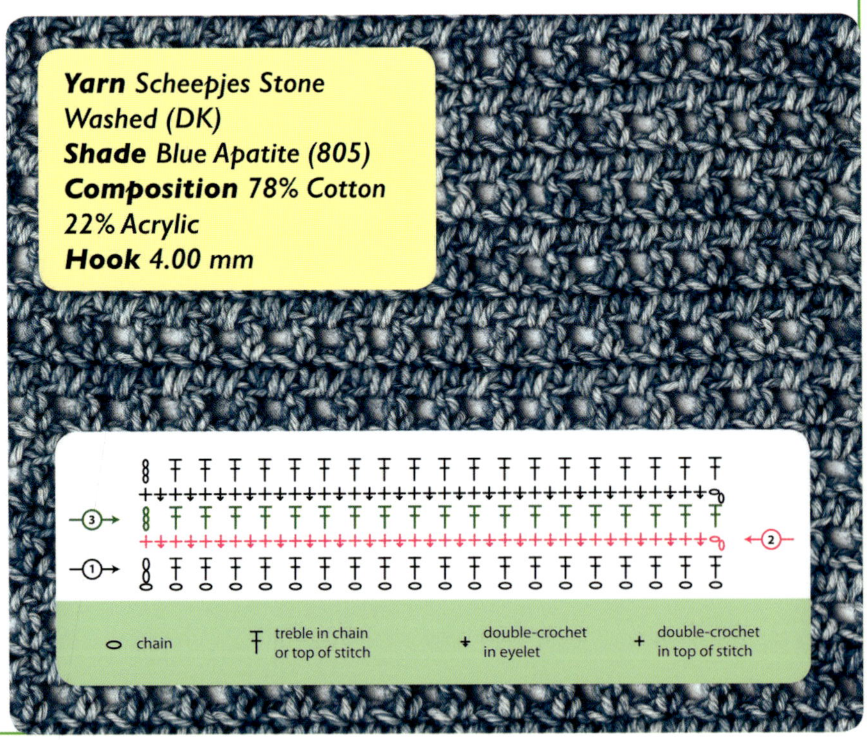

17. increase & decrease rows

See the start of this chapter for a larger photo of this stitch pattern. (This stitch pattern will "drift" to one side as it progresses.)

2 trebles together: **Yarn over. Pick up a loop in next eyelet. Yarn over and draw through 2 loops on hook.* Repeat from * to * once more. Yarn over and draw through all three loops on hook.*

3 trebles together: **Yarn over. Pick up a loop in next eyelet. Yarn over and draw through 2 loops on hook.* Repeat from * to * two more times. Yarn over and draw through all four loops on hook.*

Foundation chain Chain 22 loosely.

Row 1 1 treble in 4th chain from hook and in each of remaining 18 chains (the first 3 unworked chains count as one stitch). (20 stitches)

Row 2 Chain 2 (counts as 1 stitch). Turn. Skip next eyelet. 3 trebles in next eyelet. (Skip next 2 eyelets. 3 trebles in next eyelet) 5 times. Skip next eyelet. 1 treble in last eyelet. (20 stitches)

Row 3 Chain 2 (counts as 1 stitch). Turn. 2 trebles together. (Chain 3. 3 trebles together) 5 times. Chain 3. 2 trebles together.

Row 4 Chain 3 (counts as 1 stitch). Turn. (3 trebles in next chain-space) 6 times. 1 treble in last eyelet. (20 stitches)

Repeat Rows 3–4 as required.

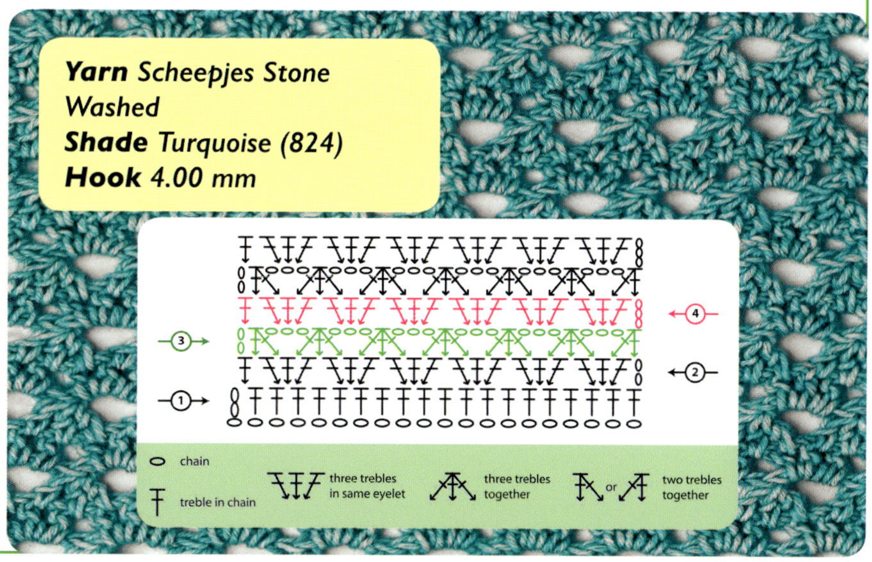

18. gathered stitch

(This stitch pattern will "drift" to one side as it progresses.)

Gathered stitch: *Pick up a loop loosely from the eyelet just worked, and from each of the next two eyelets. Yarn over and draw through all four loops on hook.*

Foundation chain Chain 22.

Row 1 1 treble in 4th chain from hook and in each of remaining 18 chains (the first 3 unworked chains count as one stitch). (20 stitches)

Row 2 Chain 2 (does **not** count as a stitch). Turn. 1 treble in next eyelet. (1 gathered stitch. Chain 1 loosely) 9 times. 1 additional treble in last eyelet. (11 stitches and 9 chain-spaces)

Row 3 Chain 2 (counts as one stitch). Turn. (1 treble in next chain-space. 1 treble in next stitch). 9 times. Skip next stitch. 1 treble in last eyelet. (20 stitches)

Repeat Rows 2–3 as required.

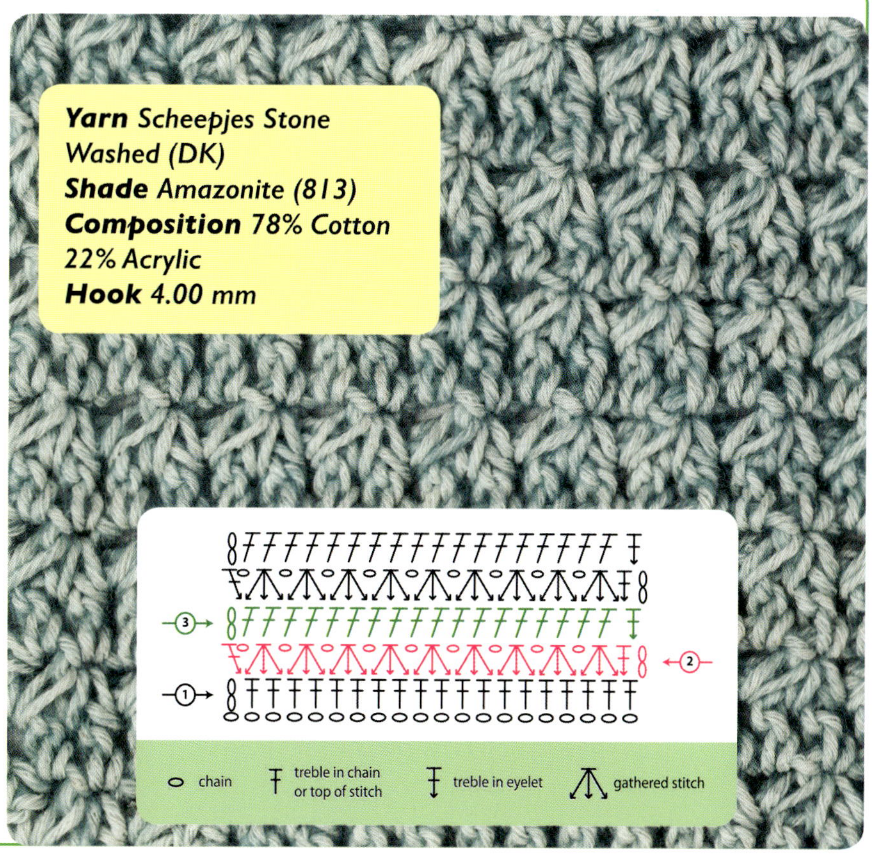

19. diamonds

***Yarn** Sublime Superfine Alpaca (DK)*
***Shade** Twill (431)*
***Composition** 100% Alpaca*
***Hook** 4.00 mm*

***2 trebles together:** *Yarn over. Pick up a loop in next eyelet. Yarn over and draw through 2 loops on hook.* Repeat from * to * once. Yarn over and draw through all three loops on hook.*

Foundation chain Chain 23 loosely.

Row 1 1 treble in 4th chain from hook and in each of remaining 19 chains (the first 3 unworked chains count as one stitch). (21 stitches)

Row 2 Chain 2 (counts as 1 stitch). Turn. 1 treble in each of next 3 eyelets. *Chain 2. Skip next two eyelets. 3 treble in next eyelet. Chain 2. Skip next two eyelets.* 1 treble in each of next 4 eyelets. Repeat from * to * once. 1 treble in each of next 3 eyelets.

Row 3 Chain 2 (counts as 1 stitch). Turn. 1 treble in each of next 2 eyelets. *Chain 2. Skip next chain-space. 2 treble in each of next 2 eyelets. Chain 2. Skip next chain-space. 1 treble in each of next 3 eyelets.* Repeat from * to * once.

Row 4 Chain 2 (counts as 1 stitch). Turn. 1 treble in each of next 2 eyelets. *Chain 2. Skip next chain-space. 2 treble in next eyelet. 1 treble in next eyelet. 2 treble in next eyelet. Chain 2. Skip next chain-space.* 2 trebles together. Repeat from * to * once. 1 treble in each of next two eyelets.

Row 5 Chain 2 (counts as 1 stitch). Turn. 2 treble in next eyelet. *Chain 2. Skip next chain-space. 1 treble in each of next 4 eyelets. Chain 2. Skip next chain-space.* 3 trebles in next stitch. Repeat from * to * once. 2 trebles in next eyelet. 1 treble in last eyelet.

Row 6 Chain 2 (counts as 1 stitch). Turn. 1 treble in next eyelet. 2 treble in next eyelet. *Chain 2. Skip next chain-space. 1 treble in each of next 3 eyelets. Chain 2. Skip next chain-space.* 2 trebles in each of next two eyelets. Repeat from * to * once. 2 trebles in next eyelet. 1 treble in last eyelet.

Row 7 Chain 2 (counts as 1 stitch). Turn. 1 treble in next eyelet. 2 treble in next eyelet. *Chain 2. Skip next chain-space. 2 trebles together. Chain 2. Skip next chain-space. 2 trebles in next eyelet.* 1 treble in next eyelet. 2 trebles in next eyelet. Repeat from * to * once. 1 treble in each of next 2 eyelets.

Row 8 Chain 2 (counts as 1 stitch). Turn. 1 treble in each of next 3 eyelets. *Chain 2. Skip next chain-space. 3 treble in next stitch. Chain 2. Skip next chain-space.* 1 treble in each of next 4 eyelets Repeat from * to * once. 1 treble in each of next 3 eyelets.

Repeat rows 3–8 as required, but end on a row 7.

Final row Chain 2 (counts as 1 stitch). Turn. 1 treble in each of next 3 eyelets. *2 trebles in next chain-space. 1 treble in next stitch. 2 trebles in next chain-space.* 1 treble in each of next 4 eyelets. Repeat from * to * once. 1 treble in each of next 3 eyelets. *Fasten off.*

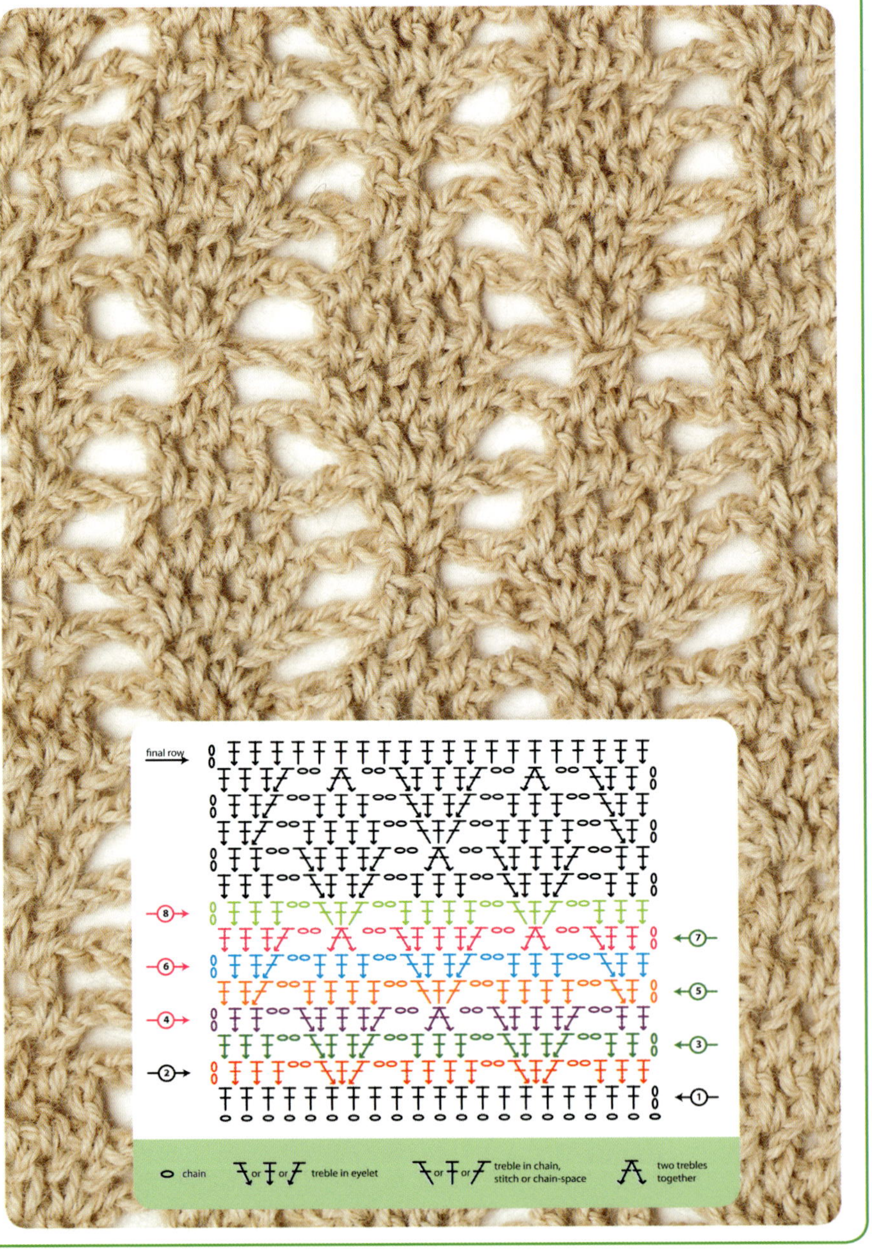

20. triplet trebles

There is a larger photograph of this stitch pattern at the start of this chapter in green yarn.

Foundation chain Chain 22 loosely.
Row 1 1 treble in 4th chain from hook and in each of remaining 18 chains (the first 3 unworked chains count as one stitch). (20 stitches)
Row 2 Chain 2 (counts as 1 stitch). Turn. Skip next eyelet. 3 trebles in next eyelet. (Skip next 2 eyelets. 3 trebles in next eyelet) 5 times. Skip next eyelet. 1 treble in last eyelet. (20 stitches)
Repeat row 2 as required.
Final row (optional) Chain 2. Turn. 1 treble in each of the next 19 eyelets.
Fasten off.

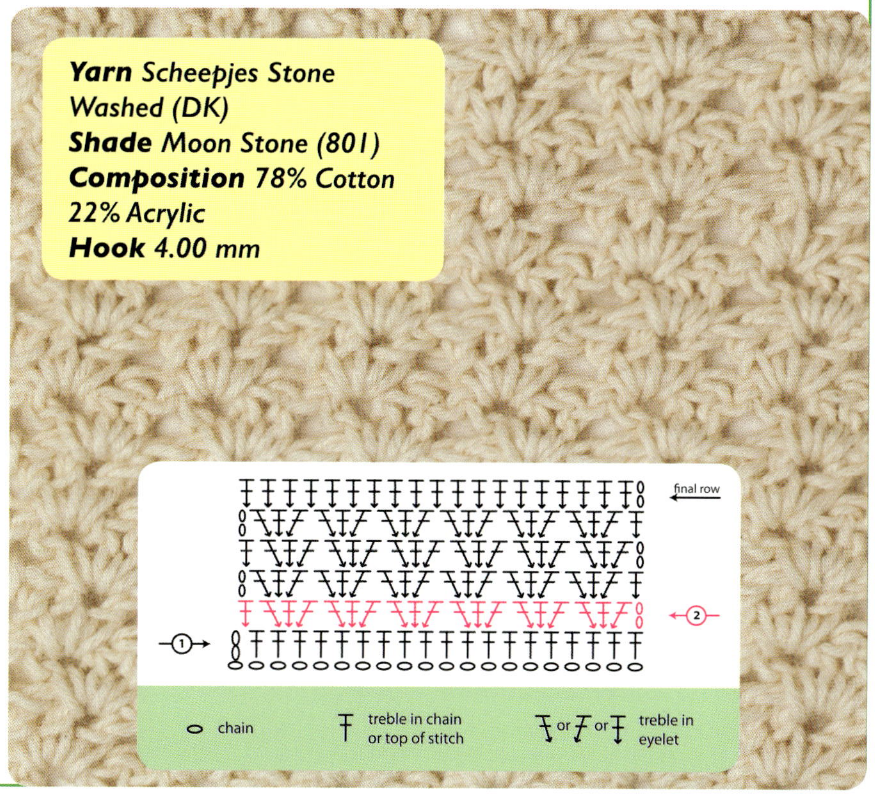

21. blackberries staggered

Blackberry stitch: *Yarn over. *Pick up a loop in eyelet specified. Yarn over and draw through 2 loops. Yarn over and draw through 1 loop.* Repeat from * to * two more times in same eyelet. Yarn over and draw through all four loops on hook.*
Foundation chain Chain 22 loosely.
Row 1 1 treble in 4th chain from hook and in each of remaining 18 chains (the first 3 unworked chains count as one stitch). (20 stitches)
Row 2 Chain 2 (counts as 1 stitch). Turn. 1 treble in next eyelet. (1 blackberry in next eyelet. 1 treble in next eyelet) 9 times. (9 blackberries, and 11 trebles)
Row 3 Chain 2 (counts as 1 stitch). Turn. 1 treble in each of 19 eyelets.
Row 4 Chain 2 (counts as 1 stitch). Turn. (1 blackberry in next eyelet. 1 treble in next eyelet) 9 times. 1 treble in last eyelet. (9 blackberries, and 11 trebles)
Row 5 Repeat row 3.
Repeat Rows 2–5 as required.

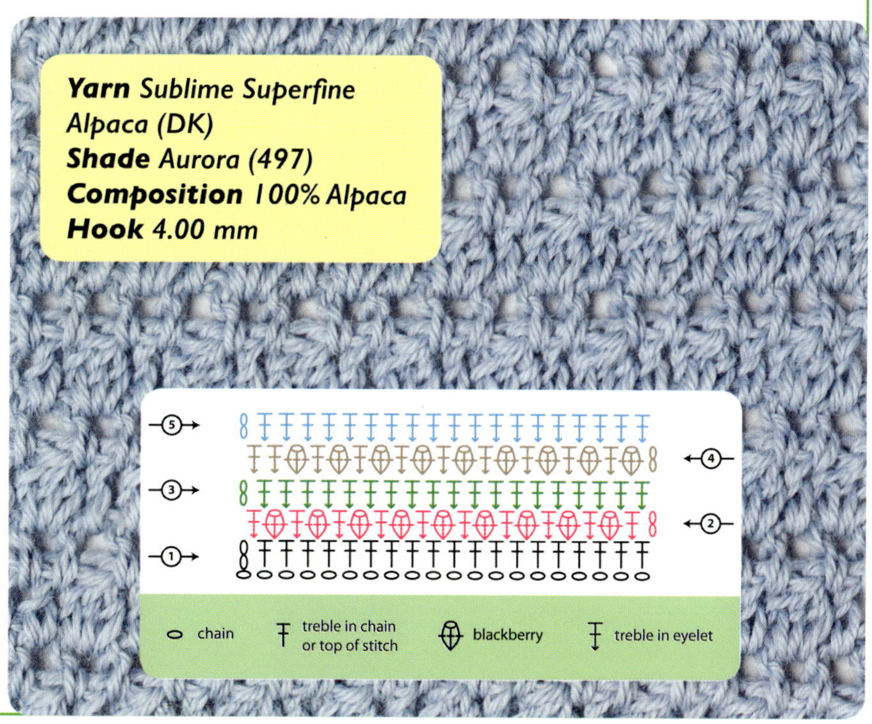

Adaptations

Create your own stitch patterns

The potential number of stitch patterns is infinite so you may want to create some of your own! Use the stitch patterns in this chapter as a starting point; adapting the patterns in small ways can make a big difference to their appearance.

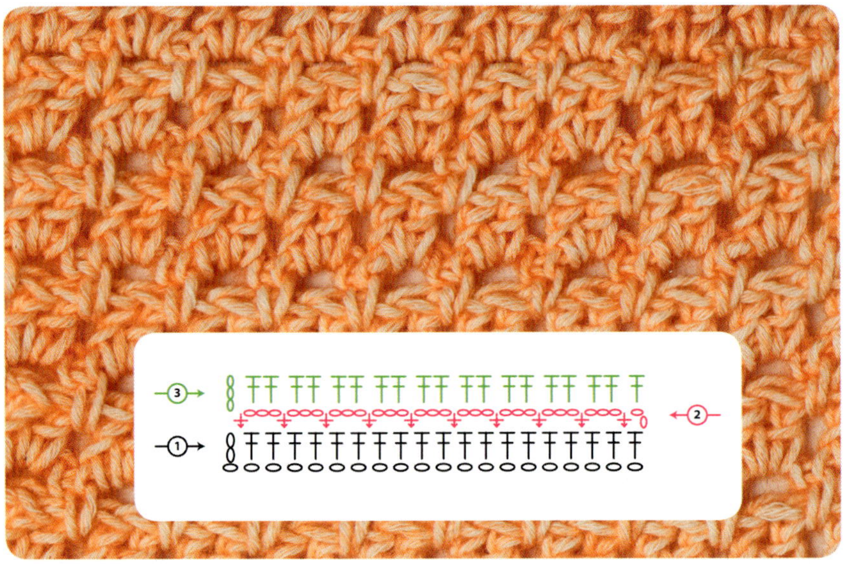

Right *In stitch pattern 5 (treble pairs & chains aligned), the 2-chain-spaces of row 2 have been increased to 3-chain-spaces.*

***Yarn** Scheepjes Stone Washed*
***Shade** Morganite (834)*

Pick 'n Mix

Texture stitch patterns that have similar tensions can be mixed and matched together. In this example one row of treble-bobbles (from stitch pattern 15) has been paired with rows of two trebles (stitch pattern 4).

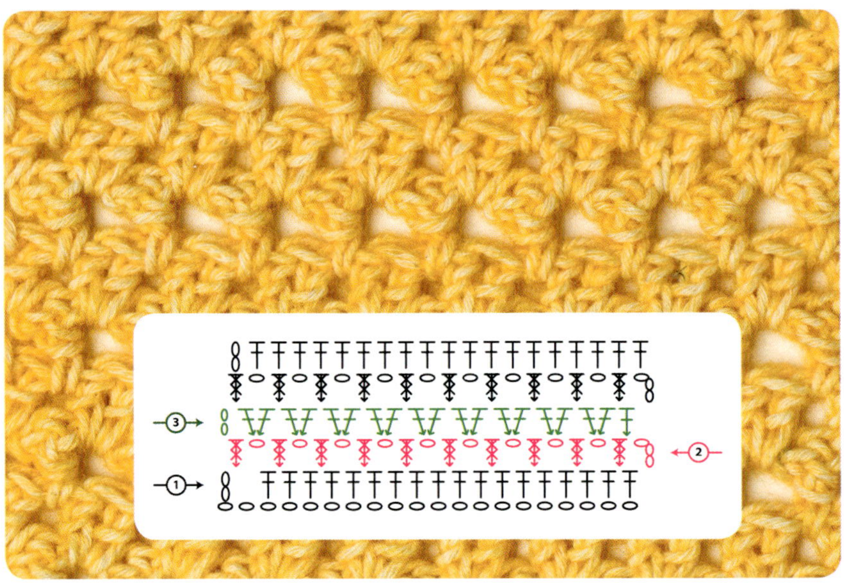

***Yarn** Scheepjes Stone Washed*
***Shade** Beryl (833)*
***Composition** 78% Cotton 22% Acrylic*
***Hook** 4.00 mm*

Rows of contrasting stitches can be used to highlight a particular stitch pattern. In this example one row of half-trebles and one row of trebles are sandwiched between two rows of woven criss-cross from stitch pattern 13.
(This stitch pattern is also shown in grey at start of chapter.)

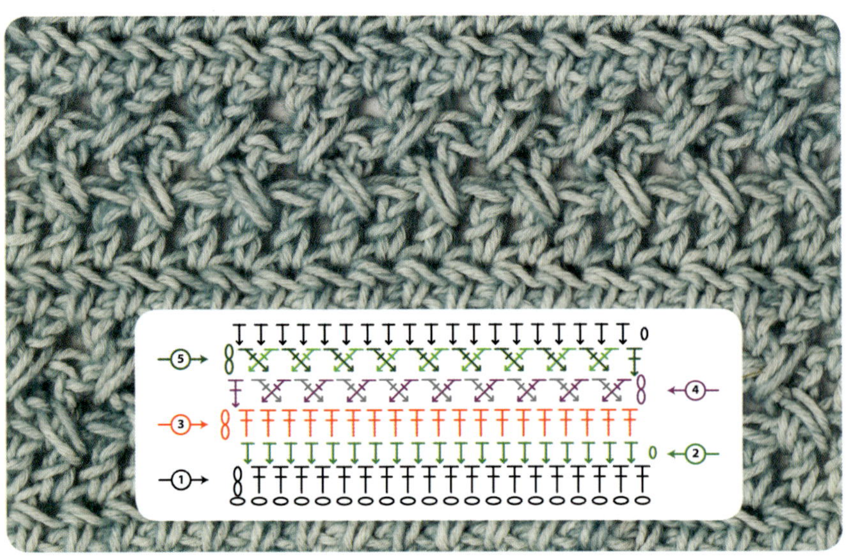

***Yarn** Scheepjes Stone Washed*
***Shade** Amazonite (813)*
***Composition** 78% Cotton 22% Acrylic **Hook** 4.00 mm*

Stripes

Stripes are ideal for showcasing this texture technique. Here are four stripe sequences and six suggested stitch patterns. (Bear in mind that not all stitch patterns will suit all sequences.)

If you want to avoid unnecessary yarn-tails when crocheting stripes, try working through the step-by-step exercise on the next page which shows how to crochet stripes by "floating" the spare yarn up the side of the work.

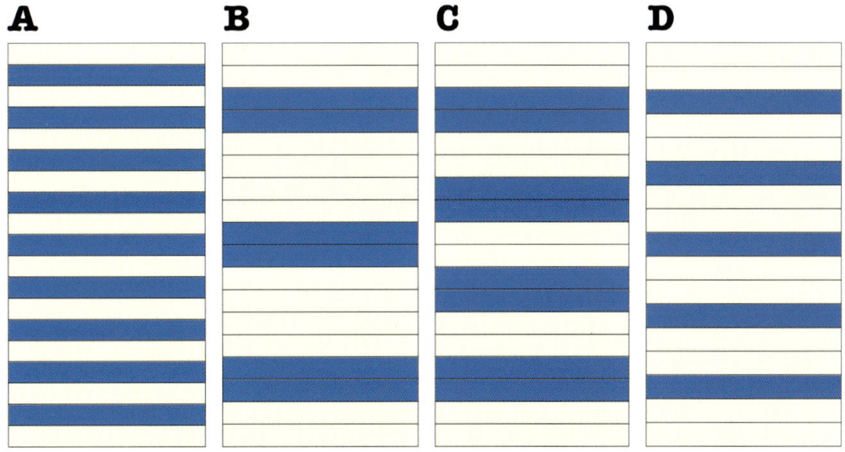

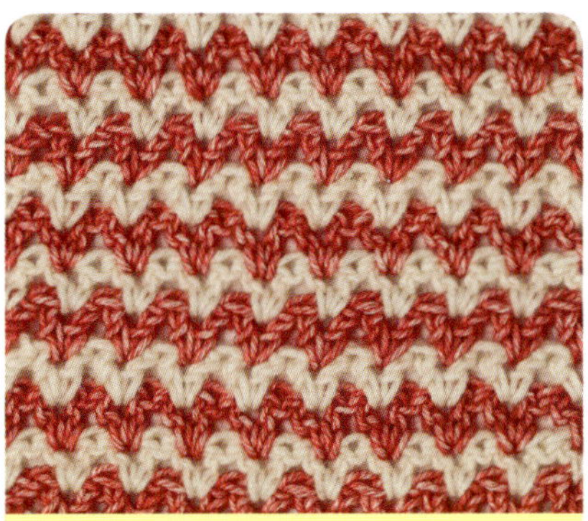

Sequence A
Stitch pattern 3 *(treble pairs aligned)*
Yarn *Scheepjes Stone Washed*
Shades *Moon Stone (801) & Red Jasper (807)*

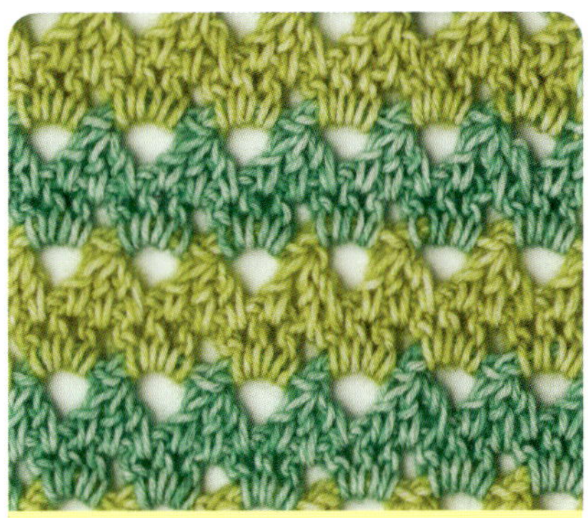

Sequence C
Stitch pattern 17 *(increase & decrease rows)*
Yarn *Scheepjes Stone Washed*
Shades *Peridot (827) & Fosterite (826)*

Sequence D
Stitch pattern 1 *(basic treble)*
Yarn *Stylecraft Alpaca DK*
Shades *Charcoal (6020) & Mistral (6013)*

Sequence B
Stitch pattern 3 *(treble pairs aligned)*
Yarn *Scheepjes Stone Washed*
Shades *Amazonite (813) & Turquoise (824)*

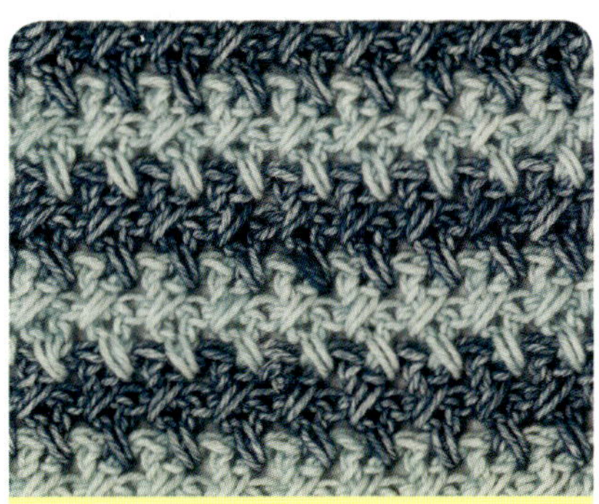

Sequence C
Stitch pattern 13 *(woven criss cross)*
Yarn *Scheepjes Stone Washed*
Shades *Amazonite (813) & Blue Apatite (805)*

Sequence D
Stitch pattern 4 *(treble pairs staggered)*
Yarn *Scheepjes Stone Washed*
Shades *Moon Stone (801) & Peridot (827)*

Stripes – floating the yarn

If you are in the habit of cutting the yarn every time you change colour when crocheting stripes, you might like to try "floating" the yarn instead. The non-working yarn is carried up and secured at the side of the work until it is needed again. Floating the yarn takes a bit of practice and won't suit every circumstance, but it does help to reduce the number of yarn ends to sew in when crocheting two-colour stripes.

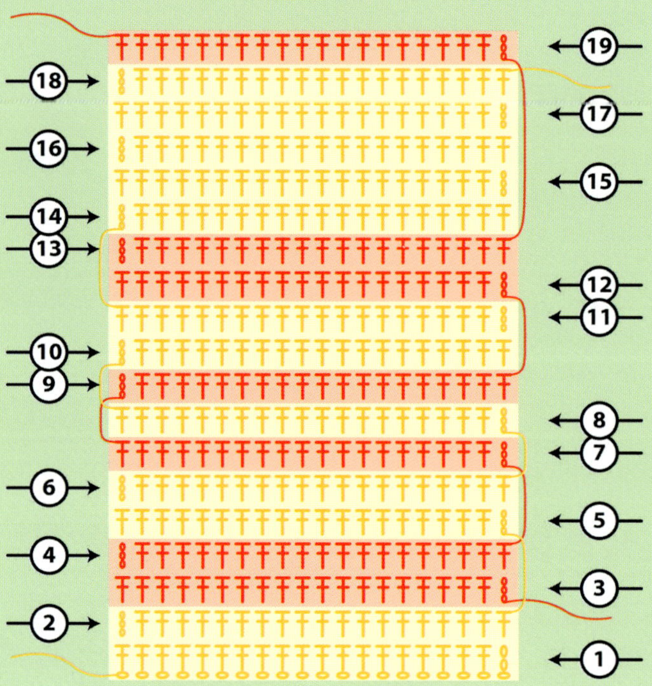

__Right__ When the __floating yarn__ method is used to crochet these random stripes, there are only four yarn-tails to sew in (whereas cutting the yarn after each colour swap would result in 19 yarn-tails).

Floating the yarn: step-by-step exercise

The exercise on these pages will give you practice in floating the non-working yarn up the side of the work. The design is intentionally random so that you can practice floating the yarn up over a various number of rows.

> **TIPS**
> - This exercise has been written for the standard method of working into the top of a stitch, but the techniques can be applied to working in between stitches as well.
> - The exercise refers to "light" and "dark" yarn, but any two contrasting colours can be used.
> - Use the chart above to help you if necessary.

Foundation chain With light yarn chain 22.
Row 1 1 treble in 4th chain from hook (the first 3 unworked chains count as one stitch). 1 treble in each of remaining 18 chains. (20 stitches)
Row 2 Chain 3 (counts as one stitch). Turn. 1 treble in each of next 19 stitches. (20 stitches)
Row 3 Swap to dark yarn (see page 7) then repeat row 2.
Row 4 Repeat row 2.
Row 5 Float and swap to light yarn *(see steps 1–4 below)* then repeat row 2.

Left-handed

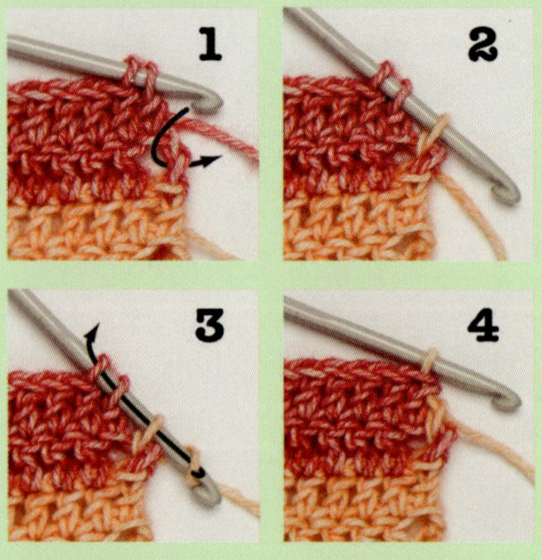

Float and swap to different yarn

- *Undo the final pull through of last stitch in row, so that there are two loops on hook. Insert hook into eyelet of row below (1).*
- *Pick up a loop of yarn specified (2).*
- *Yarn over and draw through all three loops on hook (3).*
- *Step 4 shows completed float and swap.*

Right-handed

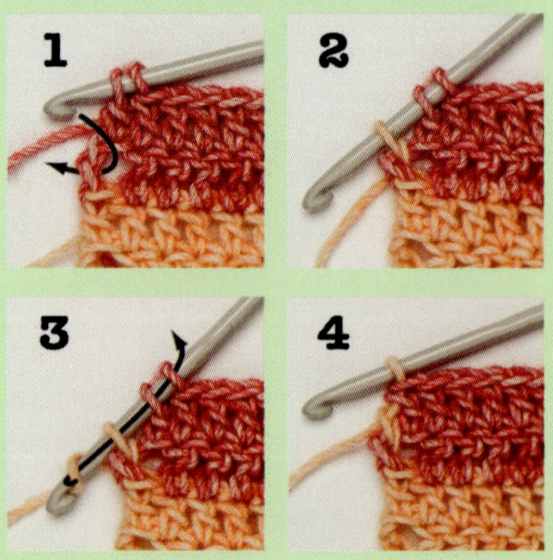

Row 6 Repeat row 2.
(Repeat rows 3–6 for extra practice in floating the yarn up over two-row stripes.)
Row 7 Float and swap to dark yarn ***(see steps 1–4 but with colours reversed)*** then repeat row 2.
Row 8 *This row requires the light yarn which is at the opposite side of the work. The light yarn can be floated up and the row worked in the same direction as the previous row, as follows:* extend the loop of dark yarn that is on the hook and pull it right out so that it won't unravel. Turn. Insert the hook into the first eyelet of previous row and pick up a loop of light yarn ***(see step 5 below)***. Then repeat row 2. *(Note: you will be working in the same direction as the previous row.)*

Float the yarn for a row worked in the same direction as the previous row

Left-handed

Right-handed

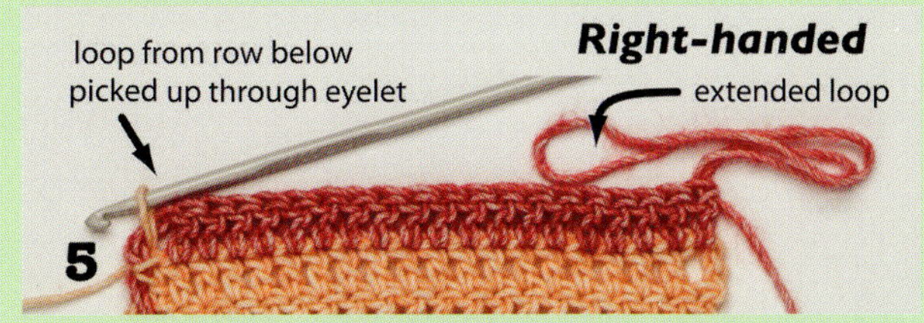

Row 9 *This row requires dark yarn. Float and swap to the extended loop of dark yarn as follows.* Undo the last pull through of the previous row so that there are two loops on the hook. Place the extended loop of dark yarn on the hook and tighten it to a normal tension. With the dark yarn, yarn over and draw through all 3 loops on hook ***(see steps 6 and 7 below)***. Then repeat row 2.
(Repeat rows 8–9 for extra practice in floating the yarn up over one-row stripes.)

Left-handed | **Float and swap with an extended loop** | **Right-handed**

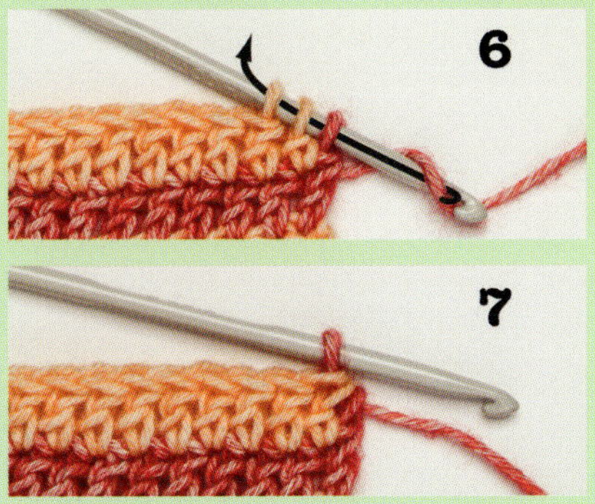

- ***Undo the final pull through of last stitch in row, so that there are two loops on hook.***
- ***Place extended loop on hook. Adjust tension of loop.***
- ***Yarn over and draw through all three loops on hook (6).***
- ***Step 7 shows completed float and swap.***

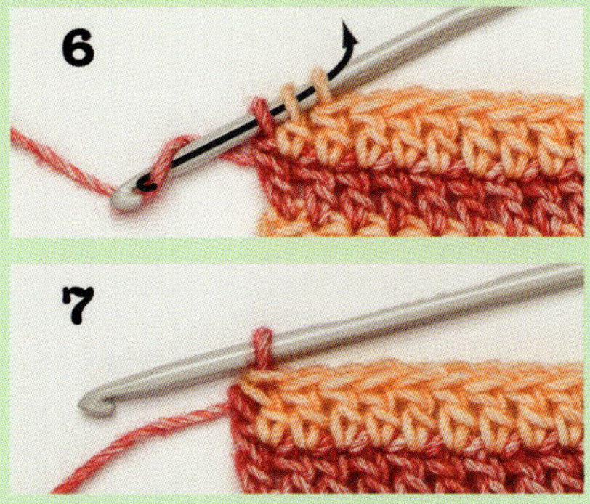

Row 10 Repeat row 8.
Row 11 *Before starting this row, take the opportunity to secure the extended loop of dark yarn as follows:* undo the last pull through of the previous row so that there are two loops on the hook. Place the extended loop of dark yarn on the hook and tighten it to a normal tension. With dark yarn, yarn over and draw through all three loops on hook ***(see step 6 above). Now release the dark yarn, pick up the light yarn and repeat row 2.***
Row 12 *This row is the same as row 8 but with the colours reversed:* extend the loop of light yarn that is on the hook and pull it right out so that it won't unravel. Turn. Insert the hook into the first eyelet of previous row and pick up a loop of dark yarn ***(see step 5 but with colours reversed)***. Then repeat row 2.
Row 13 *Before starting this row, take the opportunity to secure the extended loop of light yarn:* undo the last pull through of the previous row. Place the extended loop of light yarn on the hook and tighten it to a normal tension. With light yarn, yarn over and draw through all three loops on hook ***(step 6 but with colours reversed)***. Release the light yarn, pick up the dark yarn and repeat row 2.
Row 14 Repeat row 8.
Row 15 Repeat row 11.
Row 16 Repeat row 2.
Row 17 *Float the dark yarn up so that it is kept secured at the side of these five light-yarn rows:* Float and swap to dark yarn ***(steps 1–4 but with colours reversed)***. Release dark yarn, pick up light yarn and repeat row 2.
Row 18 Repeat row 2.
Row 19 Repeat row 7.
Either repeat rows 8–19 or try any of the stripe sequences on the previous page for extra practice.

Triangular crochet makes practical use of the many facinating and intriguing patterns associated with the humble triangle.

The rugged and hard wearing nature of this technique makes it the ideal choice for vibrant sofa throws, especially when you need to incorporate modern designs and colours into your crochet.

Plenty of design suggestions are included in this chapter, as well as two complete patterns and advice on adapting this technique to meet your own particular triangular requirements!

Triangular
Crochet

What is triangular crochet?

Triangular crochet is a way of crocheting triangle based designs.

How is triangular crochet done?

Triangles of different colours are crocheted-as-you-go to form rectangular strips. The strips are then arranged in order and sewn together.

Left *Four strips of crochet-as-you-go triangles.*

Right *The same four strips of triangles are re-arranged and sewn together.*

TIP There is no "right" side to the strips, so they can be flipped horizontally, vertically and back to front when being arranged.

How to crochet a strip of triangles

1 A strip of triangles begins with a ***starting triangle***. This is crocheted from the narrow end upwards.

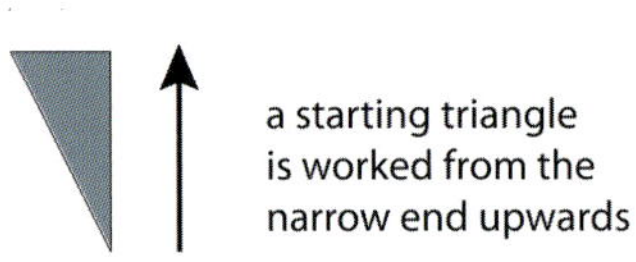

2 After crocheting a triangle, the yarn is swapped to a new colour and a foundation chain is made for the next triangle.

3 Because each triangle is crocheted from the narrow end upwards, the work is effectively turned upside down at the start of each triangle.

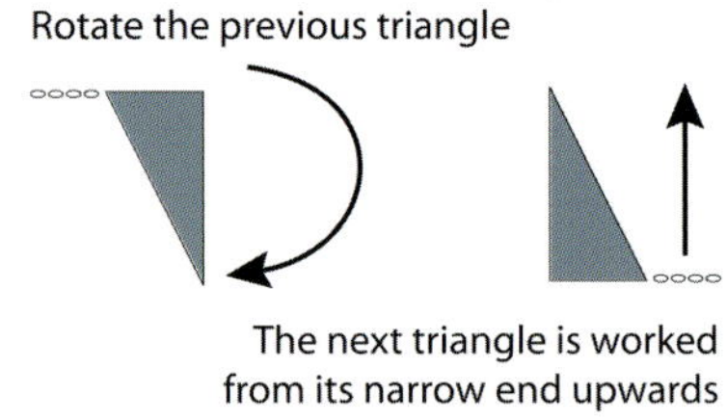

4 After making a ***starting triangle***, work a ***full-width triangle***. This triangle is joined to the previous triangle with slip-stitches as you crochet.

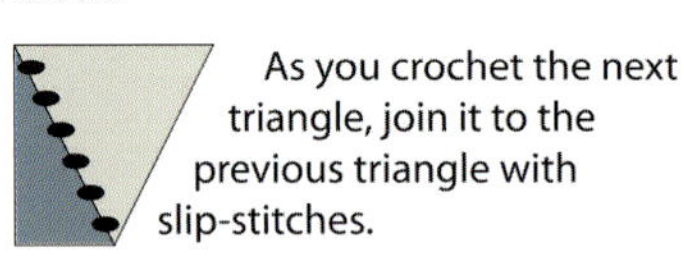

5 Keep adding ***full-width triangles*** in the same way.

6 To complete the strip, work an ***ending triangle***.

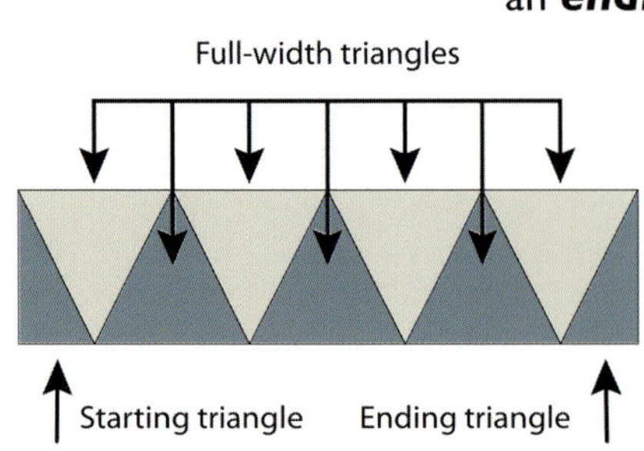

Treble in eyelet

Triangular crochet is worked in treble stitch. Apart from the first row, all the trebles are worked in the gap ***between*** *the stitches. In this chapter the gap between the stitches is called an* ***"eyelet"****.*

Left-handed

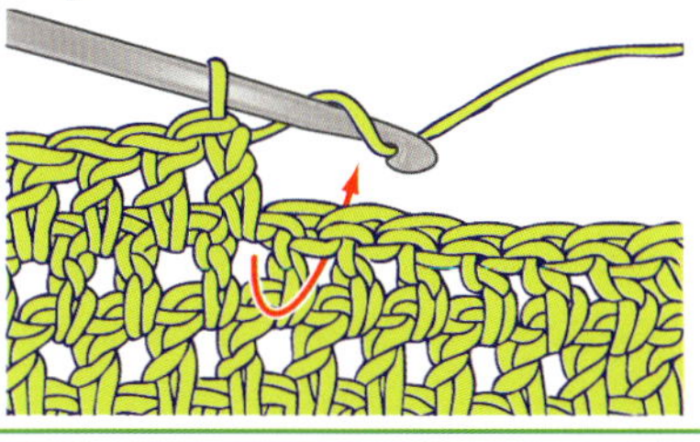

"1 treble in next eyelet" ***means working a stitch in the gap between two stitches in the row below.***

= treble in eyelet

Right-handed

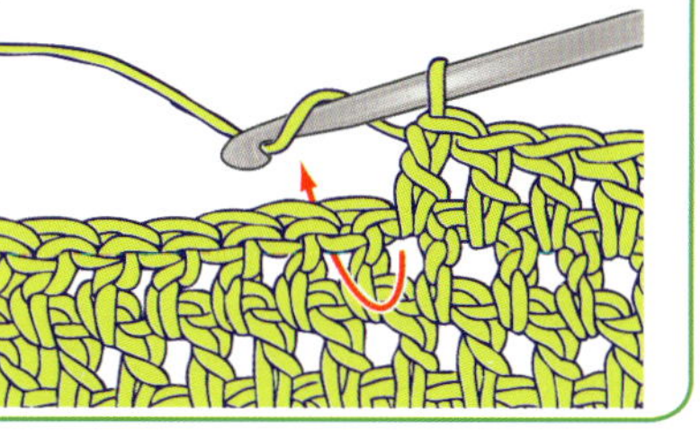

Crocheting a strip of triangles step-by-step exercise

Like all crochet techniques, learning triangular crochet will take a little practice, so before embarking on a large project, start by making strips of triangles with some left-over yarn and sew them together. You could follow the simple blue, black and grey design shown opposite with any three colours you have to hand, or try one of the multi-coloured patterns at the top of page 94. The blank template can be used for your own ideas.

Starting triangle

Foundation chain With specified shade, and leaving a 15 cm starting yarn-tail, chain 4.

Row 1 1 treble in 3rd chain from hook (first two unworked chain count as one stitch). 1 treble in last chain. (3 stitches)

Row 2 Chain 2 (counts as 1 stitch). Turn. 1 treble in next eyelet. 2 treble in last eyelet (4 stitches).

Row 3 Chain 2 (counts as 1 stitch). Turn. 1 treble in each of next 3 eyelets.

Row 4 Chain 2 (counts as 1 stitch). Turn. 1 treble in each of next 2 eyelets. 2 treble in last eyelet (5 stitches).

Row 5 Chain 2 (counts as 1 stitch). Turn. 1 treble in each of next 4 eyelets.

Row 6 Chain 2 (counts as 1 stitch). Turn. 1 treble in each of next 3 eyelets. 2 treble in last eyelet (6 stitches).

Row 7 Chain 2 (counts as 1 stitch). Turn. 1 treble in each of next 5 eyelets.

Row 8 Chain 2 (counts as 1 stitch). Turn. 1 treble in each of next 4 eyelets. 2 treble in last eyelet (7 stitches).

Row 9 Chain 2 (counts as 1 stitch). Turn. 1 treble in each of next 6 eyelets.

Row 10 Chain 2 (counts as 1 stitch). Turn. 1 treble in each of next 5 eyelets. 2 treble in last eyelet (8 stitches).

Swap to next yarn shade (see below).

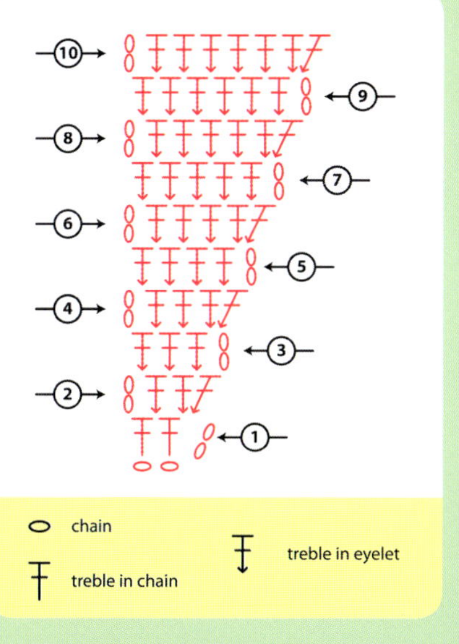

Swap to next yarn shade

The yarn is always swapped after each triangle, because adjacent triangles on a strip must be different colours.

**Leave suitably long starting and ending yarn-tails for sewing up (see tip box on page 97).*

Left-handed

"swap to next yarn shade"

Undo the last draw through of the previous stitch and re-do draw through with new shade leaving a suitably long starting yarn-tail*.

Cut previous triangle yarn leaving a suitably long ending yarn-tail.*

Right-handed

Crocheting a strip of triangles (continued)

Full-width triangle

After making a starting triangle and swapping to a new yarn, the foundation chain for the next triangle is made. Then the previous triangle is rotated and the new triangle is worked. The new triangle is joined to the previous triangle with slip-stitches as it progresses.

TIP Count the number of stitches, especially at the end of the final row.

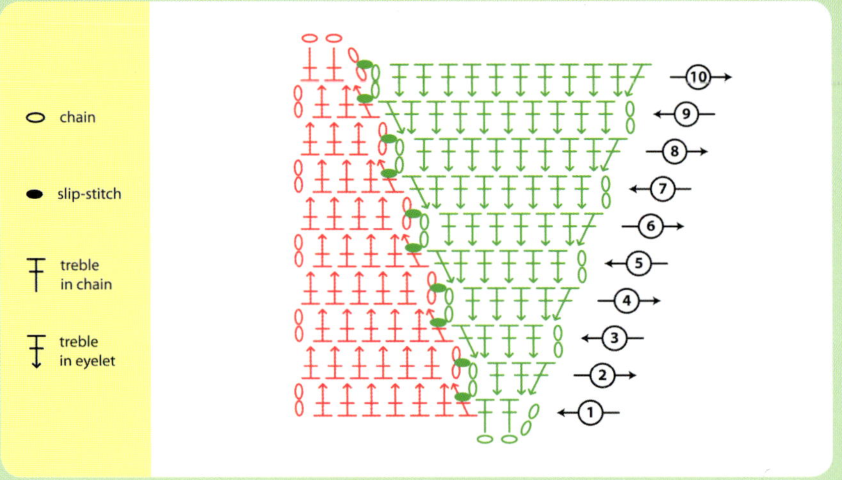

Left-handed

1 At the end of row 1, slip-stitch into edge eyelet of row 10 of previous triangle

2 After the row 2 turning chain, (but before turning) slip-stitch into edge eyelet of row 9 of previous triangle

3 Row 2 After turning, bring the yarn behind the hook. It will wrap around the edge of the previous triangle.

Right-handed

1 At the end of row 1, slip-stitch into edge eyelet of row 10 of previous triangle

2 After the row 2 turning chain, (but before turning) slip-stitch into edge eyelet of row 9 of previous triangle

3 Row 2 After turning, bring the yarn behind the hook. It will wrap around the edge of the previous triangle.

Foundation chain With specified shade, and leaving a suitably long starting yarn-tail, chain 4.

Row 1 1 treble in 3rd chain from hook (first two unworked chain count as one stitch). 1 treble in next chain. Slip-stitch into the edge eyelet of row 10 of previous triangle ***(see step 1)***. (3 stitches)

Row 2 Chain 2 (counts as 1 treble). Slip-stitch into the edge eyelet of row 9 of previous triangle ***(see step 2)***.Turn. (The yarn wraps around the edge of the previous triangle: ***see step 3***). 1 treble in next eyelet. 2 treble in last eyelet. (4 stitches)

Row 3 Chain 2 (counts as 1 treble). Turn. 1 treble in each of next 2 eyelets. 2 treble in last eyelet. Slip-stitch into the edge eyelet of row 8 of previous triangle. (5 stitches)

Row 4 Chain 2 (counts as 1 treble). Slip-stitch into the edge eyelet of row 7 of previous triangle Turn. 1 treble in each of next 3 eyelets. 2 treble in last eyelet. (6 stitches)

Row 5 Chain 2 (counts as 1 treble). Turn. 1 treble in each of next 4 eyelets. 2 treble in last eyelet. Slip-stitch in the edge eyelet of row 6 of previous triangle. (7 stitches)

Row 6 Chain 2 (counts as 1 treble). Slip-stitch into the edge eyelet of row 5 of previous triangle Turn. 1 treble in each of next 5 eyelets. 2 treble in last eyelet. (8 stitches)

Row 7 Chain 2 (counts as 1 treble). Turn. 1 treble in each of next 6 eyelets. 2 treble in last eyelet. Slip-stitch in the edge eyelet of row 4 of previous triangle. (9 stitches)

Row 8 Chain 2 (counts as 1 treble). Slip-stitch into the edge eyelet of row 3 of previous triangle Turn. 1 treble in each of next 7 eyelets. 2 treble in last eyelet. (10 stitches)

Row 9 Chain 2 (counts as 1 treble). Turn. 1 treble in each of next 8 eyelets. 2 treble in last eyelet. Slip-stitch in the edge eyelet of row 2 of previous triangle. (11 stitches)

Row 10 Chain 2 (counts as 1 treble). Slip-stitch into the edge eyelet of row 1 of previous triangle Turn. 1 treble in each of next 9 eyelets. 2 treble in last eyelet. (12 stitches)

Swap to next shade leaving a suitably long yarn-tail for sewing up.

*Continue adding the required number of **full-width triangles**.*

Ending triangle

*Once the required number of **full-width triangles** have been made, finish with an **ending triangle**.*

Foundation chain With specified shade, and leaving a suitably long starting yarn-tail, chain 4.

Row 1 1 treble in 3rd chain from hook (first two unworked chain count as one stitch). 1 treble in next chain. Slip-stitch into the edge eyelet of row 10 of previous triangle. (3 stitches)

Row 2 Chain 2 (counts as 1 treble). Slip-stitch into the edge eyelet of row 9 of previous triangle. Turn. 1 treble in next eyelet. 2 treble in last eyelet. (4 stitches)

Row 3 Chain 2 (counts as 1 treble). Turn. 1 treble in each of next 2 eyelets. 2 treble in last eyelet. Slip-stitch into the edge eyelet of row 8 of previous triangle. (5 stitches)

Row 4 Chain 2 (counts as 1 treble). Slip-stitch into the edge eyelet of row 7 of previous triangle Turn. 1 treble in each of next 4 eyelets. (5 stitches)

Row 5 Chain 2 (counts as 1 treble). Turn. 1 treble in each of next 3 eyelets. 2 treble in last eyelet. Slip-stitch in the edge eyelet of row 6 of previous triangle. (6 stitches)

Row 6 Chain 2 (counts as 1 treble). Slip-stitch into the edge eyelet of row 5 of previous triangle Turn. 1 treble in each of next 5 eyelets. (6 stitches)

Row 7 Chain 2 (counts as 1 treble). Turn. 1 treble in each of next 4 eyelets. 2 treble in last eyelet. Slip-stitch in the edge eyelet of row 4 of previous triangle. (7 stitches)

Row 8 Chain 2 (counts as 1 treble). Slip-stitch into the edge eyelet of row 3 of previous triangle Turn. 1 treble in each of next 6 eyelets. (7 stitches)

Row 9 Chain 2 (counts as 1 treble). Turn. 1 treble in each of next 5 eyelets. 2 treble in last eyelet. Slip-stitch in the edge eyelet of row 2 of previous triangle. (8 stitches)

Row 10 Chain 2 (counts as 1 treble). Slip-stitch into the edge eyelet of row 1 of previous triangle Turn. 1 treble in each of next 7 eyelets. (8 stitches) *Fasten off leaving a suitably long yarn-tail for sewing up.*

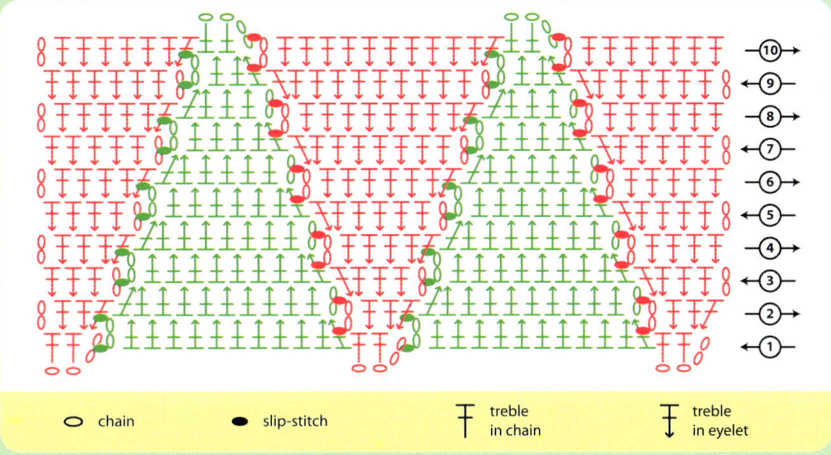

Sewing up

The strips are sewn together with a double seam of running stitch.

Sew two strips together at a time using the yarn-tails.

Step 1 Starting with the yarn-tails on one strip, use each triangle's ending yarn-tail to sew it to the corresponding triangle on the other strip. Use running stitch (see page 8) and sew through **one** of the teardrop shaped threads from each strip along the triangles' wide edges.

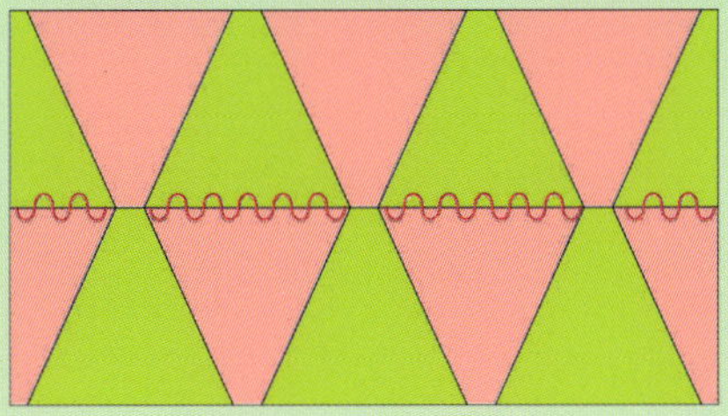

Step 2 Then use the starting yarn-tails to sew the short triangle edges together by weaving the tail up and down between the V–shaped threads as shown below.

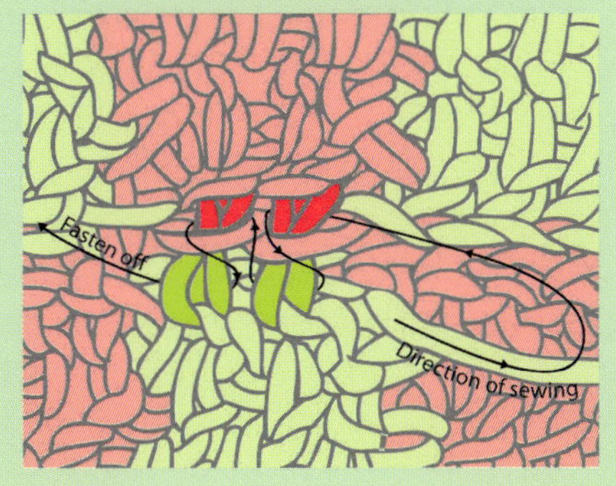

TIP It's a good idea to leave the final fastening off until all the seams have been sewn, just in case you've missed a stitch or seam somewhere.

TIP A yarn-tail 3 times the width of the triangle in length (unstretched) should be long enough to sew up and fasten off, but check that this formula works for you before embarking on a project.

Step 3 Once one side has been sewn, flip the work over and repeat steps 1 and 2 on the other side with the other strip's yarn-tails. This creates a double seam of running stitch (see page 9).

Multi-Coloured Sofa Throw

Triangular crochet makes a rugged, textured fabric making it perfect for hard-wearing sofa throws. This multi-coloured throw (photographed at the start of this chapter) is easy to adapt to the size of any sofa.

Instructions

Familiarise yourself with ***all*** *the information on pages 94–97 before starting. In particular you will need to have practised making and sewing together strips of triangles before embarking on this lengthy project.*

Make four of each of the two strips shown below. Once the strips have been sewn together, work the edging shown opposite.

TIP As well as checking that you have the correct number of stitches at the end of each triangle, remember to check that you have the right colour sequence, too.

Materials

Yarn *Adriafil Mirage*
Composition *55% wool 45% acrylic*
Yardage *125 metres (136 yards) approximately*
Shades

- *1 x 50g Baby pink (03)*
- *2 x 50g Baby light yellow (05)*
- *1 x 50g Apricot (06)*
- *1 x 50g Sea green (08)*
- *1 x 50g Light blue (09)*
- *1 x 50g Deep azure (10)*
- *1 x 50g Cyclamen (21)*
- *2 x 50g Light green (30)*
- *1 x 50g Turquoise (36)*
- *1 x 50g Deep pink (37)*
- *1 x 50g Old pink (41)*
- *2 x 50g Light mélange grey (51)*
- *1 x 50g Green-yellow (85)*
- *1 x 50g Light mélange Beige (92)*

Hook *4.00 mm*
Finished size *116 x 83 cm (45 x 32 inches) approx*
Tension *4 rows of 4 triangles = 20 x 38 cm*

Shade key

Baby pink (03)
Baby light yellow (05)
Apricot (06)
Sea green (08)
Light blue (09)
Deep azure (10)
Cyclamen (21)
Light green (30)
Turquoise (36)
Deep pink (37)
Old pink (41)
Light mélange grey (51)
Green-yellow (85)
Light mélange beige (92)

Strip 1 (make 4)

Starting triangle
Light mélange beige (92)
Full-width triangles
Work the following 8-colour sequence two times:
Baby light yellow (05)
Deep pink (37)
Green-yellow (85)
Sea green (08)
Deep azure (10)
Light green (30)
Cyclamen (21)
Light mélange beige (92).
Then work the first ***seven*** colours of the 8-colour sequence once.
Ending triangle
Light mélange beige (92)

Strip 2 (make 4)

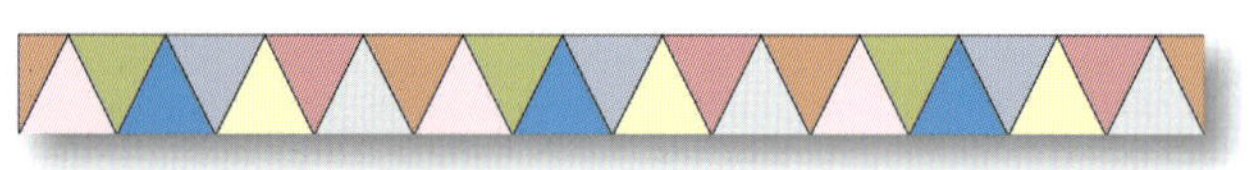

Starting triangle
Apricot (06)
Full-width triangles
Work the following 8-colour sequence two times:
Baby pink (03)
Light green (30)
Turquoise (36)
Light blue (09)
Baby light yellow (05)
Old pink (41)
Light mélange grey (51)
Apricot (06).
Then work the first ***seven*** colours of the 8-colour sequence once.
Ending triangle
Apricot (06)

Triangular Crochet

Placement diagram

Sewing up

Once the strips have been made, arrange them according to the placement diagram (left).

Remember that the strips will need to be flipped horizontally and/or vertically.

Refer to the sewing up information on pages 8–9 as well as the sewing up information specific to this technique on page 97.

The strips are sewn up with a double seam of running stitch, which helps to create a snug double-sided fabric.

Edging

Once the strips have been sewn together, a simple one-row edging can be worked. You will need approximately 17g of yarn. If the edging seems too tight, adjust to a looser tension or add extra chain stitches between the double-crochets.

With either side facing, join light mélange grey to a top corner eyelet with a slip-stitch (left-handers join to top left corner, right-handers join to top right corner). Chain 1. 1 double-crochet in same corner eyelet.

*Work **loosely** along the top edge of the throw:* 1 double-crochet in each eyelet up to and including the corner eyelet. Chain 2. 1 double-crochet in same corner eyelet.

Work along the side edge: (Chain 1. 1 double-crochet in next eyelet) up to and including the next corner eyelet. Chain 2. 1 double-crochet in same corner eyelet.

*Work **loosely** along the bottom edge:* 1 double-crochet in each eyelet up to and including the next corner eyelet. Chain 2. 1 double-crochet in same corner eyelet.

Work along the side edge: (Chain 1. 1 double-crochet in next eyelet) up to and including the next corner eyelet. Chain 2. Slip-stitch to first double-crochet. ***Fasten off.***

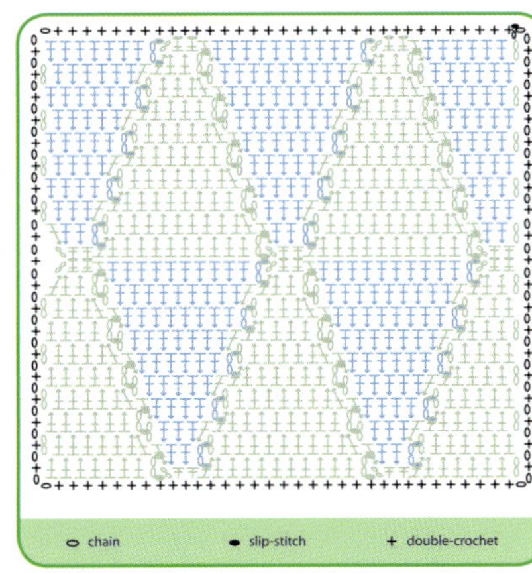

Above *Symbol chart showing the edging around a small section of triangular crochet. This simple edging can be used for all triangular crochet designs.*

Adapting the size

To increase the size of the throw, either add extra triangles as shown below, or work extra rows in each triangle (see note at bottom of page 101).

Below *To alter the width of this throw, add or remove pairs of triangles.*

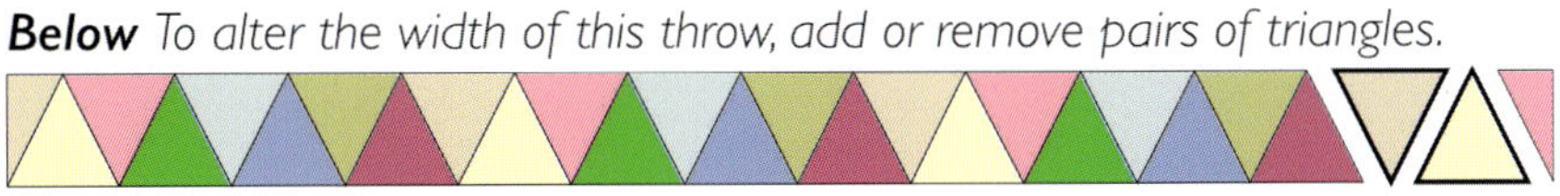

Below *To maintain the colour sequence, add or remove sets of eight triangles.*

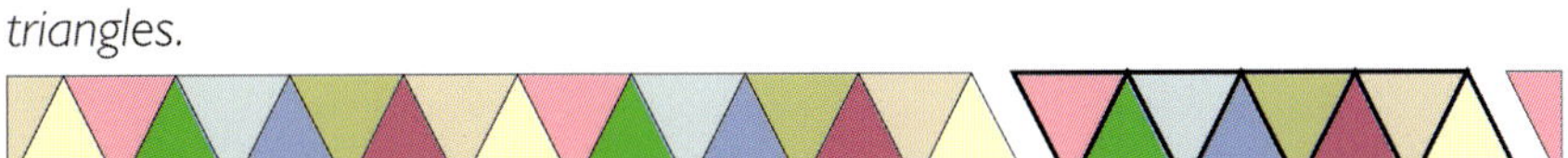

Above *To alter the height of this throw, add or remove pairs of strips.*

Navaho Inspired Throw

Instructions

*Familiarise yourself with **all** the information on pages 94–97 before starting. In particular you will need to have practised making and sewing together strips of triangles before embarking on this lengthy project.*

Make two of each of the six strips shown on these pages. Pay particular attention to obtaining the correct colour sequence. Arrange the strips according to the placement diagram (right) then sew together (refer to sewing up information on pages 8–9 and page 97). Finish by crocheting the edging.

***Below** Placement diagram for the Navaho Inspired Throw (photographed on inside front cover).*

Materials

***Yarn** Adriafil Mirage*
***Composition** 55% wool 45% acrylic.*
***Yardage** 125 metres (136 yards) approximately*

Shades

- *7 x 50g Light mélange beige (92)*
- *1 x 50g Rust (86)*
- *2 x 50g Brick (82)*
- *2 x 50g Blue fluo (74)*
- *2 x 50g Medium mélange beige (93)*
- *2 x 50g Turquoise (36)*
- *2 x 50g Mélange hazelnut (91)*
- *1 x 50g Mélange anthracite grey (54)*

***Hook** 4.00 mm*

***Finished size** 83 x 116 cm*

***Tension** 4 rows of 4 triangles = 20 x 38 cm*

Shade key

Light mélange beige
Medium mélange beige
Mélange hazelnut
Mélange anthracite grey
Turquoise
Blue fluo
Rust
Brick

Strip 1 (make 2)

Starting triangle:
light mélange beige
Full width triangles:
rust
light mélange beige
brick
light mélange beige
blue fluo
light mélange beige,
medium mélange beige
turquoise
medium mélange beige
light mélange beige
blue fluo
light mélange beige
brick
light mélange beige
rust
Ending triangle:
light mélange beige

Strip 2 (make 2)

Starting triangle:
rust
Full width triangles:
light mélange beige
brick
light mélange beige
blue fluo
light mélange beige
medium mélange beige
turquoise
light mélange beige
turquoise
medium mélange beige
light mélange beige
blue fluo
light mélange beige
brick
light mélange beige
Ending triangle:
rust

Strip 3 (make 2)

Starting triangle:
light mélange beige
Full width triangles:
brick
light mélange beige
blue fluo
light mélange beige
medium mélange beige
turquoise
light mélange beige
mélange hazelnut
light mélange beige
turquoise
medium mélange beige
light mélange beige
blue fluo
light mélange beige
brick
Ending triangle:
light mélange beige

Strip 4 (make 2)

Starting triangle:
brick
Full width triangles:
light mélange beige
blue fluo
light mélange beige
medium mélange beige
turquoise
light mélange beige
mélange hazelnut
brick
mélange hazelnut
light mélange beige
turquoise
medium mélange beige
light mélange beige
blue fluo
light mélange beige
Ending triangle:
brick

Strip 5 (make 2)

Starting triangle:
light mélange beige
Full width triangles:
blue fluo
light mélange beige
medium mélange beige
turquoise
light mélange beige
mélange hazelnut
brick
light mélange beige
brick
mélange hazelnut
light mélange beige
turquoise
medium mélange beige
light mélange beige
blue fluo
Ending triangle:
light mélange beige

Strip 6 (make 2)

Starting triangle:
blue fluo
Full width triangles:
light mélange beige
medium mélange beige
turquoise
light mélange beige
mélange hazelnut
brick
light mélange beige
mélange anthracite grey
light mélange beige
brick
mélange hazelnut
light mélange beige
turquoise
medium mélange beige
light mélange beige
Ending triangle:
blue fluo

Edging

Once the strips have been sewn together, a simple one-row edging can be worked. If the edging seems too tight, adjust to a looser tension or add extra chain stitches between the double-crochets. (There is a symbol chart for this edging on page 99.)

With either side facing, join mélange anthracite grey to a top corner eyelet with a slip-stitch (left-handers join to top left corner, right-handers join to top right corner). Chain 1. 1 double-crochet in same corner eyelet.
Work ***loosely*** *along the top edge of the throw:* 1 double-crochet in each eyelet up to and including the corner eyelet. Chain 2. 1 double-crochet in same corner eyelet.
Work along the side edge: (Chain 1. 1 double-crochet in next eyelet) up to and including the next corner eyelet. Chain 2. 1 double-crochet in same corner eyelet.
Work ***loosely*** *along the bottom edge:* 1 double-crochet in each eyelet up to and including the next corner eyelet. Chain 2. 1 double-crochet in same corner eyelet.
Work along the side edge: (Chain 1. 1 double-crochet in next eyelet) up to and including the next corner eyelet. Chain 2. Slip-stitch to first double-crochet.
Fasten off.

Adapting the size

To increase the size of the throw, work pairs of additional rows in each triangle, increasing the number of stitches in the extra rows accordingly.
Adding two rows to each standard 10 row triangle will increase the size of the throw by approximately 20%. (The amount of yarn required will increase proportionally.)

Below *A standard 10 row triangle produces a 83 x 116 cm throw.*

Right *A 12 row triangle produces a 100 x 140 cm throw.*

Triangular Crochet Inspiration

Here are some ideas to get you started with your own triangular crochet designs. Most triangle patterns are suitable for this technique, but avoid having two triangles of the same colour immediately next to each other horizontally, because this can be difficult to crochet (triangles can be the same colour vertically).

Below *Arranging a few single triangles in different colours can help when designing your own projects.*

To make a single triangle follow the instructions on page 96 for the full width triangle but omit all the slip-stitches.

Abstract

Linear

Accent

Diamond/Hexagonal

Cushions!

Cushions are a great way to try out a triangular crochet design. Four strips of nine triangles will cover one side of a cushion pad measuring between 38 to 42 cm square, depending on individual tension.

Right and below These designs can be used with the colours of the Navaho inspired throw on page 100.

TIP 50g of double knitting yarn will make approximately 12 full width triangles.

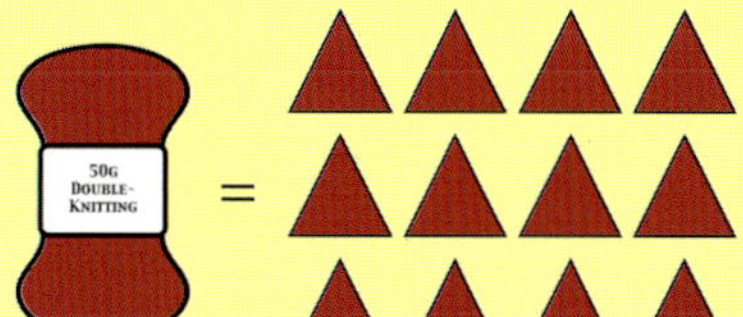

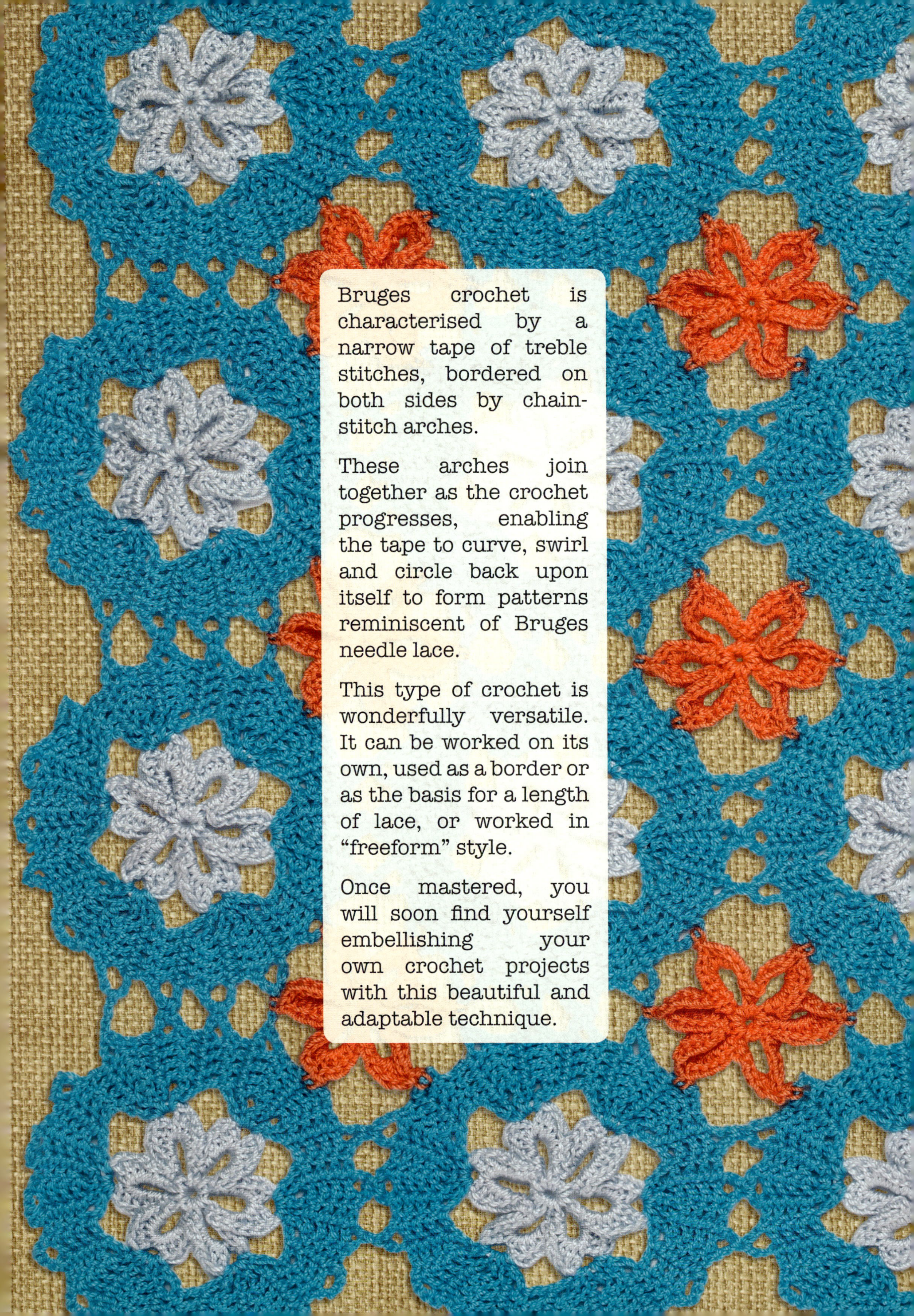

Bruges crochet is characterised by a narrow tape of treble stitches, bordered on both sides by chain-stitch arches.

These arches join together as the crochet progresses, enabling the tape to curve, swirl and circle back upon itself to form patterns reminiscent of Bruges needle lace.

This type of crochet is wonderfully versatile. It can be worked on its own, used as a border or as the basis for a length of lace, or worked in "freeform" style.

Once mastered, you will soon find yourself embellishing your own crochet projects with this beautiful and adaptable technique.

Bruges
Crochet

How to do Bruges Crochet step-by-step

The following four pages take you through the basics of Bruges crochet while making the sample photographed (right). This sample was made using DMC Petra No 3 crochet cotton and a 2.50 mm hook, but any plain yarn and a suitably sized hook will do.

Bruges tape

Bruges crochet comprises a tape bordered with chain-stitch arches. The tape used here is four treble stitches wide and the arches are five chains long.

Foundation chain Chain 9.

Row 1 1 treble in 6th chain from hook (missed 5 chain count as an arch). 1 treble in each of next 3 chain. (1 arch and 4 stitches) ***The five missed chain stitches make the first arch*** *(see Row 1 photo)*.

Row 2 Chain 5 (counts as an arch). Turn. 1 treble in each of next 4 stitches. ***The arch also functions as a turning chain but it does not count as a stitch, so you need to crochet all four trebles.*** *(see Row 2 photo)*.

Row 2 is the standard Bruges row:

Standard row *= Chain 5 (counts as an arch). Turn. 1 treble in each of next 4 stitches.*

Rows 3–18 Standard rows. *(see Rows 1–18 photo)*

Left-handed

Right-handed

Rows 1–18 (18 rows of Bruges tape)

Schematic diagrams

Because of the simplicity of Bruges crochet it is usually represented with schematic diagrams rather than symbol charts.

To help you follow these diagrams, the arches are numbered and traditional crochet symbols are used where necessary for added clarity.

Right *a schematic diagram for Bruges tape compared to a traditional symbol chart.*

Rows 1–18

Schematic diagram

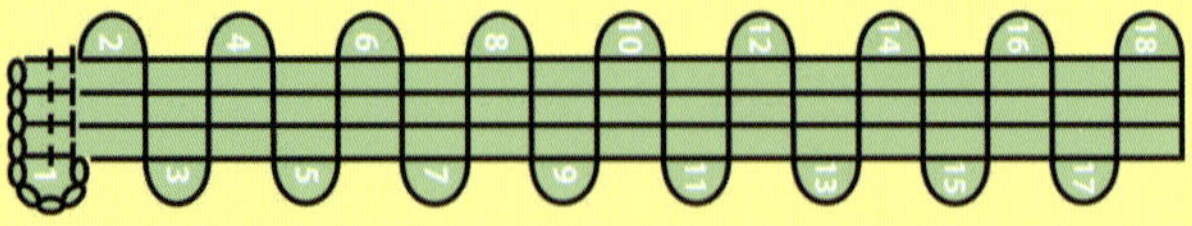

Symbol chart

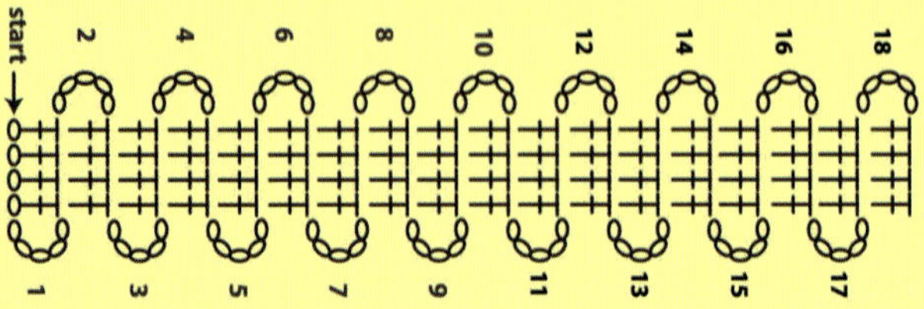

Key

o chain

ǂ treble

Adding a curve

Previously worked arches can be used to anchor the tape together as it curves round:

Row 19 ***The arch at the beginning of this row is joined to five arches down the side of the tape to form a six-arch-curve:*** Chain 2. Work down the side of the tape: pick up a loop in each of the next ***five*** arches. Yarn over and draw through all 6 loops on hook ***(see Row 19 Step 1 photo)***. Chain 2. Turn. 1 treble in each of next 4 stitches ***(see Step 2 photo)***.

Row 20 Standard row.

Joining arches

Continue to anchor the tape to itself by joining adjacent arches:

Row 21 ***The arch at the beginning of this row is joined with a double-crochet to the opposite arch:*** Chain 2. 1 double-crochet in opposite arch ***(see Row 21 photo).*** Chain 2. Turn. 1 treble in each of next 4 stitches.

Row 22 Standard row.

Row 23 Repeat row 21.

Row 24 Standard row.

Row 25 Repeat row 21.

Row 26 Standard row.

Arches can be joined with a variety of stitches. In row 27 the arches are joined with a triple-treble:

Triple-treble = *yarn over three times Pick up loop in arch specified (five loops on hook). (Yarn over and draw through 2 loops) 4 times.*

Row 27 Chain 2. 1 ***triple-treble*** in opposite arch. Chain 2. Turn. 1 treble in each of next 4 stitches.

Rows 28–33 Standard row (6 rows).

Rows 34–108 Repeat rows 19–33 five times.

Rows 109–117 Repeat rows 19–27 once.

(Exercise continues on the next page.)

Left-handed

Row 19 Step 1

Right-handed

Row 19 Step 1

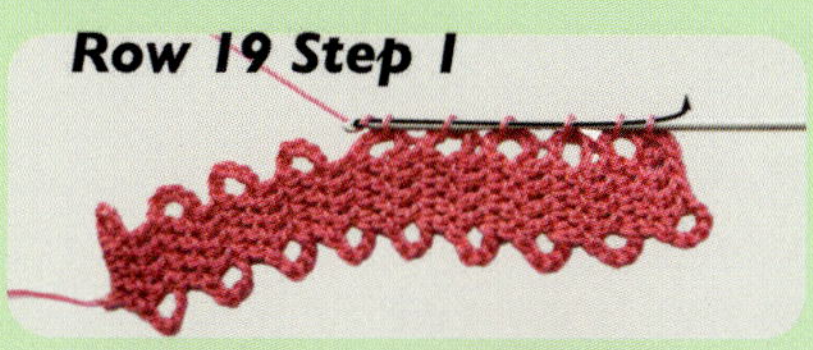

Row 19 Step 2

Row 19 Step 2

Rows 1–19

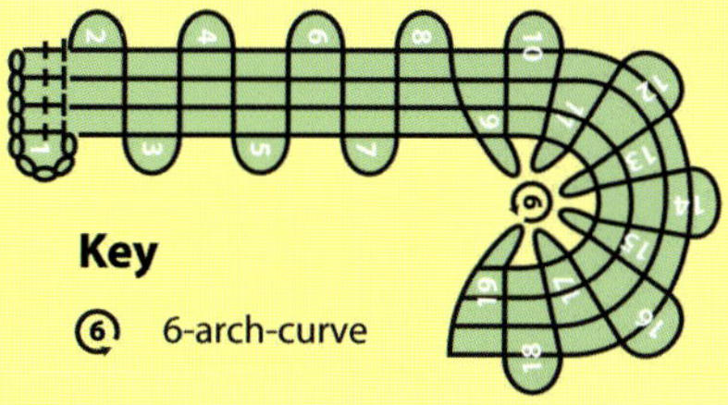

Key

6-arch-curve

Row 21 (left-handed)

Row 21 (right-handed)

Rows 1–117 **Key** + double-crochet triple-treble

4 Retaining & grafting

(The exercise from the previous page continues here.)

Rows 118–136 Standard row (19 rows).
Row 137–144 Repeat rows 19–26.

Retaining

*You can see from the schematic diagram (right) that the arch of row 145 is joined to both arch 119 **and** to the triple-treble connecting arches 117 and 91.*
To do this you will crochet a special "retained" stitch formation.
This involves starting a stitch in arch 119, but leaving it half-finished on the hook while another stitch is worked into the triple-treble between arches 117 and 91, before finally finishing off the first stitch:

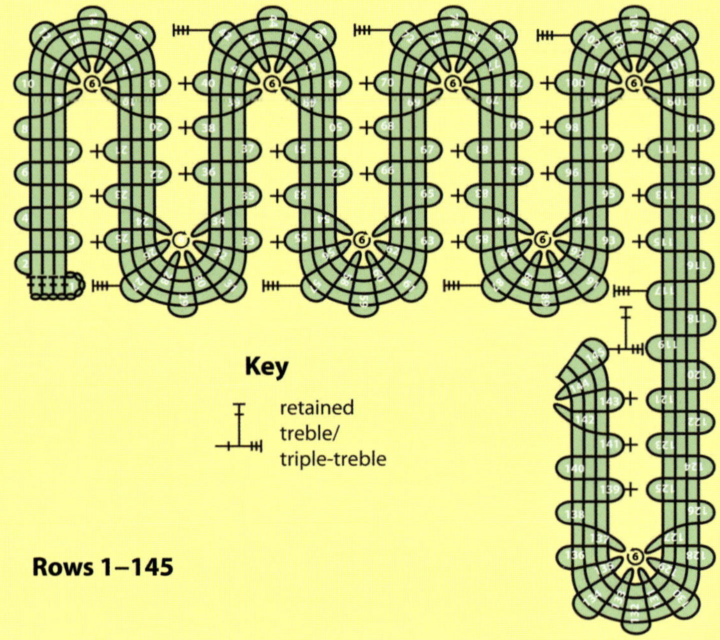

Left-handed

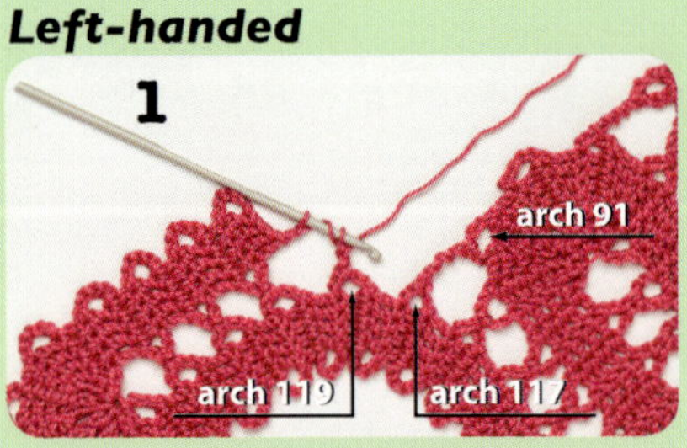

Row 145 Chain 2. Yarn over 3 times. Pick up a loop in arch 119 (5 loops on hook). (Yarn over and draw through 2 loops) two times. (3 loops remain on hook) ***(step 1)***.

Right-handed

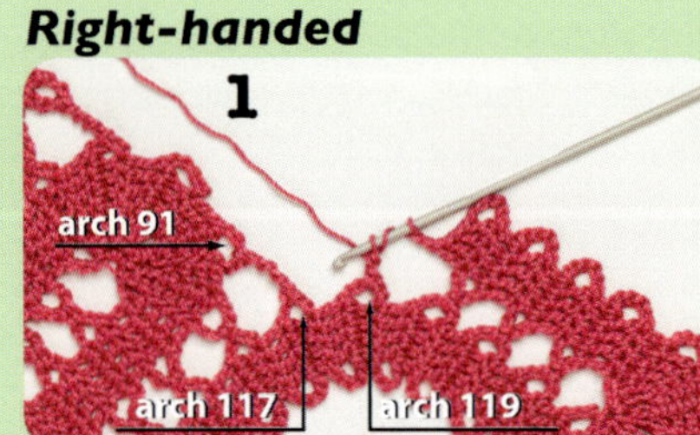

Yarn over. Pick up a loop in space made by the triple-treble connecting arches 117 & 91 (5 loops on hook) ***(step 2)***.

(Yarn over and draw through 2 loops) 4 times ***(step 3)***.

Chain 2. Turn. 1 treble in each of next 4 stitches ***(step 4)***.

Row 146 Standard row.

Row 147 Chain 2. 1 slip-stitch in arch 89. Chain 2. Turn. 1 treble in each of next 4 stitches.

Rows 148–151 Standard row (4 rows).

Row 152–174 Repeat rows 19–41 once.

Rows 175–234 Repeat rows 145–174 two more times *(use diagram below for relevant retained stitch arch numbers if necessary)*.

Row 235 Repeat row 145.

Row 236 Standard row. *Then graft rows 1 and 236 together:*

Grafting

Left-handed

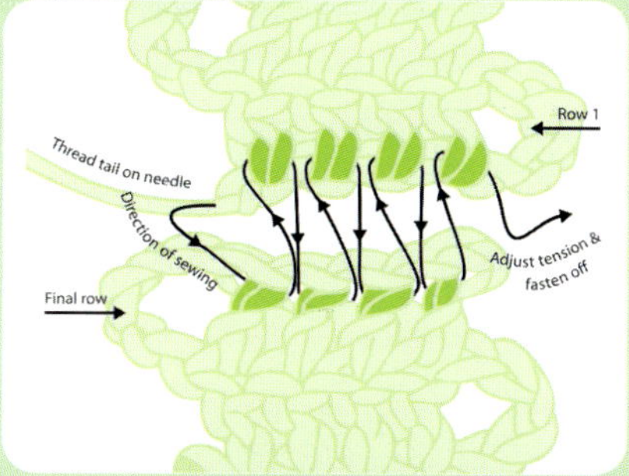

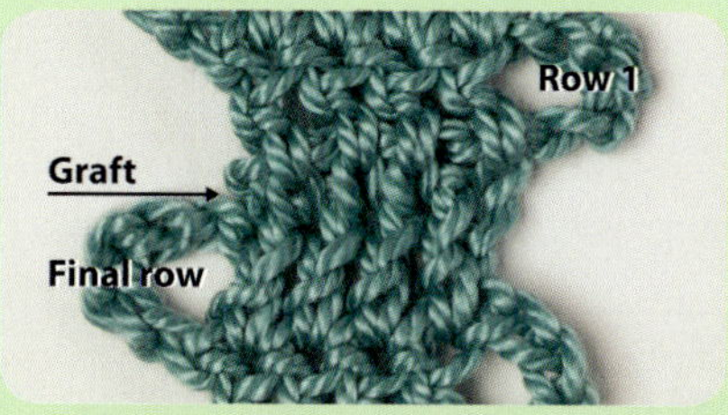

Grafting is a special way of sewing together the first and final rows of Bruges crochet.

Thread the starting yarn-tail onto a yarn needle. Pass the needle around the topmost part of the first treble of the final row. Then pass the needle under the corresponding two V-shaped threads of row 1. *Pass the needle around the next treble of the final row, then under the next two V-shaped threads of row 1. * Repeat from * to * two more times. Adjust the tension of the sewing to close up the gap between the first and final rows, then fasten off securely.

Right-handed

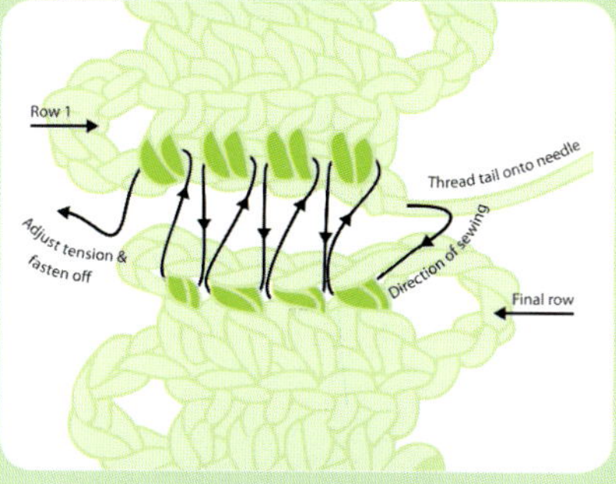

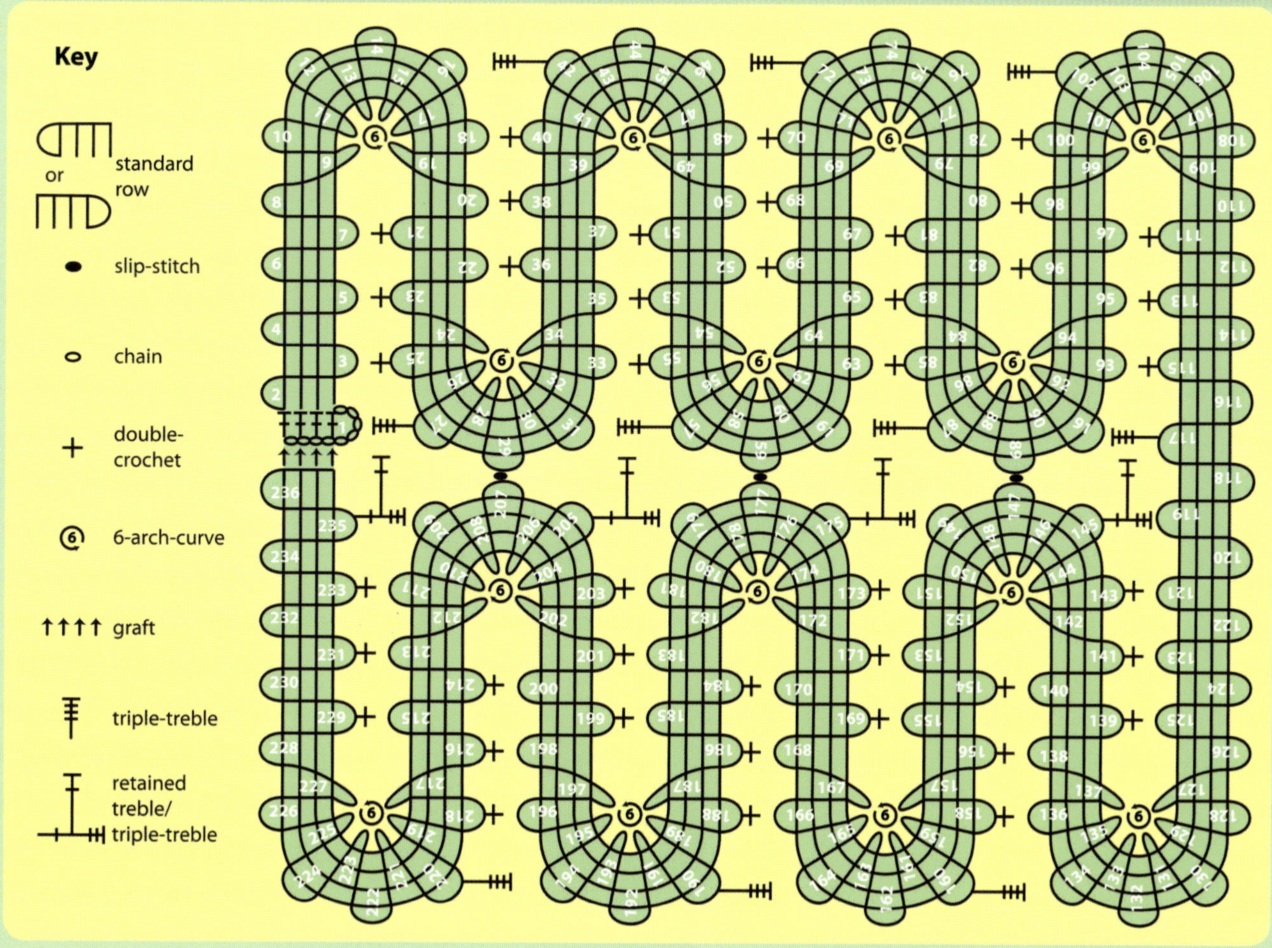

Bruges Crochet Lace Strips

Bruges crochet can be used to make strips of lace. Bruges tape is crocheted to the length required, then a decorative edging is added along the arches of one or both sides.

These edgings can also be used to finish other pieces of Bruges crochet.

Bruges tape

Foundation chain Chain 9.

Row 1 1 treble in 6th chain from hook (first 5 chain count as an arch). 1 treble in each of next 3 chain. (1 arch and 4 stitches)

Row 2 Chain 5 (counts as an arch). Turn. 1 treble in each of next 4 stitches.

Repeat row 2 until desired length is reached. Fasten off.

Bruges edging no 1 (5 dc)

Thread *DMC Petra No 3*
Composition *100% cotton*
Shade *(5745) {light yellow}*
Hook *2.50 mm*

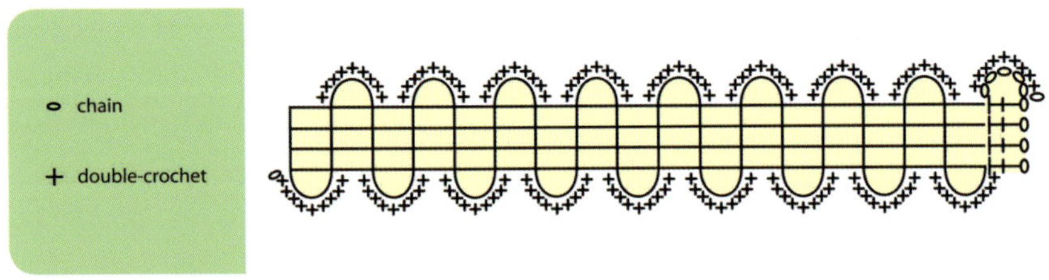

Join thread to first arch with a slip-stitch. Chain 1. 9 double-crochet in same arch. (9 double-crochet) in each arch to end.

Bruges edging no 2 (fan)

Thread *DMC Petra No 3*
Composition *100% cotton*
Shade *(5608) {peachey orange}*
Hook *2.50 mm*

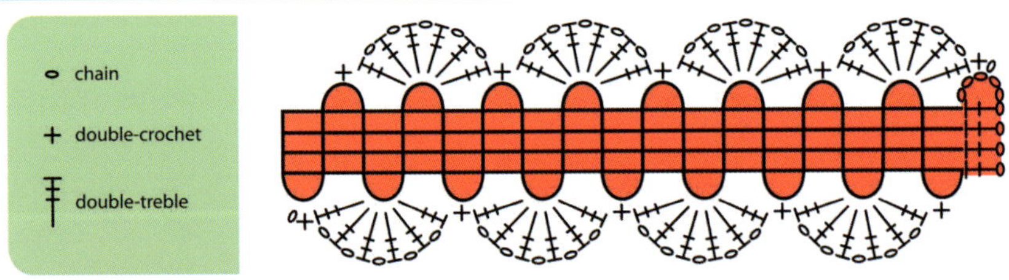

Double-treble = *yarn over two times. Pick up a loop in arch specified. (Yarn over and draw through 2 loops) 3 times.*

Join thread to first arch with a slip-stitch. Chain 1. 1 double-crochet in same arch. *1 double-treble in next arch. (Chain 1. 1 double-treble) 5 times in same arch. 1 double-crochet in next arch.* Repeat from * to * to end.

Bruges edging no 3 (points)

Thread *DMC Petra No 3*
Composition *100% cotton*
Shade *(5772) {light green}*
Hook *2.50 mm*

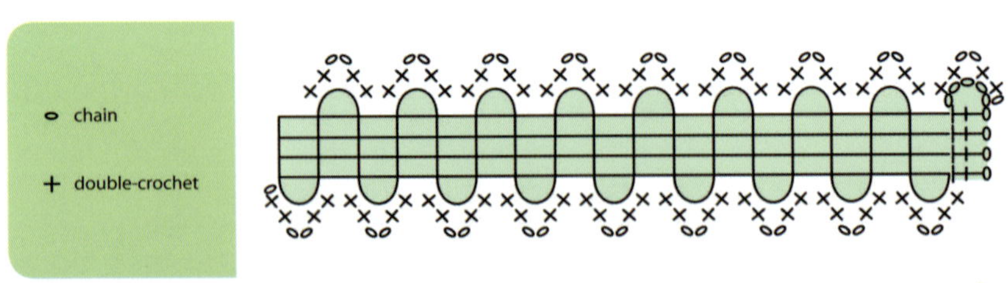

Join thread to first arch with a slip-stitch. Chain 1. (2 double-crochet. Chain 2. 2 double-crochet) in same arch. *(2 double-crochet. Chain 2. 2 double-crochet.) in each arch to end.

Bruges edging no 4 (half-treble picots)

Thread DMC Petra No 3
Composition 100% cotton
Shade (53805) {dark pink}
Hook 2.50 mm

Picot: *Chain 3. 1 half-treble in 3rd chain from hook.*

Join thread to first arch with a slip-stitch. Chain 1. 1 double-crochet in same arch. *(1 treble. 1 picot) 3 times in next arch. 1 treble in same arch. 1 double-crochet in next arch.* Repeat from * to * to end.

- chain
- double-crochet
- treble
- half-treble picot

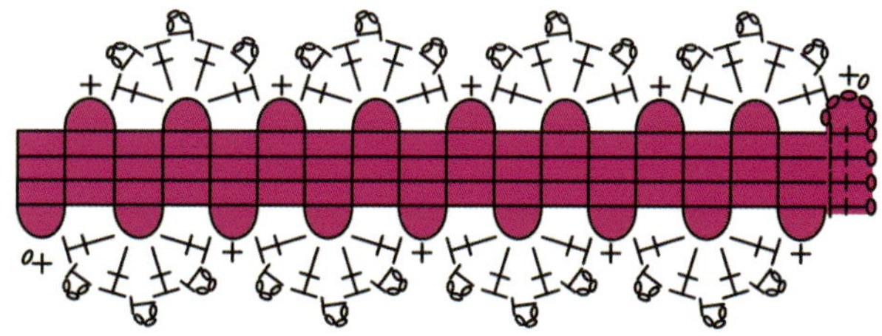

Bruges edging no 5 (half-flowers)

Two trebles together: *Yarn over, pick up a loop in arch specified. (3 loops on hook.) Yarn over and draw through 2 loops. (2 loops remain on hook.) Yarn over. Pick up a loop in same arch. (4 loops on hook.) Yarn over and draw through 2 loops. Yarn over and draw through remaining three loops.*

Join thread to first arch with a slip-stitch. Chain 1. 1 double-crochet in same arch. *2 trebles together in next arch. (Chain 3. 2 trebles together) 3 times in same arch. Slip-stitch in next arch.* Repeat from * to * to end.

Thread DMC Petra No 3
Composition 100% cotton
Shade (53845) {turquoise}
Hook 2.50 mm

TIP Use a finer crochet thread for a more delicate lace.

- slip-stitch
- chain
- double-crochet
- two trebles together

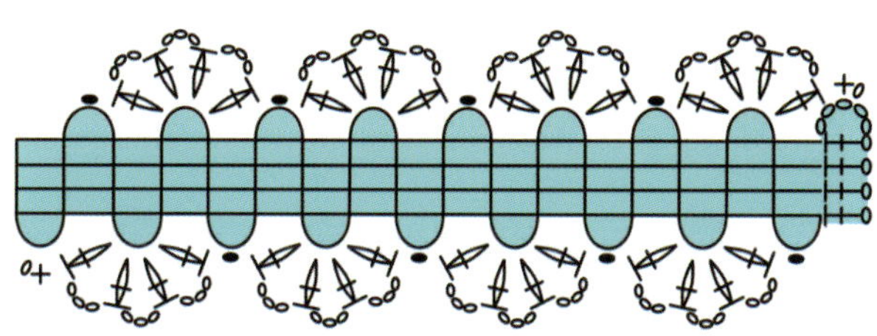

Open lace

Thread DMC Petra No 3
Composition 100% cotton
Shade (53608) {dusky pink}
Hook 2.50 mm

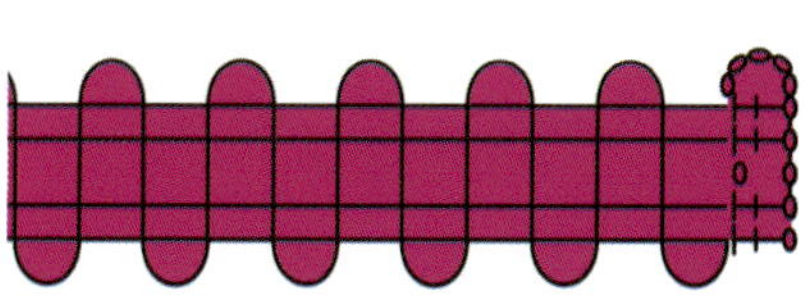

To make a more open lace, add one chain stitch in the middle of the trebles on every row of the Bruges tape (edging no 5 is shown below).

Bordering

Bruges tape makes an interesting border for all types of crocheted items from small motifs to full scale throws. You can practise this technique now by making a decorative flower coaster. Any yarn will do for this exercise, but the thread used here is listed below. *Familiarise yourself with* ***all*** *the information on pages 106–109 before starting.*

Materials

Thread *DMC Petra No 3*
Composition *100% cotton*
Hook *2.50 mm*

Shades
- *53845 {turquoise}*
- *54463 {pale blue}*
- *5608 {peachey orange}*

Loopy-flower

The side facing you as you work is the right side

Foundation chain With pale blue, chain 5. Join with a slip-stitch to form a ring.

Round 1 Chain 1. (1 double-crochet into ring. Chain 7) 6 times. Slip-stitch into first double-crochet (6 seven-chain loops).

Round 2 (2 double-crochet. 2 half-treble. 2 treble. Chain 2. 2 treble. 2 half-treble. 2 double-crochet) in each seven-chain-loop. *Slip-stitch to first double-crochet and fasten off securely.*

Bruges border

As with other Bruges patterns, you may find it easier to follow the schematic diagram (bottom right) than the written instructions.

Foundation chain With turquoise, chain 9.

Row 1 1 treble in 6th chain from hook. 1 treble in each of next 3 chain. (4 trebles and 1 arch)

Row 2 Chain 2. With right side of loopy-flower facing, 1 double-crochet into any 2-chain-space of Round 2 of loopy-flower *(when making the double-crochet keep the thread at the back of work and insert the hook from front to back into chain-space).* Chain 2. Turn. 1 treble in each of next 4 stitches.

Row 3 Standard row.

Row 4 Chain 2. With right side of loopy-flower facing, 1 double-crochet into same 2-chain-space of loopy-flower. Chain 2. Turn. 1 treble in each of next 4 stitches.

Row 5 Standard row.

Row 6 Repeat row 4.

Row 7 Standard row.

Row 8 Chain 2. With right side of loopy-flower facing, 1 double-crochet into next 2-chain-space of Round 2 of loopy-flower. Chain 2. Turn. 1 treble in each of next 4 stitches.

Row 9 Standard row.

Row 10 Repeat row 4.

Row 11 Standard row.

Row 12 Repeat row 4.

Row 13 Standard row.

Rows 14–31 Repeat rows 8–13 three more times.

Rows 32–36 Repeat rows 8–12 once.

Graft rows 1 and 36 together and fasten off securely.

Loopy-flower symbol chart

Round 1

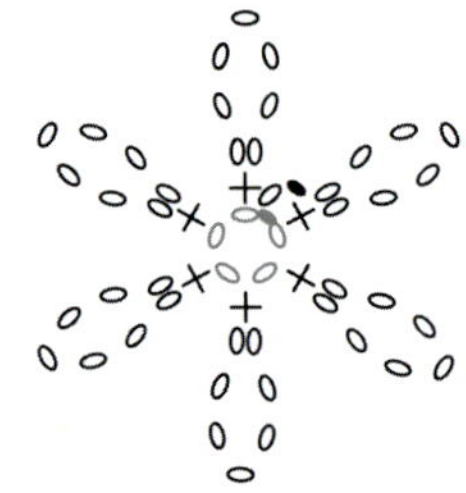

Round 2

Bruges border

TIP Left-handers can refer to the first coaster on the ***left-handed schematic diagram*** on the facing page for this border.

Symbol	Meaning
○	chain
●	slip-stitch
+	double-crochet
T	half-treble
treble symbol	treble
triple-treble symbol	triple-treble

Joining

Separate pieces of Bruges can be joined as-you-crochet. Challenge yourself by bordering a flower while simultaneously joining coasters together!

dc = double-crochet

Coaster Number 1 *Follow the instructions on the previous page to make the first coaster.*

Coaster Number 2 *Follow the instructions for Coaster Number 1 substituting the following rows:*

Rows 31, 33 and 35 *(refer to schematic diagram for specific arch numbers)* Chain 2. With loopy-flowers of both coasters wrong side facing, 1 dc in arch specified on Coaster No 1. Chain 2. Turn. 1 treble in each of next 4 stitches.

Coaster Number 3

Double-treble: *Yarn over twice. Pick up a loop from arch indicated (4 loops on hook). (Yarn over and draw through 2 loops) 3 times.*

Follow the instructions for Coaster Number 1 substituting the following rows:

Row 29 Chain 2. With loopy-flowers of both coasters wrong side facing, 1 double-treble in arch 21 of Coaster Number 1. Chain 2. Turn. 1 treble in each of next 4 stitches.

Row 31 Chain 2. 1 dc in arch 19 of Coaster Number 1. Chain 2. Turn. 1 treble in each of next 4 stitches.

Row 33 Chain 2. 1 dc in arch 17 of Coaster Number 1. Chain 2. Turn. 1 treble in each of next 4 stitches.

Row 35 Chain 2. 1 double-treble in arch 15 of Coaster Number 1. Chain 2. Turn. 1 treble in each of next 4 stitches.

Coaster No 4

Follow the instructions for Coaster Number 1, substituting the following rows:

Rows 21, 23 and 25 *(refer to schematic diagram for specific arch numbers)* Chain 2. With loopy-flowers of both coasters wrong side facing, 1 dc in arch specified on Coaster Number 3. Chain 2. Turn. 1 treble in each of next 4 stitches.

Row 29 Chain 2. 1 double-treble in arch 27 of Coaster Number 2. Chain 2. Turn. 1 treble in each of next 4 stitches.

Row 31 Chain 2. 1 dc in arch 25 of Coaster Number 2. Chain 2. Turn. 1 treble in each of next 4 stitches.

Row 33 Chain 2. 1 dc in arch 23 of Coaster Number 2. Chain 2. Turn. 1 treble in each of next 4 stitches.

Row 35 Chain 2. 1 double-treble in arch 21 of Coaster Number 2. Chain 2. Turn. 1 treble in each of next 4 stitches.

Right-handed Joining Exercise Schematic Diagram

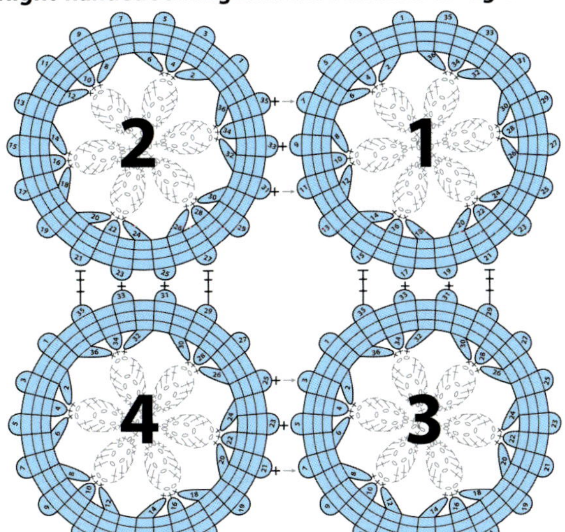

Left-handed Joining Exercise Schematic Diagram

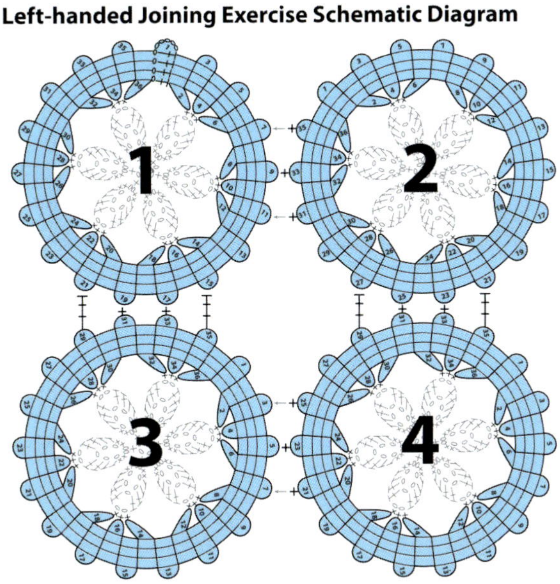

Filling

Joining four coasters together has left a gap in the centre. Gaps in Bruges crochet can be filled by joining motifs as you crochet to the vacant arches or stitches. Practise this technique by filling the gap with a loopy-flower (see the start of this chapter for a photo of this exercise).

Gap filling loopy-flower:

Foundation chain With peachey orange chain 5. Join with a slip-stitch to form a ring.

Round 1 Chain 1. (1 double-crochet into ring. Chain 7) 6 times. Slip-stitch into first double-crochet (6 seven-chain loops).

Round 2 ◊(2 double-crochet. 2 half-treble. 2 treble. Chain 1) in next 7-chain-loop. With right side facing, 1 double-crochet in double-treble indicated on diagram. (2 treble. 2 half-treble. 2 double-crochet) in same 7-chain-loop. *(2 double-crochet. 2 half-treble. 2 treble. Chain 1) in next 7-chain-loop. 1 double-crochet in arch shown on diagram. (2 treble. 2 half-treble. 2 double-crochet) in same 7-chain-loop.*◊ Repeat from * to * once. Repeat from ◊ to ◊ once. Slip-stitch to first double-crochet and fasten off securely.

Bruges Crochet Freeform Cushion

Bruges crochet is wonderfully simple yet potentially complex, as illustrated by this "freeform" design. You may not want to follow this pattern row by row, but studying the photograph, schematic diagram and instructions will give you an idea as to how Bruges lends itself to the freeform style of crochet.

Bruges Freeform Cushion Schematic Diagram

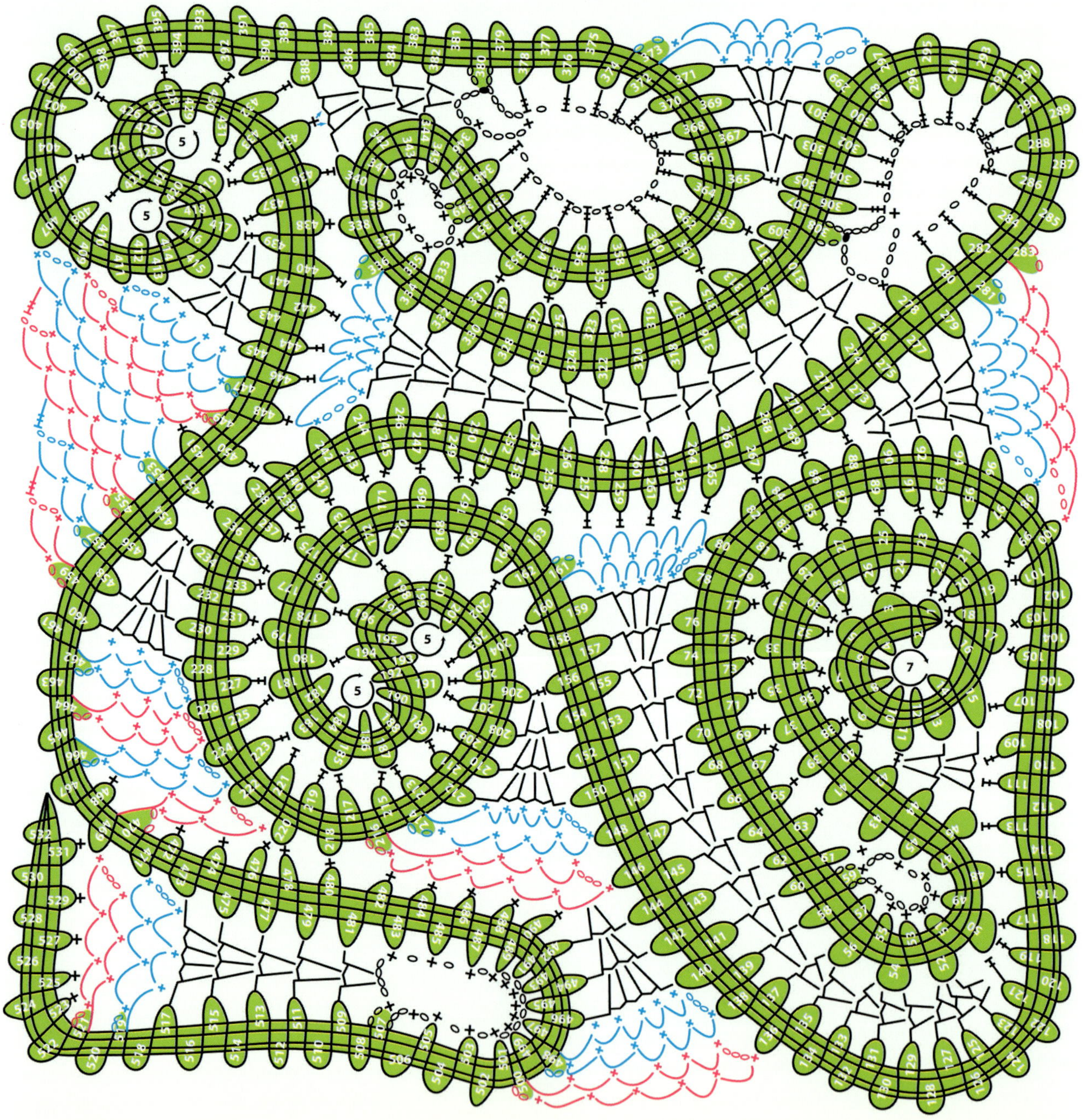

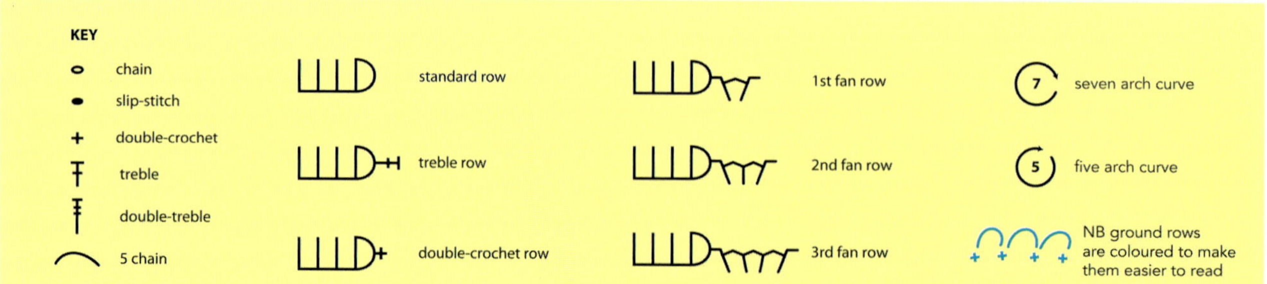

Bruges Crochet

Materials
Yarn *2 x 100g DMC Petra No 3 (100% cotton)*
Shade *(53849) {sea green}*
Hook *2.50 mm*
Cushion pad *41 x 41 cm (16 x 16") or appropriate size*

Key terms and abbreviations

YO = *yarn over*

DC = *double-crochet*

Double treble: *YO twice. Pick up a loop in arch specified (4 loops on hook). (YO and draw through 2 loops) 3 times.*

Standard row: *Chain 5. Turn. 1 treble in each of the next 4 stitches.*

DC join: *Chain 2. 1 double-crochet in arch or chain-space specified. Chain 2. Turn. 1 treble in each of the next 4 stitches.*

Treble join: *Chain 2. 1 treble in arch or chain-space specified. Chain 2. Turn. 1 treble in each of the next 4 stitches.*

Treble two arches together: *Chain 2. Yarn over. Pull up one loop in each of the two arches specified (4 loops on hook). (YO and draw through 2 loops) 3 times. Chain 2. Turn. 1 treble in each of next 4 stitches.*

Treble three arches together: *Chain 2. Yarn over. Pull up one loop in each of the three arches specified (5 loops on hook). YO and draw through 3 loops (3 loops remain on hook). (YO and draw through 2 loops) twice. Chain 2. Turn. 1 treble in each of next 4 stitches.*

DC two arches together: *Chain 2. Pull up one loop in each of the two arches specified (3 loops on hook). YO and draw through all 3 loops. Chain 2. Turn. 1 treble in each of the next 4 stitches.*

Five-arch-curve row: *Chain 2. Work down side of tape. Pick up a loop in each of next 4 arches. YO and draw through all 5 loops on hook. Chain 2. Turn. 1 treble in each of next 4 stitches.*

Place/space indicated: *refer to the schematic diagram to see where to place the stitch.*

Initial ground row: *(see row 161)*

Ground row: *(Chain 5. 1 dc) in each 5-chain-space. Chain 3. 1 dc in arch specified. Turn. Skip next 3-chain-space. (Chain 5. 1 dc) in each 5-chain-space. Chain 2. 1 treble in each of next 4stitches.*

1st fan row: *(see row 44)*

2nd fan row: *(see row 46)*

3rd fan row: *(see row 159)*

2 trebles together: *YO. Pick up a loop in next stitch. YO and draw through 2 loops. YO and pick up a loop in next stitch (4 loops on hook) YO and draw through 2 loops. YO and draw through 3 loops.*

Note this design does not lie flat; it has been designed to stretch over a cushion pad.

Bruges Crochet Freeform Cushion – 2

Instructions (make two)

Familiarise yourself with all the information on pages 106–109 before starting. In general you may find it easier to follow the schematic diagram on page 114.

Foundation chain Chain 6.
Row 1 4 treble in 6th chain from hook.
Rows 2–13 Standard row. (12 rows).
Row 14 Chain 2. Work down side of tape. Pick up a loop in each of next 6 arches. YO and draw through all 7 loops on hook. Chain 2. Turn. 1 treble in each of next 4 stitches.
Row 15 Standard row.
Row 16 DC join to arch 1.
Row 17 Standard row.
Row 18 DC join to arch 1.
Row 19 Standard row.
Row 20 DC join to arch 1.
Row 21 Standard row.
Row 22 DC join to arch 1.
Row 23 Standard row.
Row 24 DC join to arch 3.
Row 25 Standard row.
Row 26 DC join to arch 3.
Row 27 Standard row.
Row 28 DC join to arch 5.
Row 29 Standard row.
Row 30 DC join to arch 5.
Row 31 Standard row.
Row 32 DC join to arch 5.
Row 33 Standard row.
Row 34 DC join to arch 7.
Row 35 Standard row.
Row 36 DC join to arch 7.
Row 37 Standard row.
Row 38 DC join to arch 9.
Row 39 Standard row.
Row 40 DC join to arch 9.
Row 41 Standard row.
Row 42 Treble join to arch 11.
Row 43 Standard row.
Row 44 1st fan row to arch 13 ***(see photo and description below)***.

Completed 1st fan row to arch 13
Left-handed

Fan rows are made with the retaining technique. Loops are pulled up from the space below.

1st fan row Chain 2. YO 3 times. Pick up a loop from space below (5 loops on hook). (YO and draw through 2 loops) twice (3 loops on hook). YO over 3 times. Pick up a loop from same place (7 loops on hook). (YO and draw through 2 loops) twice (5 loops on hook). YO once. Pick up a loop from arch specified (7 loops on hook). (YO and draw through 2 loops) 6 times. Chain 2. Turn. 1 treble in each of the next 4 stitches.

Completed 1st fan row to arch 13
Right-handed

Row 45 Standard row.
Row 46 2nd fan row to arch 15 ***(see photo and description below)***.

Completed 2nd fan row to arch 15
Left-handed

2nd fan row Chain 2. YO 3 times. Pick up a loop from the centre space of the previous 1st fan row (5 loops on hook). (YO and draw through 2 loops) twice. YO 3 times. Pick up a loop from same space (7 loops on hook). (YO and draw through 2 loops) twice (5 loops on hook). YO 3 times. Pick up a loop from same space (9 loops on hook). (YO and draw through 2 loops) twice (7 loops on hook). YO once. Pick up a loop from arch specified (9 loops on hook). (YO and draw through 2 loops) 8 times. Chain 2. Turn. 1 treble in each of the next 4 stitches.

Completed 2nd fan row to arch 15
Right-handed

Rows 47–58 Standard row. (12 rows).
Row 59 Chain 3. Work down side of tape: (1 dc in next arch. Chain 1.) 7 times. Chain another 2. Turn. 1 dc in first 3-chain-space. Chain 2. 1 treble in each of next 4 stitches.
Row 60 Standard row.
Row 61 Chain 2. Pick up a loop from the 3-chain-space which joins rows 59 and 45. Pick up a loop from arch 43. YO and draw through all 3 loops on hook. Chain 2. Turn. 1 treble in each of next 4 stitches.
Row 62 Standard row.
Row 63 DC join to arch 41.
Row 64 Standard row.
Row 65 DC join to arch 39.
Row 66 Standard row.
Row 67 DC join to arch 37.
Row 68 Standard row.
Row 69 DC join to arch 37.
Row 70 Standard row.
Row 71 DC join to arch 35.
Row 72 Standard row.
Row 73 DC join to arch 33.
Row 74 Standard row.
Row 75 DC join to arch 33.
Row 76 Standard row.
Row 77 DC join to arch 31.
Row 78 Standard row.
Row 79 DC join to arch 31.
Row 80 Standard row.
Row 81 DC join to arch 29.
Row 82 Standard row.
Row 83 DC join to arch 29.
Row 84 Standard row.
Row 85 DC join to arch 27.

Row 86 Standard row.
Row 87 DC join to arch 27.
Row 88 Standard row.
Row 89 DC join to arch 25.
Row 90 Standard row.
Row 91 DC join to arch 23.
Row 92 Standard row.
Row 93 DC join to arch 23.
Row 94 Standard row.
Row 95 DC join to arch 21.
Row 96 Standard row.
Row 97 DC join to arch 21.
Row 98 Standard row.
Row 99 DC join to arch 19.
Row 100 Standard row.
Row 101 DC join to arch 19.
Row 102 Standard row.
Row 103 DC join to arch 17.
Row 104 Standard row.
Row 105 DC join to arch 17.
Row 106 Standard row.
Row 107 Treble join to arch 15.
Row 108 Standard row.
Row 109 Treble join to space indicated.
Row 110 Standard row.
Row 111 Treble join to space indicated.
Row 112 Standard row.
Row 113 Treble join to arch 46.
Row 114 Standard row.
Row 115 DC join to arch 48.
Row 116 Standard row.
Row 117 DC join to arch 50.
Row 118 Standard row.
Row 119 Treble join to arch 50.
Row 120 Standard row.
Row 121 Treble join to arch 50.
Row 122 Standard row.
Row 123 1st fan row to arch 52.
Row 124 Standard row.
Row 125 1st fan row to arch 52.
Row 126 Standard row.
Row 127 1st fan row to arch 52.
Row 128 Standard row.
Row 129 1st fan row to arch 54.
Row 130 Standard row.
Row 131 1st fan row to arch 54.
Row 132 Standard row.
Row 133 1st fan row to arch 54.
Row 134 Standard row.
Row 135 1st fan row to arch 56.
Row 136 Standard row.
Row 137 1st fan row to arch 56.
Row 138 Standard row.
Row 139 1st fan row to arch 58.
Row 140 Standard row.
Row 141 1st fan row to arch 60.
Row 142 Standard row.
Row 143 1st fan row to arch 62.
Row 144 Standard row.
Row 145 1st fan row to arch 64.
Row 146 Standard row.
Row 147 1st fan row to arch 66.
Row 148 Standard row.
Row 149 1st fan row to arch 68.
Row 150 Standard row.
Row 151 1st fan row to arch 70.
Row 152 Standard row.
Row 153 1st fan row to arch 72.
Row 154 Standard row.
Row 155 1st fan row to arch 74.
Row 156 Standard row.
Row 157 2nd fan row to arch 76.
Row 158 Standard row.
Row 159 3rd fan row to arch 78 ***(see photo and description below)***.

Completed 3rd fan row to arch 78
Left-handed

3rd fan row Chain 2. YO 3 times. Pick up a loop from the first space of the previous 2nd fan row (5 loops on hook). (YO and draw through 2 loops) twice. YO 3 times. Pick up a loop from same space (7 loops on hook). (YO and draw through 2 loops) twice (5 loops on hook). YO 3 times. Pick up a loop from 2nd space of the previous 2nd fan row (9 loops on hook). (YO and draw through 2 loops) twice (7 loops on hook). YO 3 times. Pick up a loop from same space (11 loops on hook). (YO and draw through two loops) twice (9 loops on hook). YO once. Pick up a loop from arch specified (11 loops on hook). (YO and draw through 2 loops) 10 times. Chain 2. Turn. 1 treble in each of the next 4 stitches.

Completed 3rd fan row to arch 78
Right-handed

Row 160 Standard row.
Ground rows A "ground" is an open pattern use to fill space between denser areas of crochet. In this design the ground is a simple one consisting of five chains and one double-crochet. A single row of this ground pattern involves crocheting across to the opposite arch, joining to that arch with a double-crochet, turning and then crocheting back.
Row 161 Initial ground row to arch 80 ***(see illustration and description below)***.

Row 161 ***initial ground row to arch 80***
Left-handed

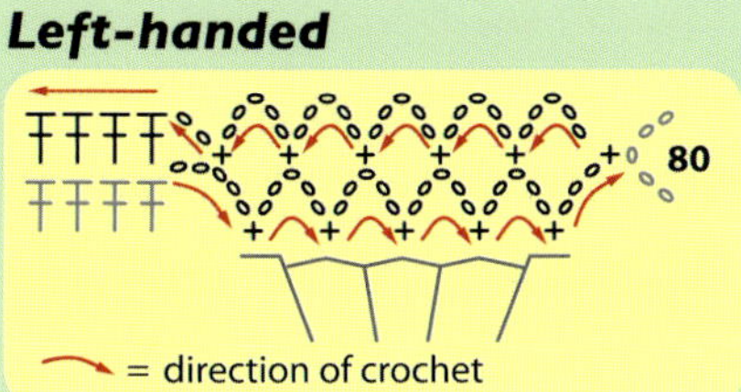

Initial ground row: (Chain 5. 1 dc in place indicated) 5 times. Chain 3. 1 dc in arch specified. Turn. Skip next 3-chain-space. (Chain 5. 1 dc in next 5-chain-space) 5 times. Chain 2. 1 treble in each of the next 4 stitches.

Row 161 ***initial ground row to arch 80***
Right-handed

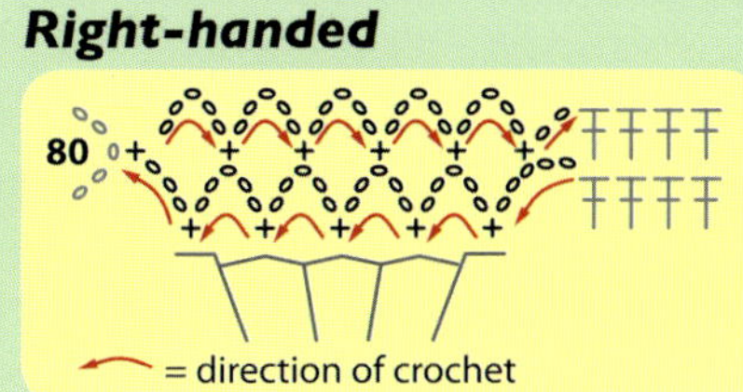

Rows 162–191 Standard row (30 rows).
Rows 192 Five-arch-curve row.
Row 193 Standard row.
Row 194 Treble two arches together (arches 182 and 180).
Row 195 Standard row.
Row 196 Treble two arches together (arches 178 and 176).
Row 197 Standard row.
Row 198 Treble three arches together (arches 174, 172 and 170).
Row 199 Standard row.

Bruges Crochet Freeform Cushion – 3

Row 200 Treble two arches together (arches 168 and 166).
Row 201 Five-arch-curve row.
Row 202 Treble two arches together (arches 164 and 162).
Row 203 Treble join to arch 191.
Row 204 Treble two arches together (arches 160 and 158).
Row 205 Treble join to arch 191.
Row 206 Treble join to arch 156.
Row 207 Treble join to arch 191.
Row 208 1st fan row to arch 154.
Row 209 Treble join to arch 189.
Row 210 2nd fan row to arch 152.
Row 211 Treble join to arch 189.
Row 212 Third fan row to arch 150 (see instructions for row 159).
Row 213 Treble join to arch 187.
Row 214 Initial ground row to arch 148 (see instructions for row 161).
Row 215 Treble join to arch 187.
Row 216 Ground row to arch 146.
Row 217 Treble join to arch 185.
Row 218 Standard row.
Row 219 Treble join to arch 185.
Row 220 Standard row.
Row 221 Treble join to arch 183.
Row 222 Standard row.
Row 223 Treble join to arch 183.
Row 224 Standard row.
Row 225 Treble join to arch 181.
Row 226 Standard row.
Row 227 Treble join to arch 181.
Row 228 Standard row.
Row 229 Treble join to arch 179.
Row 230 Standard row.
Row 231 DC join to arch 179.
Row 232 Standard row.
Row 233 DC join to arch 177.
Row 234 Standard row.
Row 235 DC join to arch 177.
Row 236 Standard row.
Row 237 DC join to arch 175.
Row 238 Standard row.
Row 239 DC join to arch 175.
Row 240 Standard row.
Row 241 DC join to arch 173.
Row 242 Standard row.
Row 243 DC join to arch 171.
Row 244 Standard row.
Row 245 DC join to arch 171.
Row 246 Standard row.
Row 247 DC join to arch 169.
Row 248 Standard row.
Row 249 DC join to arch 167.
Row 250 Standard row.
Row 251 DC join to arch 167.
Row 252 Standard row.
Row 253 DC join to arch 165.
Row 254 Standard row.
Row 255 DC join to arch 163.
Row 256 Standard row.
Row 257 Treble join to space indicated.
Row 258 Standard row.
Row 259 Treble join to space indicated.
Row 260 Standard row.
Row 261 Treble join to space indicated.
Row 262 Standard row.
Row 263 Treble join to space indicated.
Row 264 Standard row.
Row 265 Treble join to space indicated.
Row 266 Standard row.
Row 267 DC together arches 82 and 84.
Row 268 Standard row.
Row 269 DC join to arch 86.
Row 270 Standard row.
Row 271 Treble join to arch 88.
Row 272 Standard row.
Row 273 1st fan row to arch 90.
Row 274 Standard row.
Row 275 1st fan row to arch 92.
Row 276 Standard row.
Row 277 2nd fan row to arch 94.
Row 278 Standard row.
Row 279 3rd fan row to arch 96.
Row 280 Standard row.
Row 281 Initial ground row to arch 98 (see instructions for row 161).
Row 282 Standard row.
Row 283 Ground row to arch 100.
Row 284–307 Standard row (24 rows).
Row 308 Chain 7. Work down side of tape, working in arches as follows: (1 double-treble in next arch. Chain 1.) 14 times. Turn. 1 dc in first double-treble. Chain 4. Turn. 1 dc in arch 278. Turn Chain 5. Slip-stitch to 2nd chain of first 7 chain. Chain 2. 1 treble in each of next 4 stitches.
Row 309 Standard row.
Row 310 1st fan row to two arches as follows: Chain 2. *YO 3 times. Pick up a loop from the chain-space below. (YO and draw through 2 loops) twice.* Repeat from * to * once. YO Pull up one loop each from arches 276 and 274 (8 loops on hook). (YO and pull through 2 loops) 7 times. Chain 2. Turn. 1 treble in each of the next 4 stitches.
Row 311 Standard row.
Row 312 1st fan row to arch 272.
Row 313 Standard row.
Row 314 1st fan row to two arches (arches 270 and 268) {see row 310}.
Row 315 Standard row.
Row 316 1st fan row to arch 266.
Row 317 Standard row.
Row 318 1st fan row to arch 264.
Row 319 Standard row.
Row 320 1st fan row to two arches (arches 262 and 260).
Row 321 Standard row.
Row 322 1st fan row to arch 258.
Row 323 Standard row.
Row 324 1st fan row to arch 256.
Row 325 Standard row.
Row 326 1st fan row to two arches (arches 254 and 252).
Row 327 Standard row.
Row 328 1st fan row to arch 250.
Row 329 Standard row.
Row 330 1st fan row to arch 248.
Row 331 Standard row.
Row 332 2nd fan row to arch 246.
Row 333 Standard row.
Row 334 3rd fan row to arch 244.
Row 335 Standard row.
Row 336 Initial ground row to arch 242.
Row 337–348 Standard row (12 rows).
Row 349 Chain 3. Work down side of tape: (1 dc in next arch. Chain 1.) 7 times. Chain another 2. Turn. 1 dc in first 3 chain-space. Chain 2. 1 treble in each of next 4 stitches.
Row 350 Standard row.
Row 351 Chain 2. Pick up a loop from the 3-chain-space which joins rows 349 and 335. Pick up a loop from arch 333. YO and draw through all 3 loops on hook. Chain 2. Turn. 1 treble in each of next 4 stitches.
Row 352 Standard row.
Row 353 DC two arches together (arches 331 and 329).
Row 354 Standard row.
Row 355 DC two arches together (arches 327 and 325).
Row 356 Standard row.
Row 357 DC two arches together (arches 323 and 321).
Row 358 Standard row.
Row 359 DC two arches together (arches 319 and 317).
Row 360 Standard row.
Row 361 DC two arches together (arches 315 and 313).
Row 362 Standard row.
Row 363 DC two arches together (arches 311 and 309).
Row 364 Standard row.
Row 365 Treble two arches together (arches 307 and 305).
Row 366 Standard row.
Row 367 1st fan row to arch 303.
Row 368 Standard row.
Row 369 2nd fan row to arch 301.
Row 370 Standard row.
Row 371 3rd fan row to arch 299.
Row 372 Standard row.
Row 373 Initial ground row to arch 297.
Rows 374–379 Standard row (6 rows).
Row 380 Chain 7. Work down side of tape working to arches as follows: (1 double-treble in next arch. Chain 1) 16 times. Turn. 1 dc in first double-treble. Chain 4. Turn. 1 dc in arch 346. Turn. Chain 5. Slip-stitch to 2nd chain of first 7 chain. Chain 2. 1 treble in each of next 4 stitches.
Row 381 Standard row.
Row 382 1st fan row to arch 344.

Row 383 Standard row.
Row 384 1st fan row to arch 344.
Row 385 Standard row.
Row 386 1st fan row to arch 342.
Row 387 Standard row.
Row 388 2nd fan row to arch 340.
Row 389–419 Standard row (31 rows).
Row 420 Five-arch-curve row.
Row 421 Standard row.
Row 422 Treble two arches together (arches 410 and 408).
Row 423 Standard row.
Row 424 Treble two arches together (arches 406 and 404).
Row 425 Standard row.
Row 426 Treble three arches together (arches 402, 400 and 398).
Row 427 Standard row.
Row 428 Treble two arches together (arches 396 and 394).
Row 429 Five-arch-curve row.
Row 430 Treble two arches together (arches 392 and 390).
Row 431 Treble join to arch 419.
Row 432 Treble join to arch 388.
Row 433 Treble join to arch 419.
Row 434 Chain 2. YO. Pull up one loop in each space marked with an arrow on diagram (4 loops on hook). (YO and draw through 2 loops) 3 times. Chain 2. Turn. 1 treble in each of next 4 stitches.
Row 435 Treble join to arch 419.
Row 436 Treble join to arch 340.
Row 437 Treble join to arch 417.
Row 438 DC join to arch 388.
Row 439 Treble join to arch 417.
Row 440 Treble join to space indicated.
Row 441 1st fan row to arch 415.
Row 442 Treble join to space indicated.
Row 443 1st fan row to arch 415.
Row 444 Treble join to space indicated.
Row 445 2nd fan row to arch 413.
Row 446 Treble join to space indicated.
Row 447 Initial ground row as follows: (Chain 5. 1 dc in place indicated) 4 times. Chain 3. 1 dc in arch 411. Turn. Skip next 3-chain-space. (Chain 5. 1 dc in next 5-chain-space) 4 times. Chain 2. 1 treble in each of the next 4 stitches.
Row 448 DC join to space indicated.
Row 449 Ground row to arch 409.
Row 450 Treble 2 arches together (arches 240 and 238).
Row 451 Chain 2. 1 dc in next 5-chain-space. Chain 2. Turn. 1 treble in each of next 4 stitches.
Row 452 DC join to arch 236.
Row 453 (Chain 5. 1 dc in next 5-chain-space) 4 times. Chain 5. 1 dc in arch 409. Chain 3. 1 dc in arch 407. Turn. Skip next 3-chain-space. (Chain 5. 1 dc in 5-chain-space) 5 times. Chain 2. 1 treble in each of next 4 stitches.
Row 454 Treble join to arch 234.
Row 455 (Chain 5. 1 dc in next 5-chain-space) 4 times. Chain 3. 1 double-treble in next 5-chain-space. Turn. (Chain 5. 1 dc in next 5-chain-space) 4 times. Chain 2. 1 treble in each of next 4 stitches.
Row 456 1st fan row to arch 232.
Row 457 (Chain 5. 1 dc in next 5-chain-space) 2 times. Chain 3. 1 double-treble in next 5-chain-space. Turn. (Chain 5. 1 dc in next 5-chain-space) 2 times. Chain 2. 1 treble in each of next 4 stitches.
Row 458 2nd fan row to arch 230.
Row 459 Chain 5. 1 dc in next 5-chain-space. Chain 3. 1 double-treble in next 5-chain-space. Turn. Chain 5. 1 dc in next 5-chain-space. Chain 2. 1 treble in each of next 4 stitches.
Row 460 3rd fan row to arch 228.
Row 461 Standard row.
Row 462 (Chain 5. 1 dc in place indicated) 3 times. Chain 3. 1 dc in arch 226. Turn. Skip next 3-chain-space. (Chain 5. 1 dc in next 5-chain-space) 3 times. Chain 2. 1 treble in each of the next 4 stitches.
Row 463 Standard row.
Row 464 Ground row to 224.
Row 465 Standard row.
Row 466 Ground row to 222.
Row 467 Standard row.
Row 468 Chain 2. 1 dc in next 5-chain-space. Turn. Chain 2. 1 treble in each of next 4 stitches.
Row 469 Standard row.
Row 470 Chain 5. Skip first 5-chain-space. 1 dc in next 5-chain-space. Chain 5. 1 dc in next 5-chain-space. Chain 3. 1 dc in arch 220. Turn. Skip next 3-chain-space. (Chain 5. 1 dc in next 5-chain-space) 2 times. Chain 2. 1 treble in each of the next 4 stitches.
Row 471 Standard row.
Row 472 DC join to space indicated.
Row 473 Standard row.
Row 474 DC join to space indicated.
Row 475 Standard row.
Row 476 DC join to arch 220.
Row 477 Standard row.
Row 478 DC join to arch 220.
Row 479 Standard row.
Row 480 DC join to arch 218.
Row 481 Standard row.
Row 482 DC join to space indicated.
Row 483 Standard row.
Row 484 DC join to space indicated.
Row 485 Standard row.
Row 486 DC join to space indicated.
Row 487 Standard row.
Row 488 DC join to space indicated.
Row 489 Standard row.
Row 490 DC join to space indicated.
Row 491 Standard row.
Row 492 1st fan row to arch 144.
Row 493 Standard row.
Row 494 2nd fan row to arch 142.
Row 495 Standard row.
Row 496 3rd fan row to arch 140.
Row 497 Standard row.
Row 498 Initial ground row to arch 138.
Row 499 Standard row.
Row 500 Ground row to arch 136.
Row 501–506 Standard row (6 rows).
Row 507 Chain 3. Work down side of tape. (1 dc in next arch. Chain 1.) 12 times. Chain another 4. Turn. DC in first 3-chain-space. Chain 2. 1 treble in each of next 4 stitches.
Row 508 Standard row.
Row 509 1st fan row to arch 481.
Row 510 Standard row.
Row 511 1st fan row to arch 479.
Row 512 Standard row.
Row 513 1st fan row to arch 477.
Row 514 Standard row.
Row 515 2nd fan row to arch 475.
Row 516 Standard row.
Row 517 3rd fan row to arch 473.
Row 518 Standard row.
Row 519 (Chain 5. 1 dc in place indicated) 3 times. Chain 3. 1 dc in arch 471. Turn. Skip next 3-chain-space. (Chain 5. 1 dc in next 5-chain-space) 3 times. Chain 2. 1 treble in each of the next 4 stitches.
Row 520 Standard row.
Row 521 Ground row to 469.
Row 522 Standard row.
Row 523 Dc join to space indicated.
Row 524 Standard row.
Row 525 Dc join to space indicated.
Row 526 Standard row.
Row 527 Dc join to space indicated.
Row 528 Standard row.
Row 529 Dc join to space indicated.
Row 530 Standard row.
Row 531 Chain 2. Dc in arch 469. Chain 2. Turn. 2 trebles together. 1 treble in each of next 2 stitches. (3 trebles)
Row 532 Chain 5. Turn 2 trebles together. 1 treble in next stitch. 1 dc in arch 467. Fasten off securely.

Join the two pieces together

*Lay one piece on top of the other, aligning the design so that they match. Starting at any corner, I double-crochet in an arch or chain-space of first piece. Chain 2. I double-crochet in corresponding arch or chain-space of second piece. *Chain 2. I double-crochet in next arch or chain-space of first piece. Chain 2. I double-crochet in next arch or chain-space of second piece.* Repeat from * to * around three sides. Insert appropriately sized cushion pad and gently stretch out so that it covers the pad. Repeat from * to * along fourth side and fasten off securely. (This technique makes it easy to remove the cover should it need to be cleaned.)*

Luxury Bruges

Bruges need not be limited to cotton crochet threads. It adapts very well to all kinds of different fibres, from economic acrylic to delicious luxury yarns, like the six featured here. Luxury yarns can be challenging to work with so always practise first on a small piece like the Bruges exercise on pages 106–109. The open nature of Bruges crochet ensures that a small amount of luxury yarn goes a long way, so it is an ideal technique to use for accessories such as scarves and stoles.

Merino, silk & cashmere

Yarn Sublime Baby Cashmere Merino Silk DK (50g)
Composition 75% Extra Fine Merino, 20% Silk, 5% Cashmere
Yardage 116 metres (126 yards) approximately
Shade Little Liberty (458)
Hook 4.00 mm

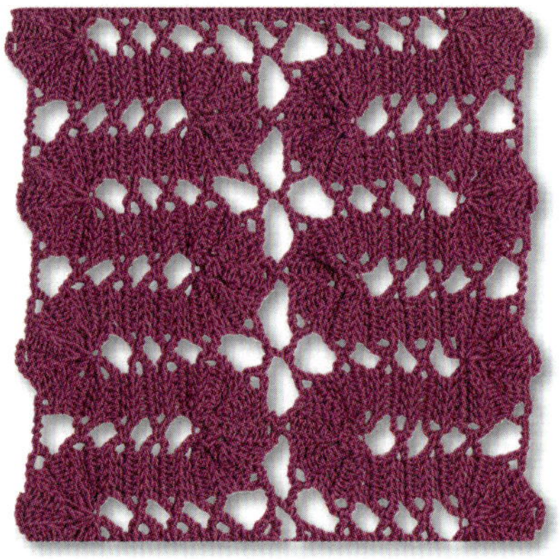

Wool, silk & alpaca

Yarn Mirasol Sulka Nina (50g)
Composition 60% Wool, 20% Silk, 20% Alpaca
Yardage 150 metres (164 yards) approximately
Shade Songbird (7117)
Hook 4.00 mm

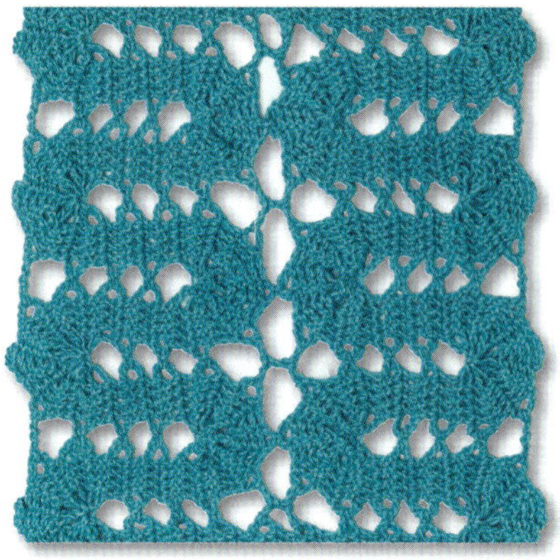

Yak blend

Yarn Rowan Softyak (50g) DK
Composition 76% Cotton, 15% Yak, 9% Nylon
Yardage 135 metres (147 yards) approximately
Shade Pampas (235)
Hook 4.00 mm

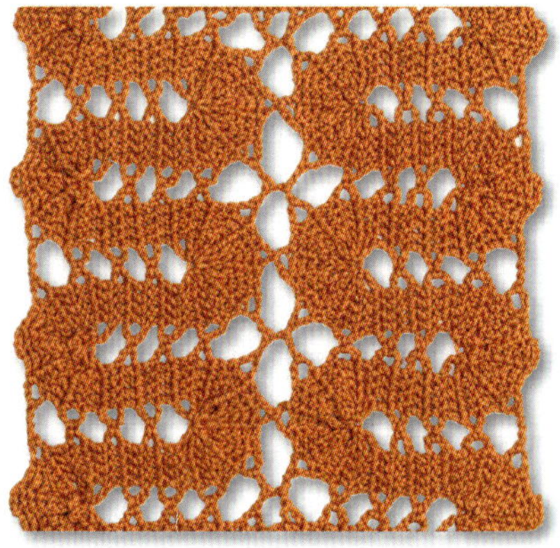

Mohair & lurex

Yarn Lana Grossa Splendid (25g)
Composition 72% Mohair, 21% Nylon, 7% Lurex
Yardage 167 metres (183 yards) approximately
Shade Jeans/silver (26)
Hook 3.50 mm

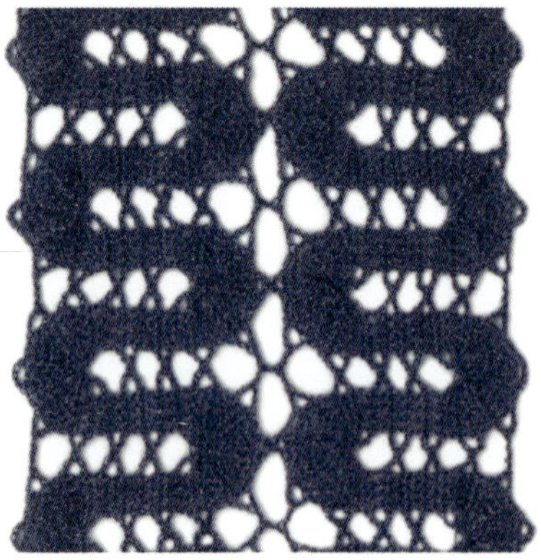

Wool

Yarn West Yorkshire Spinners Wensleydale Fleece Gems Hank DK (100g)
Composition 100% wool
Yardage 225 metres (246 yards) approximately
Shade Jadeite (385)
Hook 3.50 mm

Alpaca & silk

Yarn Lana Grossa Lace Seta (50g)
Composition 70% Alpaca, 30% Silk
Yardage 250 metres (273 yards) approximately
Shade Orchid (0018)
Hook 3.50 mm

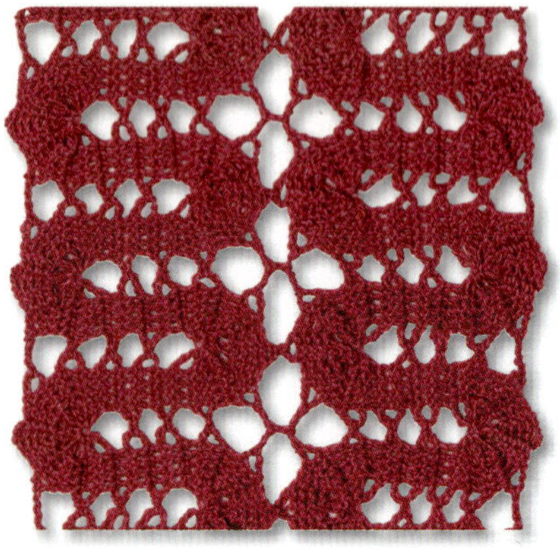